POLITICS
AS THE MASTER
SCIENCE:
FROM PLATO
TO MAO

POLITICS AS THE MASTER SCIENCE: FROM PLATO TO MAO

Herbert J. Spiro

PROFESSOR OF POLITICAL SCIENCE
University of Pennsylvania

WITHDRAWN

HARPER & ROW, PUBLISHERS
New York, Evanston, and London

Politics as the Master Science: From Plato to Mao
Copyright © 1970 by *Herbert J. Spiro*.

LIBRARY OF CONGRESS CATALOG CARD NUMBER: 70-98203

234381

For
Alexander C. S. Spiro

CONTENTS

PREFACE

This little book grew out of an experimental Introduction to Political Science that I offered at the University of Pennsylvania in 1966–1967. It is not intended as a comprehensive introduction to the ancient, recently rejuvenated discipline of political science, but rather as a companion to such an introduction. The variety of introductory courses given by American departments of political science is perhaps exceeded only by our general dissatisfaction with them. This entirely healthy attitude has generated experimentation and innovation and continues to do so. As a result, students are introduced to political science by way of courses that concentrate upon American or comparative government and politics, the history of political philosophy, and empirical theory, singly or in various combinations. My hope in writing this book was that it could be used as an integral and integrative companion to any of these, whatever their format or length.

A word about the unusual sequence. I begin with Plato and Aristotle because they are the founders of politics in every sense, but especially as the men who forged the tools of the profession, its basic vocabulary and method. Aristotle in particular was above all a "comparativist," so that I thought it logical to move from his comparison of 157 polities to my comparison of two sets of major contemporary developed political systems: Great Britain-France-Germany and the United States-Soviet Union. The latter analysis involves that rarity, a genuinely new concept, *totalitarianism*, and its critique. Consideration of totalitarianism and of the Soviet Union also leads to Marxism-Leninism-Maoism, all concerned with, and indeed designed to advance, economic and social modernization and political development. Hence the focus moves from the expansion of consciousness to the development of politics in the "new nations," and from there back to the founders, or refounders, of political science in the seventeenth and eighteenth centuries. In my own teaching I have found students more receptive to the ideas, ideals, and concepts of Thomas Hobbes, John Locke, and Jean Jacques Rousseau after prior exposure to contemporary problems of instability in new-modeled communities. In the two concluding chapters, finally, I try to ask some simple and classic questions that may help to move political science out of the *cul de sac* in which it seems at times to have gotten stuck.

Since this is a *short* companion to an introduction to political science, I have generally confined the argument to, and drawn illustrations from, only the most influential works of thinkers and the most widely remarked and criticized political phenomena in countries: Machiavelli's *Prince*, not his *Discourses*; the thought of Mao Tsetung applied to the Cultural Revolution, not to the "glory of the Hans."

Wherever possible, I give references to paperback editions of books available in the United States.

H.J.S.

POLITICS AS THE MASTER SCIENCE: FROM PLATO TO MAO

If then, there is some end to the things we do, which we desire for its own sake (everything else being desired for the sake of this), and if we do not choose everything for the sake of something else (for at that rate the process would go on to infinity, so that our desire would be empty and vain), clearly this must be the good and the chief good. Will not the knowledge of it, then, have a great influence on life? Shall we not, like archers who have a mark to aim at, be more likely to hit upon what is right? If so we must try, in outline at least, to determine what it is, and of which of the sciences or faculties it is the object. It would seem to belong to the most authoritative science and to that which is most truly the master science. And politics appears to be of this nature; for it is politics that ordains which of the sciences should be studied in a state, and which each class of citizens should learn and up to what point they should learn them; and we see even the most highly esteemed of faculties to fall under this, e.g., strategy, economics, rhetoric; now since politics uses the rest of the sciences, and since again it legislates as to what we are to do and what we are to abstain from doing, the goal of this science must include those of the others, so that this end must be the good for man. For even if the end is the same for a single man and for a state, that of the state seems at all events something greater and more complete whether to attain or to preserve; though it is worthwhile to attain the end merely for one man, it is finer and more god-like to attain it for a nation or for city-states. These, then, are the goals at which our inquiry aims, since it is political science, in one sense of that term.

Aristotle, *Nicomachean Ethics*, book I, 2.

POLITICS AS THE MASTER SCIENCE 1

CLASSICAL ATHENS AND
THE UNITED STATES TODAY

Politics is the master science, in the Aristotelian sense of the term, as much today as it was in classical Greece more than two thousand years ago. That is the thesis which we will try to demonstrate and whose meaning we will try to explore.

If politics is the master science now, its position at the pinnacle of human activities and as the most important discipline that can be a subject of systematic study has a much wider impact today than it could have had in classical Greece. Plato and Aristotle, for example, would have excluded from the politics of Athens the majority of the population: slaves, resident foreigners, women, and of course children. Aristotle would not even have admitted most of the readers of this book to the study of politics:

> Now each man judges well the things he knows, and of these he is a good judge. And so the man who has been educated in a subject is a good judge of that subject, and the man who has received an all-around education is a good judge in general. Hence a young man is not a proper hearer of lectures on political science; for he is inexperienced in the actions that occur in life, but its discussions start from these and are about these; and further,

since he tends to follow his passions, his study will be vain and unprofitable, because the end aimed at is not knowledge but action. And it makes no difference whether he is young in years or youthful in character; the defect does not depend on time, but on his living, and pursuing each successive object, as passion directs. For to such persons, as to the incontinent, knowledge brings no profit; but to those who desire and act in accordance with a rational principle, knowledge about such matters will be of great benefit.[1]

Aristotle thought that young men should be excluded from the study of politics, because they lack the maturity of judgment that can be gained only from experience. He would have had men study politics only *after* they had studied all the other subjects. Today, by contrast, it is becoming existentially impossible to exclude any human being who has reached the age of reason from an awareness of politics or from some thought of participation, however passive, in politics. Everyone, everywhere on earth, belongs not only to the political system of his immediate local community but also to the complex, interdependent, emergent global political system. And it is only through the politics of this most comprehensive of communities, the community of mankind, that either progress or stagnation or the extermination of humanity will be brought about.

Politics was the queen of the sciences and the most important of human activities in the days of Plato and Aristotle, the founders of political science. Today it has become that again, in a very concrete sense. The most important events in the lives of individuals and of communities, whatever their scope or location, are all shaped more by politics than by anything else, even so-called acts of nature or of God, such as earthquakes or epidemics. Science, whose development is certainly shaped by politics, cannot yet prevent earthquakes, though it has gone far toward preventing epidemics. However, both the issuance of warnings about and the control of the effects of such natural disasters are almost wholly within the realm of the political. The same is true of all the other activities cited by Aristotle in the passage that opens this chapter. This selection, characteristically, is taken not from the first book of his *Politics* but from the first book of his *Nicomachean Ethics*.

---

[1] Aristotle, *Nicomachean Ethics*, book I, 2.

Some of our own contemporaries deny this ubiquity and primacy of politics. Others admit but bemoan it, and some try to reverse, or at least to reduce, the dominance of politics in our lives. In this respect, our own period differs from the age in which political science was born, for at that time, everyone accepted the supremacy of politics. (The philosophers known as the Cynics were a possible exception, because they rejected politics in its conventional meaning; that is, they rejected the politics of the *polis*, or city-state, for they considered it too restricted a community to be capable of providing generally valid norms of behavior. However, while they rejected conventional politics, they at the same time laid the foundations for the cosmopolitanism of the Stoic philosophers who followed them. According to the Stoics, the universe was governed by one law, and all human beings were members of the great cosmopolitan community.) Politics in the classic age of Hellas was self-evidently more important than anything else.

This obviousness of the primacy of politics was due to the one crucial difference, among many important ones, between ancient Athens and contemporary United States. The Athenian community, life within it, and people's perception of this life were almost wholly undifferentiated in comparison with the contemporary American community, life within it, and our perceptions of this life. All of us today are members of (we say that we "belong to") a whole welter of functionally differentiated associations, organizations, and other formal and informal groupings. We belong to economic interest groups, each of us usually to several of them; to cultural groupings, including religious and educational ones; to the partly biological association of the family; and to other organizations that are politically defined. Some of the groups of which we are members—that is, some of the systems of which we are components or sub-systems—are understood to have geographical boundaries, like the state and the nation-state; others cut across geographical boundaries in a complex pattern of crisscrossing affinities and affiliations.

CLAIMS TO LOYALTY

None of these groupings to which we belong either claims, or is normally permitted to claim, our whole person or being: neither the nation-state, which in the United States operates under fairly strict constitutional restraints, safeguarding, for example, the individual's religious personality or his right not to be forced to incriminate himself; nor the various churches, since even priests can and do leave the most tightly disciplined religious orders; nor economic organizations, including both powerful business corporations and trade unions; nor professional associations or universities; nor even "political organizations" (in the strict sense of the term) that model themselves on fascist or communist movements outside the United States. None of these groupings is permitted to claim all of any one of us. And each of us normally feels that he belongs to several, and usually to many, of these groups.

This more or less institutionalized pluralism was lacking in ancient Athens and the other city-states of classical Greece. And if it was not wholly absent, it was at best only incipient. In Athens, the citizen belonged to the city. (The English words for *citizen* and *city* are derived from the Latin. In Greek as in Latin, the words for *citizen, politics,* and—as we will see later—*constitution* were derived from the master word, *polis,* which is usually inadequately translated into English as *city-state.*) A citizen belonged to the *polis* in his entirety, as Socrates makes clear in the *Crito.* (He had been condemned to death by a court consisting of about five hundred of his fellow-citizens of Athens. When his friends offered him an easy opportunity to flee Athens in order to seek refuge in another city, he refused. His whole being had been nourished by the *polis* and its laws and he could not picture living in another community after his own had condemned him, though unjustly, according to the procedures provided by its laws.)

In comparison with our view of the state and of ourselves, the Platonic and Aristotelian view was much less differentiated, much less mechanistic, much more holist, and much more organic. This was true of the classical view of both the *polis* and the individual: Socrates felt that he belonged to Athens, not to a party in Athens, not to the ruling class of Athens, not to what he thought was best in Athens, but simply to Athens. And he thought that it was all of Socrates that belonged in this way, not the best in him; not only his rational portion, or merely his emotional self, or the body that had been given sustenance by this *polis,* but all of Socrates belonged as one undifferentiated personality. It would have been impossible for Socrates, his disciples, or their contemporaries to "divide themselves up" intellectually into functional components, or "roles," as we frequently, and indeed usually, do. Nowadays, men identify themselves with the particular function they are performing, the role they are playing, at the time: as businessman, as husband or father, as part-time soldier, as the enjoyer of entertainment or the viewer of art, as motorist, as pedestrian, as member of an ethnic minority engaged in politics, as taxpayer, as voter, and so forth. This capacity to compartmentalize oneself was taken to its logical conclusion by some of Hitler's concentration camp commandants, who were efficient executors of Nazi terror, but at the same time loving family fathers, who after putting in a hard day's work at the gas ovens played Mozart sonatas on their violins at home.

THE CHANGE IN POLITICAL VOCABULARY

The lack of differentiation perceived in both *polis* and individual by the ancient Greeks is revealed in many ways, one of them the vocabulary of politics. As the Western political tradition grew it became increasingly differentiated, and this is shown by changes in the vocabulary of political philosophy. St. Thomas Aquinas revived Aristotelian thought in the thirteenth century and quoted "The Philosopher," as he referred to Aristotle, saying man is a "social and political animal" or being. Aristotle of course had said no such thing. His term was *zoon politikon*, "political being," his vocabulary providing no equivalent word for what St. Thomas meant by *social*.

In the nineteenth century, some philosophers began to speak of "economic man" to distinguish or differentiate the economic aspects, or functions, of the human being from the political, social, religious, and psychological ones. The word *economics* is of Greek origin, and Aristotle was one of the first authors to use it to denote the science of managing a household. But Aristotle would have found it inconceivable to compartmentalize or to segregate man's economic activities from his other functions or to deny that politics shaped and controlled economics, just as it shaped and controlled strategy, rhetoric, and all other lesser human activities.

The difference in degree of differentiation and in its perception by men between the classic past and our own day is very profound. Some readers may conclude from it that we can really learn little or nothing from the political thought of Plato, Aristotle, and their contemporaries in the comparatively undifferentiated *polis*. This conclusion would have to be based on the assumption that there is a qualitative difference between politics in classical Athens and politics in the modern world. This conclusion is erroneous, but it does point to one important cautionary imperative that students of politics must always bear in mind: Beware of false analogies!

At this point, one citation may serve to illustrate this danger, to which we will have frequent occasion to return. There is a book in which some distinguished scholars have discussed whether Plato was a totalitarian or a democrat.[2] This is a senseless question. Since the end of World War II both scholars and politicians have referred to a number of political systems as "totalitarian." Among these are Hitler's Germany, Stalin's Soviet Union, and Mao Tse-tung's China. But these so-called totalitarian systems were brought into being *after* differentiation and, equally important, after awareness of differentiation, or at least an awareness of its possibility, had become universal facts. Plato's Athens was neither the Soviet Union or China nor, at the other end of the spectrum of differentiation, Barotseland in Zambia. It is therefore a waste of time, except possibly for propaganda purposes, to ask whether Plato favored or contributed to the development of totalitarianism in this sense.

However, the basic processes of politics as the quintessential human activities were the same in Plato's time as they are in ours, and they will remain the same until men exterminate themselves or breed themselves out of existence. (In the future there are good possibilities for either of these alternatives.) That is why there is a great deal we can learn today from the political philosophizing of both ancient and modern thinkers. Political theory has been called "The Great Conversation," and it is the greatest, most important, and longest-lasting conversation ever held on earth. It is a conversation in which we can all participate, in which, indeed, we are all

---

[2] T. L. Thomson, ed., *Plato: Totalitarian or Democrat?*, Englewood Cliffs, N.J.: Prentice-Hall, 1963.

being constantly compelled to participate, almost on a day-to-day basis. It is a dialectic in which you can talk back to the greatest thinkers of all times and in which they will talk back to you; it is a debate from which you can try to withdraw at the cost of surrendering the most vital portion of your humanity, but from which there is really no effective withdrawal.

I will tell you, I replied; justice, which is the subject of our inquiry, is, as you know, sometimes spoken of as the virtue of the individual, and sometimes as the virtue of the polis.

True, he replied.

And is not the polis larger than the individual?

It is.

Then in the larger the quantity of justice is likely to be larger and more easily discernible. I propose therefore that we inquire into the nature of justice and injustice, first as they appear in the polis, and secondly in the individual, proceeding from the greater to the lesser and comparing them.

That, he said, is an excellent proposal.

And if we imagine the polis in process of creation, we shall see the justice and injustice of the polis in process of creation also.

I dare say.

When the polis is completed there may be a hope that the object of our search will be more easily discovered.

Plato, *The Republic*, book II, 368 f.

THE PROBLEM   2
OF ANALOGY:
PLATO

POLIS AND THE INDIVIDUAL

Plato's greatest and most influential work, *The Republic*, is usually interpreted as one big analogy between the state and the individual, by means of which Plato searched for the true meaning of justice. In this interpretation, Plato is believed to have concerned himself above all with finding justice for the individual. In other words, *The Republic* is considered mainly a work of "ethics," just as one of Aristotle's books is entitled *Nicomachean Ethics* (though we have already seen that, at least at the beginning of his *Ethics*, Aristotle was concerned primarily with what we today would consider politics). Against this common interpretation of Plato's *Republic*, we raise this question: Could Plato conceive of the individual apart from the *polis*? The answer must clearly be no. This answer is based upon at least two separate bits of evidence in Plato's works. We have already discussed the first of these in reference to the refusal of Socrates, in the *Crito*, to flee Athens after his unjust conviction. Plato could not conceive of anyone, not even his revered teacher Socrates, living outside of and apart from the political community to which he belonged. The second item comes from Book VIII of *The Republic*, where Plato discusses the five major forms of government and the "souls," or personality types, corresponding to each of these.[1] Here Plato tells us in effect that the essence of the constitution of a polity determines the essence of the souls, or the character, of its citizens. Plato could not conceive of the individual human being apart from the *polis*. As Aristotle said in the next generation, only gods or beasts are outside the *polis*.[2]

CIVIC VIRTUE

In one respect, however, there is a noticeable change from Plato to Aristotle. For Plato, the good man was identical with the good citizen, at least in the good *polis*. Socrates, who in Plato's judgment was the best citizen and the best man who ever lived, met his genuinely tragic fate because Athens had degenerated. Aristotle, on the other hand, begins to distinguish between the virtue, *areté*, of the citizen and that of the human being, depending on the particular *polis* in which one lives.[3] In the good *polis* the good man is also the good citizen. Under a bad constitution a bad man, as judged by universal and immutable standards, could be a good citizen if his character were in harmony with the essence of the constitution. As mentioned in Chapter 1, it was the Cynics who completely separated the virtue of citizens of the universal city, members of the cosmopolis of the wise and the good, from the mere conventions that set standards of good and evil for any particular *polis*.

Our own contemporaries, as suggested before, tend to compartmentalize man completely. Hence they have abandoned the search for the best life, for the best constitution, and for the links that exist between the nature of a constitution and the lives of the people living under it. On the other hand, both the ancient and the modern classical theorists of politics now regarded as great in the light of hindsight because of the influence they exerted on posterity, are often dismissed as "utopians," precisely because they did set up ideals, whose universal validity they were convinced of and whose pursuit by all men they advocated.

---

[1] Plato, *The Republic*, book VIII.
[2] Aristotle, *Politics*, book I, chap. I, § 14.
[3] *Ibid.*, book III, chap. IV.

THE SEARCH
FOR THE GOOD,
AND ANALOGIES

Plato dedicated himself to the search for the best: how to find it, and how to look for road signs that point toward it. In the course of this search he employed numerous analogies, in addition to the famous one already mentioned, that between the *polis* and its components and the individual and the "parts" of his soul. In this analogy, Plato compared the three classes of his *Republic*—the guardians, the auxiliaries, and the artisans—with the three elements of the individual's soul—the rational, the passionate, and the appetitive. The use of analogies in political discussions is a technique that persists to this day. It makes no sense to oppose the use of analogies in general, because all language and all thought contain them; they are necessary, albeit containing dangerous traps, and it is important to be quite clear about the limits to analogizing and the dangers of false analogies.

One analogy used by Plato is that between the pilot of a ship and the political leader.[4] This analogy necessarily leads to very one-sided conclusions, because it ignores the crucial difference between pilot and politician. The purpose of the pilot's work is clear; he guides the ship through waters with which he is familiar to a clearly defined destination over whose selection he exercises no control. The political leader, on the other hand, is in an analogous position only if one accepts that all his subjects, or fellow citizens, want to move to the same destination and believe that only he knows the best path by which to reach that predetermined goal.

Plato uses the trick of misleading analogies throughout his writings. He likens the statesman to the physician, to the athletic coach, and to other experts. For all these experts, the goal and purpose of their activity is clearly understood—for example, good health in the case of the doctor and physical fitness in the case of the coach. What, however, is the purpose of the activity or the service performed by the political leader? And even if one could find

---

[4] *Republic*, book VI, 488.

a community in which there was total consensus on goals, there would still be less agreement on the best techniques to achieve these goals than in a community of medical scientists or experts on physical education.

Plato uses still another analogy, between the beautiful statue and the perfect *polis*.[5] He says that just as the sculptor would not want to make the eyes of the statue so beautiful that they would detract from the overall beauty of the work of art, so the builder of the *polis* would not want to pay excessive attention to any of its component parts, classes, or individuals. To any critic of this approach the differences between a lifeless statue and a living political community must be obvious. For one thing, the statue has in its sculptor a single maker. For another, the statue is meant to last forever in perfect stability, without changing, whereas change is of the very essence in politics. Also, there are certain aesthetic standards that find general acceptance at least among members of a single culture. But there is no such set of standards by which even members of a single culture, like that of the West, would agree to judging the quality of political systems.

Political science in the United States and other English-speaking countries has generally been aware of the potential traps that such misleading analogies by Plato and his intellectual descendants have set for us. However, in continental Europe, political scientists are often inclined to expect too much from their discipline. This is as true of western Europe as of the communist countries, in whose universities political science as such was not taught until the mid-1960s. Even then it was often little more than a continuation under a new label of courses formerly entitled "Marxism–Leninism."

EPISTEMOLOGY AND THE LIMITS TO KNOWLEDGE

The problem of valid and misleading analogies is related to the whole question of epistemology. The word simply means theory of

---

[5] *Ibid.*, book IV, 420.

knowledge. By discussing epistemology at the beginning of a book like this one we are reversing the sequence in which students are normally introduced to problems of method in the social sciences. This reversal is deliberate. Most readers will recall the experience of being taught things as truths at the beginning of their exposure to a new subject that, toward the end of their study were revealed to be falsehoods.[6] This seems an inefficient, uneconomical, and even somewhat dishonest way of teaching and learning.

For example, the author of this book, in the political science course that he took as a freshman in 1946, was taught that the most important thing to know about a political philosopher was his "view of human nature." This view of human nature, that is, whether man is considered basically good or basically evil, was said to determine the political philosophy. Those who believed that man's basic inclinations are toward good would necessarily end up being constitutional democrats, while those who believed that man's basic inclinations are toward evil would necessarily end up as advocates of totalitarian dictatorship. Only toward the end of his college course in political science did the author discover that no such correlation in fact exists. For instance, most of the Founding Fathers of the United States held a rather dim view of human nature, in terms of this single dichotomy, largely because of their Protestant religious background. Nevertheless, men like James Madison and Alexander Hamilton did contribute successfully to the founding of what became the largest and, until now, the most enduring constitutional democracy in history. This is a problem to which we will have occasion to return later. The point here is that the alleged simplicity of a thesis like the one about human nature and political philosophy is an inadequate excuse for using it as a pedagogical device in the instruction of newcomers to the study of politics.

In any case, the following thesis, which relates epistemology to political philosophy, is no more difficult to understand, and it has the considerable advantage of greater accuracy. The thesis is a

---

[6] "You know, I said, that we begin by telling children stories which, though not wholly destitute of truth, are in the main fictitious." *Ibid.*, book II, 377.

simple one. The most useful criterion for classifying political philosophies is how they answer the following questions:

1. Does *the* truth exist?
2. Can this truth be known?
3. Should those who know the truth run things?

Plato, with whom we began our discussion of the problem of analogies, clearly believed that the truth had existence and that it was stable, permanent, and indeed eternal. For this reason, he considered it most important that the guardians in his *Republic* could, and therefore should, be educated to apprehend *the* truth. Once the guardians "possessed" the truth, and *because* they did possess it, they must rule in order to shape what ordinary mortals consider "reality" toward the true reality of Plato's truth. Plato's belief in the independent existence of the truth also explains his numerous attacks on the so-called Sophists. This was a label he applied to those teachers of philosophy, politics, rhetoric, and other "civic" subjects whom he considered advocates of democracy or anarchy and opponents of the values which he himself espoused. These Sophists would make it possible for any man to learn whatever it was they taught in the Athenian marketplace and then to deem himself in possession of the truth. (There is considerable tragic irony in the fact that it was for just such "sophistry" that Plato's great and revered teacher Socrates was condemned to death.)

His belief in the existence of the *truth* also led Plato to assert that "being" is a higher form of reality than "becoming." He said that the truth is fixed and eternal, but exceedingly hard to get at. It consists of the connections and relations and togetherness of things.[7] The learner can move toward apprehension of the truth only through a process of dialectic. The model for this kind of dialectic, or conversation between two persons, was precisely the dialectic that took place between Socrates and his disciples, Plato among them. But there is something phony about Plato's suggestion that this kind of dialectical process will lead those who do not yet

---

[7] *Ibid.*, book VII, 531.

know the truth toward it. After all, the truth that they will finally learn is the truth that he, Plato, already possesses. Hence, the expert analogies and the analogy to the statue, which we criticized above. The pilot, the physician, and the gymnastic trainer all have their body of true knowledge. The statue, in all its accomplished beauty, is already in being. Of course, even if one were to accept these analogies uncritically, he could still object that standards of navigation, of medicine, of gymnastics, and of aesthetics do change from epoch to epoch, though Plato, because of his firm belief in the eternal existence of one truth, would have rejected this view of the "unfolding," or development, of new truths from old ones.

Our suggestion about the relation between epistemology and political philosophy is this: Those who believe that a single truth exists, in a fixed and permanent way, which can be apprehended by a few, usually end up as elitists, hierarchists, and opponents of politics. They almost *have* to reach some such conclusion, because if they were to admit the multitude of men to participation in the pursuit of their single truth, its distortion would inevitably result.

Those, on the other hand, who doubt that the truth exists, who doubt that, if the truth exists, it can be reached, or who think (as John Stuart Mill did) that men benefit from arguing even about a truth that is known, generally favor politics and the development of politics for the sake of heightening what is quintessentially human in us. Since politics can best be developed through political participation, those who follow a more skeptical theory of knowledge usually tend to be anti-elitist and anti-hierarchist.

Plato was the first great writer in the Great Conversation. (This was initiated by Socrates; however, all we know of his contribution is what we can read in the writings of his disciples, principally Plato, since Socrates himself characteristically did not write—he only talked.) This means that Plato set the categories of debate and imparted to political philosophy a strong bias in favor of his kind of epistemology. Aristotle, as we will see in the next chapter, tried vigorously to redress the balance against the single-truth-in-being and in favor of truth-through-becoming, but he succeeded only in part, in the first recorded chapter of the written dialectic. As a result, Plato's antipolitical bias has been the predominant one throughout the history of political philosophy. A bias against politics, or at least an ambivalence toward politics, is still a marked characteristic of Western man. Politics is considered either corrupt, or dirty, or the better of two evils—the other being no politics—made necessary by our permanent inability to apprehend the single truth. It is remarkable of political science among all the social sciences that this ambivalence about politics also characterizes much of the discipline. For example, economists are not nearly so ambivalent about economics or sociologists about social processes as are most political scientists about the subject matter of their discipline. The origins of this bias cannot be understood without going back to Plato, and ignorance of these origins can be a barrier to understanding both the politics and the political science of our own day.

Selected Bibliography

Plato, *The Great Dialogues*, W. H. D. Rouse, trans., Eric H. Warmington and Philip G. Rouse, eds., New York: New American Library, 1956.

Plato, *The Last Days of Socrates: Euthyphro, The Apology, Crito, Phaedo*, Hugh Tredennick, trans., Baltimore, Md.: Penguin Books, 1954.

Plato, *The Republic*, Francis M. Cornford, ed. and trans., New York: Oxford University Press, 1941.

Plato, *The Republic*, Benjamin Jowett, trans., New York: Scribner's, 1928.

Plato, *The Republic*, I. A. Richards, ed. and trans., Cambridge, Eng.: Cambridge University Press, 1966.

Plato, *Selections*, Raphael Demos, ed., New York: Scribner's, 1927.

Plato, *The Sophist and the Statesman*, A. E. Taylor, trans., Raymond Klibansky and Elizabeth Anscomb, eds., New York: Thomas Nelson, 1961.

Popper, K. R., *The Open Society and Its Enemies.* vol. 1, *The Spell of Plato*, New York: Harper & Row, 1962.

Thomson, T. L., ed., *Plato: Totalitarian or Democrat?* Englewood Cliffs, N.J.: Prentice-Hall, 1963.

It is as difficult a matter to reform an old constitution as it is to construct a new one; as hard to unlearn a lesson as it was to learn it initially. The true statesman, therefore, must not confine himself to the matters we have just mentioned: he must also be able, as we said previously, to help any existing constitution. He cannot do so unless he knows how many different kinds of constitutions there are. As things are, we find people believing that there is only one sort of democracy or oligarchy. This is an error. To avoid that error, we must keep in mind the different varieties of each constitution; we must be aware of their number, and of the number of different ways in which they are constituted.

Aristotle, *Politics*, book IV, chap. I, 7–8.

THE IMPORTANCE OF METHOD: ARISTOTLE

3

QUESTIONS AND ANSWERS

The Greek word *method* means "following after." The method we use in studying a subject matter simply consists of our approach to its problems. In political science perhaps more than in any other discipline method is of supreme importance. Nor is this a matter of "merely academic" importance or interest. Method is something of whose importance those who are responsible for day-to-day domestic and foreign policy may be, and certainly should be, aware. This is so, because our method shapes the questions we ask about the problems that we confront, and the form of our questions usually shapes the content of the answers to them. For example, during the brief war between Israel and the Arab states, in June 1967, the questions policy-makers in different countries asked made all the difference in the world for the policies pursued by their countries. These questions, whether or not they and others were aware of it, revealed their basic approaches to politics. A really orthodox communist of the Marxist-Leninist persuasion, and few of these are left among active policy-makers in the Soviet Union or other communist countries, would have asked questions about the national and international class position of the Israeli and Arab participants involved. These questions would have predetermined the answers and the policies based upon these answers. Similarly, a rigid anti-communist American ideologue in the Department of State, and there are few of these left too, would have inquired into the connections of the various politicians involved with the "international communist conspiracy," and his policy recommendations would have been preshaped by these questions. In both these extreme cases, incidentally, commitment to an epistemology that assumes the existence of a single truth would have led naturally to a pair of entirely predictable but opposed answers and policies. Our point here is that one's method, or approach, in politics as in everything else, is of supreme practical importance.

That is why Aristotle's impact upon the development of politics, philosophy, and science in the West has been tremendous and permanent. He, much more than his great teacher Plato, presented all his works within the systematic framework of a single, clearly rationalized, and relatively easily understandable method. And Aristotle's method has had a much greater and more enduring influence than the particular substantive policies that he advocated in his writings.

Aristotle's lasting influence may be considered under four headings: (1) he continued the dialectical method and tradition that Socrates, his intellectual grandfather as it were, and Plato, his immediate teacher, initiated; (2) he was the first to formulate systematically the general laws of logic, which have governed rational discussion in the West ever since; (3) he was the first to advance a systematic theory of causality; and (4) he was the one to cast those criteria by which Western man has since distinguished, with few exceptions, between that which is natural and that which is not.

DIALECTICS

Aristotle continued the Great Conversation by beginning his works, especially those on politics and ethics, by attacking his teacher Plato. Aristotle explicitly apologizes for the attack when he says that piety requires, when we must choose between what our teachers taught us and the truth, that we opt for the truth. This position, whether explicitly or implicitly, has governed the thought and writings of all honest philosophers about politics from Aristotle's time to our own. Socrates taught Plato, Plato taught Aristotle, Cicero learned from Aristotle, St. Augustine acknowledged the teachings of Cicero, St. Thomas Aquinas referred to all these predecessors and especially to Aristotle, "The Philosopher," Thomas Hobbes attacked Aquinas and the other Scholastics, and John Locke acknowledged the teachings of both Hobbes and all the others just mentioned. And so on through the ages, from Rousseau through Bentham and Mill to Marx, Lenin, and even Mao Tse-tung. All state their understanding of the positions of their predecessors, and each attacks, often vigorously and even viciously, what he dislikes and disapproves of in the previous statements about politics. But each assumes that the way toward a better understanding of the truth or truths is through this kind of dialectic. Socrates used the dialectical method in real life, but he never wrote down his thoughts; Plato used the dialectical method in his great dialogues, but he never reflected upon the dialectical method itself in a systematic fashion; and Aristotle did just that, thereby giving dialectics scholarly respectability.

ARISTOTELIAN LOGIC

Aristotle was also the first to give systematic formulation to Greek dialectical logic. This is the logic of the categorical syllogism and of the excluded middle. It has been described as an oppositional logic. Every individual in the universe must be either A or not-A, and that is that. By contrast, the non-Aristotelian logic of Oriental philosophies, Confucianism for example, does not insist upon the absolute mutual exclusiveness of opposites. Something can be both A and B at the same or at different times. It has been suggested, initially by the philosopher Immanuel Kant, that the Western constitutionalist concept of the separation of powers (into legislative, executive, and judicial) is directly related to the three parts of the Greek syllogism.[1] This important aspect of Greek logic was first

---

[1] See Carl J. Friedrich, "Some Reflections on Constitutionalism for Emergent Political Orders," in *Patterns of African Development*, Herbert J. Spiro, ed., Englewood Cliffs, N.J.: Prentice-Hall, 1967, p. 9 ff.

articulated systematically by Aristotle. Its importance can be illustrated by the fact that many non-western countries have tried in the twentieth century to construct constitutions that are explicitly based upon the separation of powers as it is included in almost all written western constitutions, beginning with that of the United States. However, where the philosophical preconditions are lacking out of which the tradition of the separation of powers has grown, as they are in all Oriental societies, this kind of superimposition is bound to be somewhat artificial and to have results different from those intended by the authors of the constitution in question. The immediate point here, however, is that Aristotle made a great impact upon the development of politics, and especially of constitutionalist politics in the West, by being the first to articulate explicitly the logical presuppositions upon which the politics of his own era was based.

THEORY OF CAUSALITY

Aristotle's most important contribution to the understanding of politics by his intellectual descendants to this day was probably his theory of causes.[2] Today, when someone is asked what caused an event, for example, what caused the outbreak of the war between Israel and the Arab states in 1967, the answer would be given in terms of the particular action that immediately triggered the event. In this case the "cause" would be given as President Nasser's demand that the United Nations troops in the Gaza Strip on the borderline between the United Arab Republic and Israel be withdrawn, and Egypt's subsequent denial of passage to ships bound for the Israeli port through the Gulf of Aqaba. Had Aristotle been asked whether this was the cause of the war, he would have answered that it might indeed have been the efficient cause. However, in addition to the efficient cause, any event or any thing also has three other causes: the material, the formal, and the final. It is true that today we sometimes use the word *cause*, in addition to the meaning that corresponds to Aristotle's efficient cause, in the sense of a final

---

[2] Aristotle, *Physics*, book II, 3.

cause. People speak of the cause for which they are fighting—in Israel's case, for example, the preservation or the expansion of that state on behalf of the values to which it is committed. This is the ground upon which one stands, or the reason one has to engage in the good fight; it is the cause to which one is dedicated, especially in great struggles. This understanding of cause corresponds roughly to Aristotle's final cause, the goal at which a thing, an event, or a movement aims—the *telos*.[3] This is the reason why Aristotle's philosophy has been called teleological.

In addition to the efficient and the final causes, Aristotle considered two others: the material cause, that is, the substance out of which an event or a thing was made, and the formal cause, that is, its essence. In the Israeli-Arab conflict of 1967, the material cause would have been the concatenation of events, boundaries, armaments, and other material and human factors that were present at the time of its outbreak. The formal cause would have been the "definition" that the parties to the conflict, direct and indirect, gave (in their understanding of contemporary reality) to their circumstances before they caused, "efficiently," the war to break out.

Each thing, and each event, thus has, in the Aristotelian view, four causes: the material, the formal, the efficient, and the final. For example, a chair has these four causes or, to put it differently, there are four ways in which, or four positions from which, to look at a chair. First, there is the actual material from which the chair is made, the wood, the nails, the cement, and so forth. Second, there is the formal cause, that is, the essence of a chair, or "chairness," the definition of a chair, which is in the minds of those who make chairs and also of those who use them. Third, there is the efficient cause, that is, the carpenter. And fourth, there is the final cause of the chair, that is, the purpose that a chair serves, presumably as something upon which one can sit.

This is basically a simple way of looking at things and at events in order to obtain knowledge about them, or in order to get at the "why" of them. Two thousand years after Aristotle, the great British philosopher David Hume said that an explanation was the point at

---

[3] "That for whose sake a thing is done." *Loc. cit.*

which the mind came to rest. Why did the Israeli–Arab War of 1967 take place? Aristotle would have answered that one view this event by asking the four questions about the material, the formal, the efficient, and the final causes. Only after answering these four questions could, in Hume's phrase, the mind come to rest. The important thing to note here is that Aristotle could not possibly have omitted the *telos*, that is, the final cause, the purpose for which a thing was made or an event took place. Aristotle always had to consider the purpose for which men acted, the reason why they lived in the *polis*. David Hume might have disregarded this purpose, and today many if not most political scientists try to free their studies of purposes or values. They try to be value-free, *wertfrei*, in the words of Max Weber, the influential German political sociologist of the early twentieth century.

There is a large school of social scientists today who, often without knowing it, are the direct heirs of Aristotle. They are the functionalists, who look at the "functions" that are performed in a social system by its various component parts. We will have occasion later on to return to them and to their indebtedness to "The Philosopher." The remarkable thing to consider here is that Aristotle, writing in the fourth century B.C., systematically examined the 157 known *poleis*, or city-states, of his area from these four complementary points of view. In his *Politics* Aristotle first looks at the population, the geography, the economic resources, and so forth, which make up any particular political community. This is the material cause. Then he asks about the form, the essence, the parts in the definition of any particular *polis*, including its constitution, or "arrangement of offices." Third, he asks who the founders were, and why and how they founded the particular *polis* under consideration. And finally, he inquires into their purposes, goals, or the *telos* that led them to establish the city-state and guided them in its governance.

NATURE AND THE NATURAL

The best way for us today to get an understanding of Aristotle is by starting with his *Physics* and next reading his *Metaphysics* before we study his *Nicomachean Ethics* and his *Politics*. In that way we can get a clear understanding of his method for the study of all phenomena, both "natural" and political or social. Today, we would expect any thinker about politics first to formulate his general or universal method, which would correspond to his natural philosophy, or his philosophy of science, before he began to apply this method to the particular study of politics. This is the logical sequence in which we in the twentieth century would read any thinker. That does not mean, however, that this was the sequence in which Aristotle would have written his works. We must remember that Aristotle was above all a *political* philosopher, and for him the most important reality was political reality. Of course, Aristotle did make a clear distinction between politics and the political system, on the one hand, and nature, that is, the environment of the *polis*, on the other. But this was a relatively novel distinction to make, as is suggested by the origins of the idea of causality itself. For primitive man, in pre-Socratic times, no difference existed between the society in which he lived and the nature in which he lived. Anthropologists tell us that primitive man saw no such distinction. Nature, that is, the fauna and flora that surrounded him, was not differentiated clearly from society, that is, the other human beings with whom he lived or with whom his own immediate community or tribe had friendly or hostile intercourse. To put it differently, primitive people saw nature as a part of society. ("Society" was used deliberately instead of "polity" in order to emphasize that primitive people were not aware of the possibilities of shaping their lives through "politics.")

In the Greek *polis*, for the first time in history, the distinction between political society and nature was systematically developed. This happened in an unintended way. To begin with, as the great classical scholar Werner Jaeger has shown in his *Paideia*, the essentially *political* idea of justice, that is, retribution and compensation, was very gradually transferred from the *polis* itself to the gods on Mount Olympus as they ran Nature, *physis*, which was in fact viewed as part of the *polis*.[4] The Greeks, and especially the Athenians, assumed that the gods should run nature in the way they

---

[4] Werner Jaeger, *Paideia: Ideals of Greek Culture*, vol. I, New York: Oxford University Press, 1944, p. 161.

themselves, as citizens of the *polis*, ran their own affairs. The *polis* tried to achieve justice; therefore the gods *ought* to try to achieve justice in the world at large. From this view, it was only one step toward assuming, as the Stoics did, that nature and the universe, *physis* and *cosmos*, operated according to eternal, immutable, necessary, and rational laws. "Naturally," human laws should reflect the highest reason that was imbedded in the universe and in nature. This later became the ideal of the Roman Law: Law is the highest reason imbedded in nature.

For the Stoics it meant that the individual should bring himself into harmony with the cosmic "jive," as it were, according to a famous Stoic dictum, *volentem fata ducunt, nolentem trahunt*, "him who is willing, the fates guide; him who resists, the fates drag along." In the Stoics' view, life consisted of eternally repetitive cosmic cycles. Each cycle would end in a great world conflagration, whereupon a new cycle would begin to end in another conflagration; they were eternally repeated spirals within one great never-ending circle.

Christianity gave a unilineal direction to this circular vision of history, by introducing the notion of eschatology, or a divinely willed course and outcome for the history of man. But, whereas both the Greeks and the Roman Stoics saw all of nature and society governed by the same set of general laws, Christianity confused the notion of causality by introducing the concept of "free will" for human beings alone but *not* for the rest of nature. In this way, Christian thought sought to explain the existence of evil in a world governed by an omnipotent and benevolent God.

The moderns, starting in the seventeenth century, began to distinguish between prescriptive and descriptive natural law. For the classical Greeks they were one and the same thing. The gods told men how they *ought* to behave, and this at the same time told men how they and the rest of nature in fact *did* behave. Descriptive laws had to conform to prescriptive ones. In the Middle Ages descriptive laws were ignored for the sake of the prescriptive laws of Christianity, while theology, not politics, was the master science. But with the Enlightenment, in the eighteenth century, a new distinction between prescriptive and descriptive natural law was introduced. Now society was seen as a part of nature, which is governed by necessary "laws." Some of the philosophers were mechanistic and saw nature as analogous to the machine. Others were organicists and saw nature as analogous to the body. Today some are cyberneticists, and see nature and the political system as analogous to a communications system. The best contemporary political and other social scientists have taken necessity out of the descriptive "laws" of society and politics and have substituted probability for it. They try to understand society and politics in terms of the probable generalizations that result from the observation of reality, just as natural scientists also try to understand the rest, the non-social parts, of nature in terms of probability. This, however, leaves a great deal upon which human beings can act, through politics. Men can act upon both their political and social environments, and their natural environment, only after they understand the "why" of things. For politics, in the Aristotelian sense as the master science, they must understand the why's of political processes in order to be able to act upon these processes to effect their intended results. The achievement of this kind of understanding is the purpose, the *telos*, of political science.

But how do we gain this kind of understanding of politics as the most encompassing activity of men in society and nature? That is the basic and central question to which political science addresses itself. And Aristotle's answer to it constitutes another major methodological contribution of permanent validity—a contribution often ignored today by the so-called "behavioralists" or "quantitativists" in the discipline. These important "schools" within political science sometimes attempt to reduce everything to objectively quantifiable figures. Attitude surveys, voting statistics, quantifiable correlations, and the like are their chief tools. It is worthwhile at this point in our study of the Great Conversation to quote Aristotle's warning, issued two and a half millennia ago, but as valid today as in the fourth century B.C.:

> We must be content, then, in speaking of such subjects and with such premises to indicate the truth *roughly* and *in outline*, in speaking about things which are only for the most part true and with premises of the same kind to reach conclusions that are no better. In the same spirit, therefore, should each type of statement

be received; for it is the mark of an educated man to look for precision in each class of things just so far as the nature of the subject admits; it is evidently equally foolish to accept *probable* reasoning from a mathematician and to demand from a rhetorician scientific proofs.[5]

ARISTOTLE AND THE FORMS OF GOVERNMENT

Aristotle's enormous methodological impact has been general and by no means confined to political science, but his influence upon later political science has been ineradicable. His influence has been much greater than Plato's, largely because Aristotle was much more comprehensive and much more systematic than Plato. (This may also explain why Aristotle is generally considered much duller to read than Plato.) Aristotle was, in a sense, totally comprehensive and exhaustive; he dealt with everything and anticipated most that could have been anticipated, leaving little for his successors to do, or at least so it seemed for many centuries.

For example, Aristotle, virtually for all times, provided a classification of the forms of government. His classification was very similar to Plato's, but Aristotle put forward systematic criteria of classification, and therefore he appears more scholarly and has been more influential than his master. Aristotle's criteria included the number who ruled, their class, and the question of equality. But the most important criterion was the answer to this question: In whose interest and for whose good do they rule? Under the right, good forms of government, rule is in the common interest. Under the wrong, bad forms of government, rule is in the self-interest of the rulers. The right forms of government, therefore, are monarchy, aristocracy, and polity (roughly the equivalent of republican constitutionalism). The wrong forms of government are tyranny, oligarchy, and democracy.

Today, with minor exceptions, the same terms are still being used to describe different forms of political systems. The only in-

---

[5] Aristotle, *Nicomachean Ethics*, book I, 3. Italics supplied.

teresting additions to the classificatory scheme first advanced by
Aristotle over two thousand years ago are the categories of "totalitarianism" and "development." Totalitarianism is a term used to
describe "total" dictatorship, that is, a special form of *tyranny*, to use
one of Aristotle's terms. Development, on the other hand, is nowadays usually applied when the standard fixed categories of Aristotle
do not seem to fit. Actually, development was something, namely
"becoming," with which Aristotle was very much concerned. This
was due to his teleological orientation and his search for the causes
of stability and, therefore, also of political change. There is considerable irony in the fact that Aristotle called Europe, that is,
Europe north of Greece, "underdeveloped."[6] In his search for the
"causes" of change, in any direction, Aristotle gave advice to politicians, including tyrants, that does not differ substantially from that
offered seventeen centuries later by the Florentine Machiavelli.[7]
Aristotle asserts that "sedition" is always due to inequality, and
thereby he guided the way to some very modern explanations of
the great revolutions, including the French, the Russian, and the
Chinese.

Aristotle also addressed himself to the question of the prerequisites of stability. In contemporary parlance, he was asking
about the conditions that would facilitate constitutional democracy
or, in his own terms, the existence of a true "polity." Aristotle
asserted that what was needed above all was a strong middle class.[8]
In the United States today this is the prevailing view: American
constitutional democracy has been made possible above all by the
predominance in American politics, from the time of the War of
Independence, of the great American middle class. Beginning with
the Founding Fathers, many Americans have sought to explain the
success of politics in the United States, and of the United States
in the world at large, by way of the presumed predominance within
American politics of the "middle class."

Aristotle also identified in an inestimably influential way what

---

6 Aristotle, *Politics*, book VII, chap. VII, § 2.
7 *Ibid.*, book V.
8 *Ibid.*, book IV, chap. XI, § 8.

he considered the basic processes of politics. Here he made a paramount distinction between ruling and being ruled. He did not yet
distinguish, as some of his analysts have asserted, between the legislative, executive, and judicial functions.[9] However, Aristotle did
make a relatively clear distinction between the *formulation* of issues
(he refers to it as the initiation of deliberation), the deliberation
of issues, and the resolution of issues, as well as the relation between
resolution and "will."[10] Aristotle accepted the supreme importance
of deliberation in politics, the persuasiveness of deliberation, and
the possibility that deliberation be left permanently incomplete.

However, Aristotle's understanding and categorization of politics
was so comprehensive and so brilliant that its overall impact often
turned out to be stifling. It is ironic and perhaps tragic that this
comprehensiveness and brilliance prevented the innovation in thinking about politics that Aristotle himself expected. It was, after all,
Aristotle who wrote in his *Politics*: "Necessity itself, we may reason-
ably suppose, will steadily be the mother of indispensable inventions;
on that basis, and with *these* once provided, we may fairly expect
that inventions which make for the adornment and graces of life
will also steadily develop; and this general rule must be held to be
true in politics as well as in other spheres."[11] As has happened so
frequently in the history of thought, the disciples of great teachers
stagnate because they live by false analogies. It is for this reason
that we must now turn to a critique of the impact of Aristotle's
political philosophy, without, of course, in any way blaming Aristotle
himself for the way in which his ideas have been both understood
and misunderstood.

CRITIQUE OF ARISTOTLE'S IMPACT

For political science itself, probably nothing had so great an
impact as the scheme for the classification of forms of government
that Aristotle advanced. He distinguished between the three good

---

[9] *Ibid.*, book IV, chap. XIV.
[10] *Ibid.*, book VI, chap. VIII, § 17, 21; and book III, chap. XI.
[11] *Ibid.*, book VII, chap. X, § 7.

forms of government, monarchy, aristocracy, and what he called polity, or the mixed constitution, and the three bad forms of government, their perversions, tyranny, oligarchy, and democracy. Aristotle inherited these categories from Plato, but because, as usual, he advanced the scheme in a much more systematic fashion, it was his formulation that has exerted great influence through the ages to our own day. The basis for the scheme was the answer, in each case, to the question: In whose interest do the rulers rule? This makes it easy to understand why Aristotle preferred a political system governed by a predominant middle class. A middle class was more likely to govern in the "general interest" than either a large lower class or a small upper class. However, the preference cannot be understood unless one takes into account the unquestioned assumption of both Aristotle and Plato, and their contemporaries in classical Greece, about the primacy of politics. Hence the misunderstandings and distortions that result when students of the success of American politics, and also American politicians and political thinkers, transfer Aristotle's preference for the middle class polity to the United States. Instead of sharing the Aristotelian assumption of the primacy of politics, most of these Americans asserted the primacy of economics. As a result, the analogy between the Aristotelian middle class polity and the role of the middle class played in American politics since the Revolution leads to false analyses and to policies that have quite un-Aristotelian results. Similarly, some neo-Aristotelian analyses of politics in the so-called developing countries insist that stability cannot be obtained in these countries unless there is first a sound middle class. It is argued that the middle class alone will provide the economic foundation upon which democratic and constitutional politics must be based. If politics begins to develop before this economic foundation has been laid, the neo-Aristotelians accuse the leaders of the developing countries of irresponsibility: You cannot yet afford democratic politics, they say to them. While Aristotle might have agreed that these "barbarians"[1] were incapable of constitutionalism we must remember that Aristotle considered those northern Europeans, who today have highly developed political systems, also barbarians. He was so firmly committed to the assumption of the primacy of politics that he could never have accepted arguments that proceed from the contrary assumption about the primacy of economics.

Aristotle's commitment to the primacy of politics meant, among other things, that political science must be committed to certain values and that the individual political scientist is above all the advocate and creator of values. Today, on the contrary, much of political science tries to be value-free. This is alleged to be, quite mistakenly, a condition of being "scientific." We will return to this point later on. But a value-free political science is unlikely to ask the only questions that really mattered to Aristotle, his immediate forerunners, and his successors through the ages to the twentieth century, with its frequently misunderstood or misapplied scientism. For Aristotle the following were among the most important questions: What is the highest good? What is the good life? What is the best *polis*? Who is the good citizen? What is the relation between the good citizen and the good *polis*? But when political scientists who claim to be value-free apply concepts that were first forged in an age as value-laden as Aristotle's to the study of contemporary politics, then grave distortions are bound to result. This is true especially of the Aristotelian scheme for the classification of forms of government, not only because it is based upon Aristotelian values, but also because it fails to point out some of the most significant differences among political systems today. This scheme leads those who employ it to put into the same class political phenomena that are in fact quite different from one another.

Aristotle's impact has been similarly unfortunate when it comes to the study of the causes of change and the prerequisites of political stability. It leads one to overlook his basic commitment to politics and his opposition to the kind of homogeneity and internal unity that American advocates of the middle class polity usually put forward as its chief advantage, but which Aristotle precisely attacked in his critique of Plato's *Republic* and the latter's analogy between the *polis* and the beautiful statue.[12] Aristotle opposed homogeneity within the *polis*, because he favored politics and its development. Politics to him meant the development of issues and their discussion, rather than total agreement within the community. Only through

---

[12] *Ibid.*, book II, chap. II, § 2.

the generation and discussion of realistic issues limited by a good constitution could change be kept within limits that would prevent revolution, thereby insuring stability. Most contemporary advocates of the middle class polity, however, prefer consensus to the growth and development of politics, and therefore differ fundamentally from Aristotle in his commitment to politics and in his preference for diversity over homogeneity. This is revealed by another Aristotelian peculiarity that contemporary advocates of the virtues of the middle class generally overlook. According to Aristotle the good life required leisure. He persistently denigrated all those instrumental activities which engage most members of today's middle class a great deal of the time. This is of course the exact reverse of the attitude of most contemporary Americans. The kind of genuine leisure that the institution of slavery made possible in ancient Athens for a very limited proportion of the population would be denigrated by most Americans as useless and unproductive. Here again, latter-day Aristotelians are led into traps camouflaged by false analogies.

The Greek aristocratic ideal, as transmitted by Aristotle and other classical writers, did, however, have a great impact on Europe, and especially on Great Britain in the period leading up to and culminating in the nineteenth century. Great Britain was believed by outsiders and by the British themselves to have a mixed constitution on the model of Aristotle's polity. The British governing class enjoyed the kind of leisure that Aristotle considered a prerequisite of political stability, though in their case this was derived not from slavery, but from the fruits of the Industrial Revolution, a large industrial proletariat, and the yields of a vast colonial empire. The British differed from the continental Europeans in that they never accepted any political theory in a dogmatic fashion. Although the French political scientist Montesquieu thought he had discovered the separation of powers in the English constitution, British politicians in fact never recognized either the theory of the separation of powers or of functions, nor did they act on the assumption of the separability of the performance of these functions. On the contrary, they always accepted the supreme importance of deliberation, its pervasiveness throughout the political process, and its potential permanent incompleteness. In this respect there is an affinity between Aristotelian theory and British practice, because Aristotle distinguished between the initiation of deliberation, what we have called the formulation of issues, deliberation itself, and the resolution of issues in its relation to "will." And Aristotle like the British, but unlike the continental Europeans and the United States in its constitution, viewed the political process as an ever ongoing one, not as a mechanically compartmentalized succession of legislation, execution, and adjudication.

The British in practice also recognized Aristotle's distinction between constitution, *politeia*, laws, *nomoi*, and ordinary day-to-day policy, *psephismata*.[13] The distinction made by Oliver Cromwell between "fundamentals" and "circumstantials," though somewhat less refined than Aristotle's, moves in the same direction of trying to preserve more or less permanently the rules of the political game, while at the same time recognizing the more ephemeral character of ordinary legislation meant to meet the circumstances of a particular time. But then, the British did not have to worry about maintaining the fundamentals of their constitution, changing the circumstantials of their legislation, or seeing to it that circumstantials and fundamentals were not confused with one another, because the British did not suffer from any major constitutional revolutions of the kind that both the United States and France experienced in the last quarter of the eighteenth century. On the continent, on the other hand, revolutions occurred with increasing frequency after the great French Revolution. The distinction between fundamentals and circumstantials should have been maintained, but it was probably impossible to maintain it.

Selected Bibliography

Aquinas, St. Thomas, *Treatise on Law*, Stanley Parry, ed., Chicago: Gateway Editions, 1965.

Aquinas, St. Thomas, *Treatise on Law, On Truth and Falsity, On*

---

[13] Ernest Barker, ed., *The Politics of Aristotle*, New York: Galaxy, 1962, pp. 128, 168.

Human Knowledge, Stanley Parry, ed., Chicago: Gateway Editions, 1949.

Aristotle, *Constitution of Athens and Related Texts*, Kurt von Fritz and Ernst Kapp, trans. and eds., New York: Hafner, 1950.

Aristotle, *The Ethics of Aristotle*, J. A. K. Thomson, trans., Baltimore, Md.: Penguin Books, 1953.

Aristotle, *The Politics*, Sir Ernest Barker, trans. and ed., New York: Galaxy Books, 1962.

Aristotle, *The Politics*, T. A. Sinclair, trans., Baltimore, Md.: Penguin Books, 1962.

Bendix, Reinhard, *Max Weber: An Intellectual Portrait*, Garden City: Doubleday, 1960.

Charlesworth, James C., ed., *Contemporary Political Analysis*, New York: The Free Press, 1967.

Charlesworth, James C., ed., *A Design for Political Science: Scope, Objectives, and Method*, Philadelphia: The American Academy of Political and Social Science, December 1966.

Deutsch, Karl W., *The Nerves of Government: Models of Political Communication and Control*, New York: The Free Press, 1966.

Jaeger, Werner, *Paideia: Ideals of Greek Culture*, 3 vols., New York: Oxford University Press, 1944–1948.

Kaplan, Justin D., ed., Kurt von Fritz and Ernst Kapp, trans., *The Pocket Aristotle*, New York: Washington Square Press, 1958.

Lipset, S. M., *The First New Nation: The United States in Historical and Comparative Perspective*, New York: Basic Books, 1963.

Montesquieu, Charles Louis de S., *The Spirit of the Laws*, Introduction by Franz Neumann, New York: Hafner, 1949.

S cience *is the knowledge of consequences and dependence of one fact upon another: by which, out of what we can presently do, we know how to do something else when we will, or the like another time; because when we see how any thing comes about, upon what causes, and by what manner; when the like causes come into our power, we see how to make it produce the like effects.*

. . .

Causes of absurdity. *1. The first cause of absurd conclusions I ascribe to the want of method; in that they begin not their ratiocination from definitions; that is, from settled significations of their words: as if they could cast account, without knowing the value of the numeral words,* one, two, *and* three.

Thomas Hobbes,
"Of Reason and Science,"
in *Leviathan* (1651), chap. 5.

BASIC
POLITICS

4

THE OBSOLESCENCE OF CONCEPTS

Since the end of World War II, a great deal of constitution building has taken place in the world. With increasing frequency, so-called "new nations" have given themselves constitutions, often said to be modelled explicitly upon constitutions of more successful developed countries. Very few if any of these new constitutions achieved the purposes for which they were designed. Often they did not outlast the calendar year in which they were introduced, or the leaders who introduced them. These new constitutions, for whose design Western constitutional experts and other political scientists were often consulted, were sometimes literally not worth the paper on which they were printed. But this worthlessness of constitutions was not confined to the new nations or the "developing areas." Complaints about the inefficacy of the constitution were voiced also in an old nation like the France of the Fourth Republic (1945 to 1958). Spain and Greece and Belgium suffered constitutional crises at various times during the post-war period. The United States came close to a constitutional crisis in the election of 1968. And some students attributed many of the most serious difficulties of the United Nations to faults in its constitutional design, or at least to the unwillingness of some of its members to abide by the constitutional provisions of its Charter. As the twentieth century moves toward its last quarter, the need for intelligently designed and realistically practicable constitutions increases from year to year. But the principles, and the discipline providing the principles, that is, political science, upon which sound constitutional design could be based seem to be making inadequate progress toward filling this need.

The reasons are very obvious. Before constitutional design can achieve its purposes in each case, there must be not only clarity about these purposes but also a capacity to explain differences among political systems that have existed in the past and among those that exist in the present. For example, why were the responses of two otherwise very similar countries, like the United States and Canada, to perceived threats of internal communist subversion in the 1950s and to Communist China in the 1960s as different as they were? Why did Germany have its Hitler, while France, which also suffered from the aftermath of World War I and the ravages of the Great Depression in the late 1920s and early 1930s, did not? Why has postwar, post-fascist politics in West Germany been so much more successful than in Italy? Why have politics in India and Pakistan, formerly components of the same British colony, developed along such very different lines since independence? Clearly, before we can explain differences, we must be able to compare the phenomena that we wish to explain. And we can make sound comparisons only if we have categories, terms, words, and concepts with which to describe these phenomena. For instance, we cannot explain the differences between the behavior of men and monkeys, except perhaps intuitively, unless we have words with which to describe the differential behavior of these two species.

The trouble with political science, which was reflected in efforts to design new constitutions or to redesign old ones, was the poverty of its concepts. (The German word for "concept" is *Begriff*, which is derived from *Griff* which means, literally, "handle," like the handle of a suitcase. Concepts are the handles with which we pick up or grasp the reality in which we exist.) The conceptual tool-kit of political science in the period at the end of World War II still stood heavily under the persistent influence of Aristotle's impact upon the discipline, an impact more than two thousand years old. But the attempt to understand political realities in 1945 or 1950 in terms of the Aristotelian classification of forms of government would have yielded inadequate descriptions, misleading comparisons, and false explanations. Aristotle's criteria of classification were, it will be recalled, the number of those who rule and hold power, and whether they rule in behalf of the public interest or in their own selfish interest. On the basis of these two criteria, he arrived at his six-fold classification: monarchy and tyranny, aristocracy and oligarchy, polity and democracy.

But if one had looked at postwar European politics between 1945 and 1950 using Aristotle's categories, one would have found that each of these terms covered a multitude of sins. For example, there were the apparently "good" monarchies, like Great Britain, the Netherlands, Denmark, Sweden, and Norway. And then there were the questionable monarchies, like Belgium, whose King Leopold had collaborated somewhat with the German occupation forces in his country, or Greece, whose bitter civil war had eroded what little loyalty to the institutions of constitutional monarchy and the particular dynasty may have existed before the war, and whose young King fled his country in 1967, to be replaced by a military junta. In the Middle East, King Farouk of Egypt, who was once uncharitably described by *Esquire* magazine as "the ultimate in royal slobs," performed in a fashion that would have made it difficult for a neo-Aristotelian to classify him either as a king or as a tyrant. Perhaps only in Ethiopia did the Emperor Haile Selassie, who claimed direct descent from the Queen of Sheba and King David, rule in a royal way that could have been described and comprehended in terms of the Aristotelian scheme. But that scheme of classification would not have helped in comparing or explaining differences between, say, Ethiopia and Egypt, or Greece and Denmark (whose royal families were closely related).

The same is true with the tyrannies, or, in contemporary parlance, the dictatorships. After the overthrow of Hitler's and Mussolini's fascist dictatorships at the end of World War II, there were still many regimes left in Europe and the rest of the world that were so described. Foremost among them was the Soviet Union under Josef Stalin. But there were also, among others, the regimes of

Dr. Salazar in Portugal and Generalissimo Franco in Spain. Franco, incidentally, gave Spain a constitution that reestablished it as a monarchy, although he left unsettled for more than two decades, until 1969, the question of the identity of the monarch who was to sit on the throne. Although it had a constitution, Spain was clearly not a constitutional polity in the Aristotelian or indeed any other sense. Spain was a monarchy according to its formal constitution, yet its ruler did not hesitate upon occasion to describe himself as a benevolent dictator. A small upper class, which for a time consisted of a coalition among the monarchy, the fascist Falange, the Roman Catholic Church, and the wealthy landed aristocracy, supported the Generalissimo's rule. Did this make Spain more of an oligarchy than a dictatorship? The point here is that even a satisfactory answer to this question of description would not help in comparing Spain with other more or less similar political systems, nor would it facilitate explanation of the peculiarities of Spain's political development.

A similar difficulty is inherent in Aristotle's concept of oligarchy, especially in the epoch that has been heavily influenced by the thought of Karl Marx and his intellectual descendants. Many Marxists assert that all capitalist societies, regardless of their constitutional facade, are dictatorships of the bourgeoisie, which is, by definition, a minority of the total population. Any class that owns the instruments of production necessarily rules and exploits the class that owns nothing but its own labor power. For the Marxist it makes no difference in principle whether the constitution of a bourgeois capitalist society provides for universal suffrage, for equality of all before the law, and for the accountability of elected and appointed officials, the bureaucracy, and the military to a representative parliament. He would still describe the system as a dictatorship of the bourgeois minority and, therefore, to apply Aristotelian terms, as an oligarchy. On the other hand, and here there is a certain congruence between the ideas of Marx and those of Aristotle, Marxists assert that a minority, but a new and different one, rules *after* the revolution and until the establishment of full communism. This minority is the vanguard of the proletariat, that is, the communist party. The new ruling class now is the majority class, the proletariat, or working class. Since this class is as yet incapable of exercising rule, its vanguard, the most advanced and progressive section of the working class (which may, paradoxically, consist of nonworkers, for example, intellectuals) must provide leadership. In other, Aristotelian, words, Marxists might describe the rule of the communist party after the socialist revolution as an aristocracy, because here a minority is said to govern in the general interest. Again, however, these categories of description, whether Aristotelian or Marxian, are of little use in getting at the important differences between various contemporary political systems, whether they exist in the communist countries, in capitalist countries, or in those of a different persuasion. The inadequacy of this vocabulary of political science is revealed whenever scholars comment upon certain apparent similarities between the Soviet Union and the United States. These resemblances surprise them, because they are discovered in two political systems whose leaders constantly proclaim not only their opposition to one another but also their fundamentally different and antagonistic goals, structures, and operating procedures. However, in both the United States and the Soviet Union managerial elites play very important roles, and in both the evaluation of individuals tends to be based upon their capacity to produce. There are other similarities. Since both the specialist and the layman intuitively sense significant differences between the two most powerful states on earth, we may conclude that efforts to understand each of them and to explain differences between the two by means of either the Aristotelian or the Marxian vocabulary of politics are doomed to failure: These vocabularies cannot isolate the significant similarities and differences.

This brings us to the last pair of Aristotle's types of government, polity and democracy. Polity was a mixed form, whereas democracy came closer to what Plato described as "mobocracy," that is, a *polis* in which the mob rules in its own interest, not in the interest of the *polis* as a whole. In the study and categorization of what Aristotle called *polity* considerable progress has been made. Aristotle could have little objection to the contemporary tendency to call the mixed form of government "constitutional democracy." Western political systems at the end of World War II either were or aspired to be constitutional democracies. Constitutional democracy has been described by Professor Carl J. Friedrich as a system of regularized restraints upon the wielders of power.[1] Constitutional democracy in this sense has taken on a variety of forms. Much has been made of the distinction and the differences between the cabinet-parliamentary form that is found, for example, in Great Britain, and the presidential-congressional form, of which the United States is the prototype. Again, there are federal systems, like those of the United States, the Federal Republic of Germany, or Switzerland, and more unitary systems, like those of France, the United Kingdom, or Sweden. There are also many different systems of representation, through which the *democratic* part of constitutional democracy is made possible.

A relatively refined vocabulary has been developed by political scientists in order to enable them to describe such differences among political systems that are considered constitutional democracies. However, these refinements still seem inadequate for at least two reasons. In the first place, the words of this vocabulary still lead one to pay excessive attention to the formal, legal, constitutional provisions, and not enough attention to the actual realities of politics. This difficulty is similar to the one mentioned above, in which apparent resemblances between the United States and the Soviet Union came as a surprise. In the present case, a similar surprise can arise when one finds that British and American politics do not differ from one another in ways that one would be led to expect by the formal, constitutional differences between cabinet-parliamentary government and presidential-congressional government. And in the second place, there is a very real, nonacademic inadequacy in the more refined vocabulary with which contemporary constitutional democracies have been described. This results from the fact that the policy maker, as distinguished from the academic student, is not really helped very much in his purposes, when he is told, for example, that West Germany under Chancellor Adenauer was a federal system, whereas France under President DeGaulle was a unitary system. This distinction may either not tell him enough about the process by which policy, including foreign policy, is made, or it

---

[1] *Constitutional Government and Democracy*, 2nd ed., Boston: Ginn, 1950, p. 26 and *passim*.

may tell him the wrong things and mislead him into expecting events that will not actually happen. In other words, for purposes of both retrospective explanation *and* prospective forecasting, the conventional Aristotelian conceptual vocabulary, as well as more recent refinements of it, are inadequate.

FACTORS OF CAUSATION

Such dissatisfaction should have led scholars and others toward attempts to improve the tools with which they do their work, and this has often been the result. On the other hand, and perhaps more frequently, the consequence has been a reaction to the excessive and severely disappointed optimism about the feasibility of constitutional engineering. This excessive reaction has gone to the other extreme, in which the basic assumption is that man can accomplish nothing through politics, and that it is impossible to achieve one's intended purposes through the design of political institutions. Those who hold this view generally tend to explain the great disasters of the twentieth century in *non*political terms. World wars, economic depressions, massive unemployment, inflation, the forced migrations of populations numbering in the millions, the slaughter in concentration camps of other millions, and the threatened extermination of whole nations or even of all humanity—all this is being explained in terms of nonpolitical factors. Such explanations are offered especially to account for the kinds of differences between political systems that were previously mentioned: the Soviet Union and the United States, the United Kingdom and the United States, France and Germany, Pakistan and India, the League of Nations and the United Nations, and so forth.

The factors that are used for purposes of explanation—sometimes a single factor, sometimes a combination of them—cover a great variety of phenomena. There are, for example, the rigidly deterministic explanations that rely upon geography. According to these explanations, what happens in the domestic and foreign politics of a country depends entirely upon its geographical situation. Then there are the often similarly deterministic explanations that rely upon the factor of "national character." The French do things in

their way simply because they are French and because their national character has been formed by centuries of common experience. Similarly, the Germans do things their way because they are
Germans. These theories sometimes have a strongly racist bias, in
that they suggest that there is some underlying biological foundation
of Frenchness or Germanness.

Next, there are closely related cultural explanations of political
events. Some of these, for example, rely upon the structure of the
family in different countries and the shape that child rearing within
the family gives to people's attitudes. Again, there are sociological
explanations of differences between political systems, which may
focus, for instance, upon changes in social structure or in the demography of a society, and which attribute all other changes to these
allegedly more basic factors. In the United States, economic theories
have perhaps been most popular. According to such explanations,
American politics has generally been relatively successful, because
the United States is a rich country that could afford the luxury of
democracy. The Germans, on the other hand, had to resort to Hitler's
brutal rule because they had passed through the debilitating disasters of defeat in World War I, the Great Inflation in the mid-
1920s, and then the Great Depression with its accompanying mass
unemployment starting in 1929. The Fourth French Republic failed,
according to this view, because of France's failing economy in the
period between 1945 and 1958, whereas the Fifth French Republic
was successful because of the improvement in France's economy
between 1958 and 1967. There are also combinations of all or most
of these deterministic and nonpolitical explanations. For example,
one respected scholar explained Hitler's rise and his popularity with
a majority of German voters at the time of his coming to power in
1933 by asserting that the German people at that time suffered from
a castration complex, itself explained by the fact that they had
experienced so many psychologically emasculating disasters, including the ones just mentioned. They turned to Hitler because they
saw in him a phallic symbol!

This kind of explanation of political events recalls Book VIII
of Plato's *Republic*, where he describes the personality type that goes
with each type of *polis*, in the course of the degeneration of the city

from the best to the worst form of government. Similarly, some contemporary students of politics and society see a connection between
the predominant personality type and the form of government. But
there is a major difference between Plato's causal sequences and
those assumed by our contemporaries, in that today the personality
type, or the psychological predispositions of a population, or the
family and child-rearing patterns, or the social structure, or the economic determinants, is believed to be the *prime* cause, or independent variable, whereas for Plato the personality of the individual
was shaped by the political community of which he was a member.
For example, Plato tells us, in effect, that the "democratic man" has
no respect for his elders and is discourteous and unmannerly, and
that in a democracy even donkeys often take precedence on the
sidewalks over citizens, *because* this is the general atmosphere of a
democracy.[2] On the other hand, contemporary deterministic theorists
tell us that it was the psychology of the German "man in the street"
that brought about Hitler's rise to power, his initiation of World
War II, and all the other disasters that followed. For Plato, politics
shaped all other aspects of human existence. For many contemporary
students, *non*political factors determine political phenomena, which
are therefore regarded as merely dependent variables, or secondary
or tertiary phenomena in the chain of causation.

But here we must ask again whether either Plato's approach,
with its unquestioned assumption of the primacy of politics, or the
contemporary deterministic approaches, with their deliberate relegation of politics to relative insignificance, is adequate for purposes of
description, comparison, and the explanation of differences. The
answer in both cases must be no. Plato's approach, like Aristotle's
concepts, is inadequate, in part because human existence and men's
consciousness of their existence are much more highly differentiated
today than they were when political science was founded. The
approaches of the deterministic and largely antipolitical theorists of
today are inadequate, on the other hand, because they fail to consider man's more highly developed consciousness of his capacity to
shape his future through politics. This consciousness, and the self-

---

[2] Plato, *The Republic*, book VIII, 563.

confidence that it often inspires in man, may be illusory. But even *if* only geography, or only culture, or only social structure, or only economic and psychological factors did matter, then description, the first stage of scholarship, would still call for categories that enable us to describe the differences between societies in their attitudes toward politics and toward the capabilities of politics.

There is another way to point out the need for better approaches to the study of politics than those conventionally in use today. Political science, as all science and indeed all scholarship, is comparative. Explanations of differences, as well as predictions, are possible only on the basis of comparison. In the study of politics one can either compare different political systems or the same political system at different points in time. For example, in trying to get some idea about the development of politics in the United States, scholars and politicians in 1950 might have compared American politics at that time with American politics in 1900, and then they might have tried to project certain discernible trends into the future. Had they used an essentially Aristotelian approach, they probably would have emphasized certain changes in the relative importance of the "branches" of the federal government and between the federal government and the states. Had they used a combination of the various deterministic approaches, they would have emphasized trends toward economic concentration, the growth of large national interest groups or, as David Riesman has called them, "veto groups," and perhaps, with C. Wright Mills, the emergence of a "power elite."[3]

Neither of these approaches, nor some combination of them, would have been likely, in 1950, to have forecasted the central importance of racial conflict in American domestic and international politics of the succeeding two decades. And even if the forecast had made allowance for the crucial significance of the racial issue, it probably would have said little about the manner in which this issue was to be dealt with by the American political system. While it might have told us something about the respective roles to be played

---

[3] David Riesman *et al., The Lonely Crowd: A Study of the Changing American Character,* New York: Anchor Books, 1951; and C. Wright Mills, *The Power Elite,* New York: Oxford University Press, 1956.

by the executive, the legislature, and the judiciary, and perhaps even by interest groups that existed in 1950, like the NAACP, what would it have told us about the peaceful or violent character of the conflict? What could it have told us about new groups that were to be created during the next decade and a half, like CORE or SNCC or RAM or the Black Panthers or SDS? Such an approach could not, of course, have anticipated the war in Vietnam—no approach could have produced precise substantive predictions of this kind of political event. However, none of the conventional approaches was likely to have anticipated the possibility of changes in human consciousness and the political and nonpolitical consequences of these changes. And even if one had foretold the spread of the belief that men can improve the condition of their lives through politics, and only or at least mainly through politics, the forecast would have lacked the vocabulary by means of which to describe differences in the political process, in one political system over time, or between several political systems. In order to overcome these deficiencies, the need for more comprehensive, more systematic, and more nearly universally applicable approaches to the study of politics was recognized. The following section is one response to that need.

POLITICAL STYLE[4]

Politics is the process by which a human community, as small as two persons or as large as the community of mankind, deals with its problems. Politics occurs whenever two or more individuals are aware that they face problems together and try to do something about solving these problems, regardless of whether they do it in cooperation or in conflict. The political process begins with the recognition of problems. Problems are obstacles between the present condition of men and some goal they are pursuing. But the recognition of a problem itself does not yet give rise to politics, since there

---

[4] Adapted from Spiro, "Comparative Politics: A Comprehensive Approach," *American Political Science Review*, vol. 56, no. 3 (September 1962), pp. 577–595.

may be unanimous agreement on what to do about the problem, and for politics to begin, there must be disagreement, that is, *issues* must be formulated. The *formulation* of issues is the first phase of the political process. In a healthy political system this is followed by the *deliberation* of issues, that is, the weighing of alternatives. Deliberation of issues in turn normally leads to their *resolution*, that is, the selection of one of various alternatives that had been weighed for action. This finally, again in a healthy system, leads to the *solution* of the problem that was originally recognized for political processing. The sequence given here for the "flow of policy," or the political process, is not the one invariably followed in all political systems, or in any one political system with respect to all its problems. Nor does each of the four phases always receive the same degree of attention. As we will see later in the study of particular political systems, sometimes poorly formulated issues are interminably deliberated upon, in a process that leads to no resolution and does not result in the solution of the problems that originally gave rise to the issues. Other systems seem to solve successfully those problems that are the chief concern of a small governing group, but that do not interest or involve or permit the political participation of the rest of the population. Some systems have a high incidence of issues, that is, they have a large volume of politics, whereas others have very little politics. However, all political systems, no matter what their size or their location in history, process issues. They do so in a variety of sequences and with differences in attention paid and energy devoted to the four phases of the flow of policy.

All political systems also have in common their varied pursuit of the four basic goals of politics: *stability*, *flexibility*, *efficiency*, and *effectiveness*. Unless the community that is processing issues has some endurance over time, it cannot be considered a system, or at least only to the limit of its endurance. Unless a system adjusts more or less flexibly to changes in its environment and in its own makeup, it is likely to pass out of existence as a result of petrification. Unless it achieves efficiency by solving at least some of those problems considered important by some of its members, these members will seek to combine with others in new political systems for the solution of their problems. And unless the system is effective, in the sense of producing policies, that is, solutions to problems that are acceptable to those segments of its population whose opposition could lead to the end of the system, it is again unlikely to endure for very long.

Individual human beings, too, can be looked upon as systems pursuing the same basic goals. They exist within the political system, and most of what happens to them results from decisions made by others. The individual can become responsible for his own future to the extent that he has the capacity to contribute to these decisions in a way proportionate to his exposure to their consequences. He is in a sound *situation of responsibility* to the extent that the political system makes available to him *knowledge* about the consequences of his actions, alternatives among which to make his *choice*, *resources* with which to implement his choices, and *purpose* or commitment to the value of responsibility itself. Without foreknowledge of the probable consequences of his actions, he cannot achieve stability; without choice, no flexibility; without resources, no efficiency; and without purpose, no effectiveness in terms of his own pursuit of the value of individual responsibility.[5]

The four basic goals of a political system are in conflict with one another, and this conflict generates the tensions that keep politics going. Perfect stability would obviously prevent flexibility, and interfere with the efficient solution of changing problems. Constant flexibility would make stability impossible and would undermine the acceptability of policies and of the constitution to those people whose commitments to values do not change from day to day. And so forth. In different political systems and in any one political system at different times, more or less attention is paid to each of the four basic goals of politics or to varying combinations of them. These differences can be described, compared, and explained in terms of "political style."

Legalism prevails where there is exclusive preoccupation with the basic goal of stability. Here the attempt is made to predetermine the entire future, thus precluding the "necessity of choice" for all

---

[5] See Spiro, *Responsibility in Government: Theory and Practice*, New York: Van Nostrand Reinhold, 1969.

time. Where political style is legalistic, constitutional problems and other legal problems are likely to predominate.

Pragmatism results from excessive devotion to the basic goal of flexibility. Here the paramount desire is to keep the future permanently open, to be permanently in a position to avail oneself of novelty and even to create novelty for its own sake. Where political style is pragmatic, especially in developed or developing contemporary systems, economic problems are likely to predominate.

Violence results from exclusive or excessive concern with the basic goal of efficiency, or the desire to solve problems immediately. Here resources, including the means of force, are instantly brought to bear on any problem as it appears at the moment, with little regard to consistency with past or future policies, or to the acceptability of the solution on the part of those who will be affected. Where political style is violent, power problems are likely to occupy the center of the stage.

Ideologism prevails where there is excessive concern for the basic goal of effectiveness. Here the main desire is to create values and to enforce, if necessary, the population's permanent commitment to values that can offer answers to all questions and solutions to all problems, for all time, in a manner both comprehensive and consistent. Ultimately, ideologism aims at the elimination of politics. Where there is perfect agreement, there cannot be any politics. Where political style is ideological, cultural problems are likely to predominate.

Various combinations of these pathological styles are, of course, possible and indeed likely, because no political system can ever achieve total legalism or utter pragmatism or undiluted violence or perfect ideologism. But there are many instances of ideological violence, as, for example, in Nazi Germany; or of pragmatic violence, as practiced by the Mafia in the United States or in Italy; or of pragmatic legalism of the type that has often led to constitutional litigation before the United States Supreme Court; or of ideological legalism of the kind that has led, in German politics, to the almost fanatical desire on the part of some politicians to establish or maintain the perfect internal consistency of the legal code. We also find a radical oscillation from one political style to another. For example,

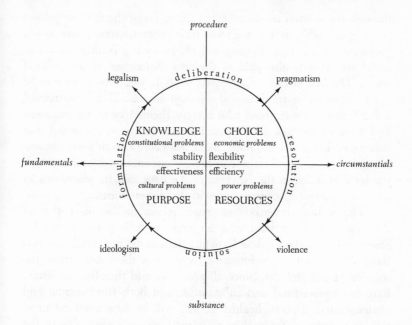

international politics in the 1950s and 1960s have frequently oscillated from the legalism of a John Foster Dulles in the Suez crisis of 1956 to the pragmatism of a Lyndon B. Johnson in the Dominican crisis of 1965.

Again, different component parts of one political system will display different styles. The military may incline toward violence, while the entrepreneurs lean toward pragmatism, the bureaucrats toward legalism, and the clergy or the intellectuals toward ideologism. The particular "mix" that emerges from a consideration of all the components of a political system gives us the "profile" of its political style. (For purposes of convenience, this could also be presented diagrammatically.)

Not all political systems have a pathological political style. In some a dynamically balanced concern for stability, flexibility, efficiency, and effectiveness leads to a healthy style, which we will describe as the "politics of purposive compromise." In such a situation, equal but alternating preoccupation with each of the four goals, through the natural tensions among them, keeps the flow of politics running smoothly and at the same time generates new issues as old problems are satisfactorily disposed of. In such a healthy situation, equal attention is also paid to the two dimensions of all political issues. The first of these dimensions refers to *time*. An issue may be perceived as either *fundamental* or *circumstantial*. If it is considered a fundamental issue, those who involve themselves in its treatment look back to the past and forward to the future in the stand that they take. Those, on the other hand, who consider an issue circumstantial, are concerned only with present circumstances and not with the relation between the outcome of the issue and its precedents in the hoary past or its consequences in the distant future.

The second dimension of issues relates to the perception of their *content*: those who view an issue as mainly *procedural* are concerned with the method by which it is to be processed, whereas those who consider it *substantive* focus upon the substance of the solution of the problem. Since all problems, and therefore all issues, have both procedural and substantive, and both fundamental and circumstantial, aspects, healthy politics will be kept centered upon the intersection of the politics of purposive compromise, due to the tensions "naturally" generated by the complexities of the human condition. However, at this point we are less concerned with the characteristics of some ideal state than with categories that can describe, both comprehensively and systematically, the differences between political systems. Our hope is that the approach that has just been sketched in outline goes further in that direction than the others previously criticized. It is the purpose of the next chapters to see whether this hope is warranted.

Selected Bibliography

Almond, Gabriel A., and G. Bingham Powell, *Comparative Politics: A Developmental Approach*, Boston: Little, Brown, 1966.

Dawson, Richard E., and Kenneth Prewitt, *Political Socialization*, Boston: Little, Brown, 1969.

Friedrich, Carl J., *Constitutional Government and Democracy*, Boston: Ginn, 1968.

Mills, C. Wright, *The Power Elite*, New York: Oxford University Press, 1956.

National Commission on the Causes and Prevention of Violence, *Violence in America: Historical and Comparative Perspectives*, Hugh Davis Graham and Ted Robert Gurr, directors, New York: Signet, 1969.

Riesman, David, *et al.*, *The Lonely Crowd: A Study of the Changing American Character*, New York: Anchor Books, 1951.

Spiro, Herbert J. "Comparative Politics: A Comprehensive Approach," *American Political Science Review*, vol. 56, no. 3 (September 1962), pp. 577–595. Also Bobbs-Merrill reprint.

Spiro, Herbert J., *Government by Constitution: The Political Systems of Democracy*, New York: Random House, 1959.

Spiro, Herbert J., *Responsibility in Government: Theory and Practice*, New York: Van Nostrand Reinhold, 1969.

Spiro, Herbert J., *World Politics: The Global System*, Homewood, Ill.: Dorsey, 1966.

"On all great subjects," says Mr. Mill, "much remains to be said," and of none is this more true than of the English Constitution. The literature which has accumulated upon it is huge. But an observer who looks at the living reality will wonder at the contrast to the paper description. He will see in the life much which is not in the books; and he will not find in the rough practice many refinements of the literary theory.

It was natural—perhaps inevitable—that such an undergrowth of irrelevant ideas should gather round the British Constitution. Language is the tradition of nations; each generation describes what it sees, but it uses words transmitted from the past. When a great entity like the British Constitution has continued in connected outward sameness, but hidden inner change, for many ages, every generation inherits a series of inapt words— of maxims once true, but of which the truth is ceasing or has ceased. As a man's family go on muttering in his maturity incorrect phrases derived from a just observation of his early youth, so, in the full activity of an historical constitution, its subjects repeat phrases true in the time of their fathers, and inculcated by those fathers, but now true no longer. Or, if I may say so, an ancient and ever-altering constitution is like an old man who still wears with attached fondness clothes in the fashion of his youth: what you see of him is the same; what you do not see is wholly altered.

Walter Bagehot,
The English Constitution (1867),
Ithaca, N.Y.: Cornell University Press,
1966, p. 59.

THE TEST OF METHODS I: GERMANY, FRANCE, GREAT BRITAIN

5

For the political scientist, as for any other scientist, the best test for any method is the results it yields: Does it explain the past? Has it predicted the future? How adequately? How accurately? How do different methods compare with each other, when they are applied to the same set of phenomena?

Natural and physical scientists usually apply an additional test of convenience to the methods they use: Can the method be replicated in the laboratory, so that another investigator applying it to the same material can verify or falsify the results previously obtained? Political scientists cannot use a direct equivalent of the physicist's or the chemist's laboratory. When they use simulation techniques, for example, the participants' awareness that they are engaged in simulation, instead of the "real thing," in which real values, including human lives, have to be risked, makes their behavior "unreal" to varying degrees. As a result, political scientists must rely upon the data of history as the functional equivalent of the laboratory, and they compare the explanations yielded by competing methods. They also rely upon history when they compare the accuracy of the predictions made in the past on the basis of different methods. Did subsequent events confirm these predictions? Of course, when sufficient time and patience are available, one can wait to see if events predicted now and based upon competing methods are confirmed or refuted. But in that case, too, the comparison of the methods' accuracy is made retrospectively, that is, *after* its fulfillment or failure.

For the political scientist in his explanatory work, method performs the same task that it performs for the contemporary natural scientist. It is an approach, a tool, and its job is instrumental. But the political scientist applies his method to conscious human beings, who may be persuaded *either* by its instrumental utility, since it helps them understand reality, *or* by its ultimate purpose. If ordinary people accept an approach used by political scientists because of its instrumental utility, they behave like scientists. This was generally true, for example, of those laymen who accepted Dr. Daniel Moynihan's explanation of the behavior of American Negroes in terms of the predominance of the fatherless family because they found it more satisfactory than other explanations based upon different methods. Other laymen, however, accepted or rejected his explanation, and with it his method, because they approved or disapproved of the ultimate purposes that they ascribed to Dr. Moynihan's work: to improve the living conditions of Negroes, to integrate them into white society, to subject them further to the white "power structure," and so forth. Each group of laymen may have changed their own subsequent behavior as a result of their awareness and their acceptance, or rejection, of the explanation and the method that produced it. To the extent that they reacted positively, that is, behaved in a way prescribed by Moynihan's explanation in order to alleviate the Negroes' condition, they may have contributed toward converting the explanation into a self-fulfilling prophecy. This is a result that explanations in the natural sciences are less likely to have. For instance, the behavior of iron under stress will not be affected by physicists' explanations (though, of course, the behavior of other physicists and of engineers may be affected by them).

These circumstances make it at the same time more difficult and more important to test methods in political science than in the natural and physical sciences. The difficulty is further complicated, and the importance enhanced, by the ideological or justificatory function of methods in political science. Some methods, and some theories, are devised less for instrumental, explanatory reasons, than for the purpose of rationalizing a policy, or completing the internal consistency of an ideology. Each ideology, as a comprehensive, internally consistent, closed system of knowledge, advances its own method for the study of political (as well as natural) phenomena. While this does not mean that this ideologically dictated method need be entirely false or "objectively unrealistic," it does mean that methods themselves, for the political scientist, are part of the total reality that he must seek to explain—and this is no easy job, since he himself is also a part of that reality.

WHAT TO EXPLAIN

Today, Great Britain, France, and West Germany offer an almost perfect arrangement for exercises in comparative method. The population of each is close to 50 million. Each has a highly developed industrial economy and a similar standard of living and education. Each is regarded as a constitutional democracy, with official commitment to the general values of the "Western liberal tradition" and a parliamentary system of government. All three belong to the Western European Union and to NATO, and France and West Germany are members of the European Economic Community, which Great Britain has wished to join for almost a decade against French opposition. As in this last mentioned respect, differences in this general picture of similarities can be clearly identified. We know how these three countries differ in the distribution of their populations—between city and country, Protestants and Roman Catholics, and so forth; in the distribution and sources of their gross national products—industrial, agricultural, exports, and so forth; in their school and university systems; and in their processes of politics and institutions of government. On the basis of attitude surveys and opinion polls, we also know something about the views that Britons, Frenchmen, and Germans have expressed on a variety of economic, cultural, and political questions.

What explanations does this general picture of similarities, with its particular differences, call for? There is a strong bias in the social sciences to look upon government as a dependent variable, that is, to ask how government varies as a result of independent changes in other spheres of life, like the economy, family, culture, or geography. We should not let ourselves be influenced by this bias in our comparative evaluation of methods. It is conceivable that the governments of these three countries differ mainly because they have different economies and have had different economic histories; or because their cultures, including educational institutions and family structures and values, differ today and have differed over time; or because of their geographical location. However, it seems equally conceivable that their economies differ because their governments pursue a variety of economic policies and goals; and that their cultures vary because governments have sought to achieve a variety of educational purposes and have presented different models from which families could copy their internal behavior; and even that the practical consequences flowing from their geographical location have been materially affected by the use the government has made of geography, including the technological responses made to it. Moreover, none of these explanations need be treated as mutually exclusive of any of the others. It seems more likely that these factors have reciprocal effects upon one another, that there are "feedback loops" between them.

In its search for explanations, most of the recent literature in comparative politics has focused upon differences in *stability*. Stability has also been a main concern of policy makers and their scientific advisers when they have had to make forecasts of the future behavior of foreign states acting in international politics. Stability is by our definition a fundamental matter, and scholars who have sought to account for differences between stable and unstable political systems have therefore generally also asked related questions about *effectiveness*: Why have the policies and constitutions of a particular system been more acceptable to important population groups in one country than in another? These same students of politics have less frequently inquired into achievement of the two basic circumstantial goals, efficiency and flexibility. *Efficiency* has been of greater interest to the policy maker, who wants to be able to gauge the capacity of a political system to solve the immediate problems it is confronting, the solution of which he wants to help or hinder. *Flexibility*, finally, seems sometimes almost to be condemned as a defect, especially in the established, mature Western countries, particularly when treated as identical with pure instability.

The preoccupation with stability has generally led to (and may originally have flowed from) the predominantly Anglophile outlook of studies in comparative government. This predilection can be found on both sides of the Atlantic, in the United States as well as in continental Europe. British government and the British constitution are generally admired for their stability in comparison with all other major powers, regardless of the historical starting point of a particular inquiry. The American Revolution occurred in 1776, the French Revolution in 1789, and Germany was unified as a national state only in 1871. Since then, the United States has passed through the great catastrophe of the Civil War and is passing through the grave crises of the 1960s. France experienced the Revolutions of 1830, 1848, and 1871, more than a dozen different constitutions, military defeat at the hands of Germany in 1870, 1914, and 1940, the troubles leading to the return of General DeGaulle to the Presidency of the Republic in 1958, and the threat of civil war on at least two occasions since then. Germany lost two world wars, changed from monarchy to the short-lived Weimar Republic with its tremendous instability of governments, and passed through the twelve years of Hitler's brutal National Socialist dictatorship, to be divided between the eastern Communist-ruled German Democratic Republic and the western Federal Republic, whose two decades of unprecedented political stability amount, in the view of some Germans, almost to political stagnation.

In this line-up, Britain appears as it did to Shakespeare's John of Gaunt (*King Richard the Second*, II, I, 1. 40 ff.):

> This royal throne of kings, this scept'red isle,
> This earth of majesty, this seat of Mars,
> This other Eden, demi-paradise,
> This fortress built by Nature for herself
> Against infection and the hand of war,
> This happy breed of men, this little world,
> This precious stone set in a silver sea,
> Which serves it in the office of a wall
> Or as a moat defensive to a house

Against the envy of less happier lands;
This blessed plot, this earth, this realm of England,

. . .

This land of such dear souls, this dear dear land,
Dear for her reputation through the world. . . .

Britain's last political revolution, the so-called Glorious Revolution of 1688, was a very mild affair compared with any of those that followed it in "less happier lands." The Civil Wars of the mid-seventeenth century were the last political upheavals involving major violence. Since then, the British constitution, partly because it is "unwritten," as contrasted with those of the other countries in this comparison, has changed very slowly and in timely response to demands made by those groups to whom both constitution and policies had to be acceptable for the maintenance of stability. In the present century, despite Britain's loss of its vast empire, near defeat in World War II, and relegation to the international status of a second-rate power, the stability of the British constitution, governments, and policies compares favorably with almost every other country on earth.

Because of Britain's unique history and geography, the task of explaining its stability may appear to be unusually easy. A comparison of Germany and France is much more difficult, because it calls, in the first place, for clarity about what we mean by stability. In 1871, Germany was unified in a ceremony held in the Hall of Mirrors at Versailles on the occasion of the defeat of France. This defeat ended the Second Empire of Louis Napoleon, and the French began their *Third* Republic, which persisted, with increasing instability of governments, until World War II. The monarchical and federal constitution of the Second German Reich gave that country a period of unprecedented order and economic progress. It was replaced by the very democratic Weimar Constitution of 1919, which provided Germany with a framework for enormous civic unrest, political violence, economic disaster, and the more or less legal transition to Hitler's assumption of power in 1933. Under Hitler, what little political stability the Germans enjoyed came from the dictator's own notoriously unstable mind, since he had and used the power of revamping the most basic institutions and laws at his pleasure. After World War II, both France and Germany established new constitutional orders. France's Fourth Republic lasted, with even worse cabinet instability than its Third, until 1958. The German Federal Republic has achieved great constitutional and governmental stability for West Germany, while East Germany has been firmly in the grip of its Communist boss, Walter Ulbricht, who put down with the force of Soviet arms the only effort to overthrow his regime by violence, in 1953.

Before we can explain differences in stability between Germany and France, we have to agree to a description of these differences. Which has been more stable, which less stable? It might be hard to agree on an answer to this question, but for one major difference between the two countries: Hitler. A comparison of the period beginning in 1870 does show more drastic constitutional changes in Germany than in France, especially in view of the fact that most analysts of the Fourth French Republic consider it a mere continuation of the Third, and many find a good deal of continuity even between the Fourth and the Fifth Republic, whereas hardly any scholars have regarded the Weimar Republic as a continuation of the Second German Empire. In the quarter of a century since the end of World War II, West German government and politics have undoubtedly been more stable than French government and politics, but that is too short a time span in which to view stability. In any event, and regardless of the categories of analysis one uses, Hitler's twelve-year reign of terror in Germany, containing possibly the most intensive use of deliberate violence in human history, clearly had no parallel in France. The short-lived regime of Marshal Petain, which collaborated with the Nazis and was dependent for its survival upon the German occupation forces, was much more episodic in French history than was Hitler's longer rule in German history. Therefore, the basic question for purposes of comparison is: Why did German politics turn so pathological? Why did nothing similar happen in France? (This, incidentally, is not a merely academic question. American, British, French, and Soviet military leaders and politicians with responsibility for military government in Germany after the end of World War II asked themselves basically the same question in their efforts to prevent recurrence of the phenomenon.

German politicians too asked themselves this question, after they were allowed to assume responsibility for German affairs once more, for example, when they designed their new constitutions.)

SUBSTANTIVE DETERMINISM

To answer questions about the most dramatic difference between Germany and France, as well as other less dramatic but equally important differences between them and other pairs of countries, one school of thought has focused upon comparisons of their substantive historical development and their contemporary substantive wherewithal as the foundation upon which their governmental institutions and political processes rest. The sociologist Seymour M. Lipset, for example, has proposed a theory that explains stable democracy as dependent upon the presence or absence of certain "requisites": wealth, industrialization, urbanization, and education. This kind of method has most often been applied to the so-called underdeveloped countries, like those in Asia, Africa, the Middle East, and Latin America, in order to gauge the prospects for democracy there. Lipset himself, however, began by applying it to Europe, and it seems quite suitable for purposes of our comparison of Germany and France, since in 1870 both were certainly underdeveloped countries by the retrospective standards of 1970 as well as the British standards of that time.[1]

The method contains certain obvious determinist assumptions and implications. It may suggest that Germany's economic and social development as of 1870, or the rate of development between 1870 and, say, 1914, caused political development to take the course, relative to political development in France or Britain, that it did in fact take. In this way, the approach would rule out political, and perhaps even cultural, social, or economic, creativity and inventiveness. That, however, is not the only trouble with this type of method. There is no empirical evidence that France was more highly developed in its economy or its society than Germany in 1870. Moreover, if we advance the starting point of the comparison to 1914,

---

[1] Seymour Martin Lipset, *Political Man: The Social Bases of Politics*, Garden City, N.Y.: Anchor Books, 1960, p. 31 ff.

then Germany would definitely place ahead of France on most if not all the indices that are used to gauge the requisites of stable democracy. According to different measures of national wealth, Germany may be regarded as having been wealthier at the time. Germans were more industrialized, more urbanized, and certainly better educated than Frenchmen. Especially with respect to literacy, Germany had one of the highest ratings in the world, matched among populous countries only by Japan, another country whose "democracy" was not very "stable." Yet, no matter what our definition of democracy, it did come to an end in Germany almost a decade before it was suppressed (for a much briefer period during the war) in France. And France did not produce a Hitler or a regime as outrageous as that of the Nazis. The theory of social and economic requisites of stable democracy cannot therefore provide adequate explanations, and it is equally unlikely to supply accurate forecasts, when applied to today's underdeveloped countries.

The shortcomings of this theory become even more apparent when it is applied to the country that experienced the Industrial Revolution first, Great Britain, which enjoyed political stability, though not democracy, both before and during its unprecedented economic and social development. Moreover, it would be hard to demonstrate a correlation between the growth of industrialization, urbanization, and literacy in Britain *after* World War I and up to the present and the development of British democracy however defined. This difficulty would arise when we study both the internal ups and downs of these indices for Britain and their relative standing compared to France, Germany, or other sometime democracies.

THE FAMILY

Another popular approach to explaining differences between political systems starts with the family as the basic unit of society. Since almost all human beings are born into and raised by some type of family unit, this method concludes that the political behavior of adults is shaped in large measure by family-determined patterns of child-rearing. These patterns are said to be so fundamental, that they persist over many generations, and often over centuries.

This kind of explanation was frequently offered while Adolf

Hitler was actually in power, probably because many non-Germans, as well as many Germans critical of his rule, were aware of certain peculiarities of the German family or, at least, of the caricature of the German family. In this view, the father, *pater familias*, in the German family held and exercised all authority, and the German family was said to be more "authoritarian" than families in other national societies. As a result, to simplify the explanation slightly, most Germans reacted negatively to the removal of the Kaiser, who had played the role of *pater familias* for the nation, just as the father plays it in each individual family. The founding of the Weimar Republic had destroyed authority, and therefore most Germans were eagerly yearning for a new center of authority, from which they could take their orders. Adolf Hitler responded to this yearning.

This explanation of the pathology of German politics has several weak points. To begin with, it would be easy to demonstrate that the character of the family in several other neighboring European societies was as authoritarian as that in Germany, if not more so. A reasonable case could be made for asserting that the father in France played at least as authoritarian a role as his German counterpart. Indeed, it seems likely that fathers in the United States, at least until the time of the Presidency of Woodrow Wilson, played an equally authoritarian role. But this points to a greater difficulty: What is *the* German family? And where does change in this family come from? There are millions of families in Germany, as in every large society, and these millions of families do not act in unison. They do not all suddenly somehow get together and announce that they will increase, or decrease, or maintain at an equal level the powers of the father, or of the mother, or of the children. Or, if many families did indeed act in unison in this way, they would be engaging in political action, for example, by organizing a pressure group of families whose goal it is to increase government subsidies or to suppress or encourage church schools. Sometimes, in certain countries, members of many families do get together in order to try to change their own character or that of the relations between families on the one hand and the government on the other. However, when this occurs, then the families are trying to change themselves *through political action*. It therefore makes little sense to look upon the family as the prime cause, or even as a major cause among several, of political change, especially of the kind of dramatic political change that occurred in Germany between 1929 and 1933 and resulted in such tragedy.

To illustrate this point, one might study the members of almost any German family that was split by the division of the country into the German Democratic Republic in the former Soviet zone of occupation and the Federal Republic of Germany in the former western zones of occupation. In 1945, before the division of the country, the members of this family, both parents and children, presumably held the same general values. However, after a quarter of a century, that is, a whole generation, of division, those members of the family who have been living and raising their children in West Germany will have developed values different from those of their brothers and sisters who have been living in East Germany. And this would apply as much to strictly familial values as to political ones. Indeed, some Germans today are concerned about the differential development of their language in the two parts of their divided nation. There are words that have come into use in East Germany that the ordinary West German would not understand, and there are others that have taken on quite different meanings in the two parts of the country. It therefore seems inadequate, to say the least, to look upon the family, the basic unit of society, as the source and origin of political change.

It may be true that children learn their values mainly in the family. However, "the family" does not exist in a vacuum, but rather within a political system. When the political system changes, and especially when it is being changed as a result of deliberate political action, the family and the values it instills in its members are more likely to change as a result of politics than the other way around. It is politics and people's understanding of politics that shapes behavior in this most basic of social units. Another illustration of this may be found in the transformations that have occurred in the United States in immigrant families in the course of two or three generations. If family values shaped political values, then the "political culture" of the United States at any one point in time would have been determined by the particular blending of native and immigrant families in the country and the combination of values that this blending produced. In fact, however, immigrant families have almost always taken on, for purposes of running family affairs, the political values and procedures of the American political system, as they understood or misunderstood them. As a final illustration of this point, we cite the cartoons of George Price in *The New Yorker* magazine. These usually show the harassed father of a family with many children being outvoted in family council. This family is clearly modeling its internal operations on those of the larger political system, in a way that citizens of more "authoritarian" polities either would not understand or would point to when trying to denigrate the excesses of American democracy. In other words, the effects of politics upon the family, upon its values, and upon other less basic social units and structures seem at least as important as their reverse.

PROCEDURAL VOLUNTARISM

At the other extreme of the spectrum that runs from the substantive to the procedural perception of the content of issues, some political scientists have explained the Hitler phenomenon as the consequence of a badly designed (fundamental) constitution, or a badly managed (circumstantial) economy. Here the assumption is that human reason can design institutions and procedures that will achieve their purposes, more or less, by shaping the political processing of whatever substantive problems the system may confront in certain ways, and that human skill can deliberate about and manipulate day-to-day problems and resources, especially economic ones, so as to achieve the desired ends.

The failure of the Weimar Republic to prevent Hitler's rise to power is explained, therefore, as the result of its faulty electoral system of proportional representation, its directly elected president (intended, incidentally, by its chief designer, the sociologist Max Weber, to replace the father figure of the Kaiser), or its constitutional provisions for presidential emergency powers, including the suspension of civil rights. The suggestion is clearly implied that better constitutional engineering would have prevented the collapse of the structure. On the circumstantial side of the voluntarist argument, mistaken economic policies during the Great Inflation of 1923 and the Great Depression of 1929 and the following years are blamed, along with the deliberately anticonstitutional and pro-Nazi manipulations of German finance and industrial capitalists, some of whom did for a while feed large subsidies to Hitler before he was appointed Chancellor.

The type of method that yields this kind of procedurally voluntarist explanation also motivated the refounders of German constitutionalism when between 1945 and 1948 they set about drafting the state constitutions and then the Basic Law of the Federal Republic. They were intent upon preventing a recurrence of the presumed faults of their forerunners at Weimar. There was an additional "natural" inducement for them to concentrate upon constitutional design in the simple fact that there was little they could do about the substantive historical and cultural traditions of their people or the substantive resources that were left to them after the catastrophe of their total defeat in World War II. Moreover, they wanted to insure political stability above everything else, above flexibility, efficiency, and effectiveness, because they had just passed through twelve years of Hitler's rule, which had been characterized by total instability, especially of procedures, that is, of the rules of the political game. Hitler had geared everything to the quick achievement of the ideologically dictated substantive goals of his Thousand Year Reich, the immediate realization of his vision of the single truth. He, in turn, and the millions of Germans who initially supported his ascent to power, were reacting to what they perceived as the ineffectiveness of the irresolute democracy of Weimar. His could be described as an excessively substantivist reaction to an excessively proceduralist period in German history. It points at the same time to the inadequacies of procedural voluntarism as a method of explanation and as an approach to forecasting. To use Aristotle's causal vocabulary, the focus of the procedural voluntarist is entirely upon the formal and efficient causes, whereas the substantive determinist neglects these to concentrate wholly upon the material and final causes. Each approach ignores the concerns of the other; equally important, both overlook the tensions that are always existentially generated by the conflicting preoccupations of the same or different population groups in the political process.

To avoid these complementary, dialectically contradictory, and mutually compounding shortcomings of the substantivist and the proceduralist methods, we could advance a tentative explanation of the Hitler phenomenon in Germany and its absence in France, an explanation which is based precisely upon the practical consequences of application of these two approaches with their defects. The founders of the Weimar Republic sought to correct the substantive faults of the Second German Empire, including the launching and loss of World War I, by designing the best possible procedural framework for their First republic, but this framework, the Weimar Constitution, turned out to be quite incapable of dealing with the novel sets of substantive problems that arose in the years between 1919 and 1933. The Weimar Republic was governed by coalitions that usually agreed only on a lowest common denominator of parliamentary procedures, but not on substantive goals or the policy means that could realize these goals. Those voters who, in increasing numbers during the last three years of the Republic's life, supported Hitler, did so largely because, after pointing to the ineffectiveness and inefficiency or the "Weimarer System," as he contemptuously called it, Hitler promised the effectiveness of total if enforced consensus and the efficiency of quick if violent solutions to the nation's substantive internal and external problems. In place of Weimar's legalistic and pragmatic political style, he offered ideologism and violence. His offer was accepted and he fulfilled his promise over the short run.

His successors at Bonn in 1948 did not overreact to excessive substantivism with the same kind of excessive proceduralism and the unrealistic expectations based upon it that had prevailed at Weimar in 1919. As a result, the Federal Republic has come closer toward achieving its authors' purposes than any of the earlier constitutional blueprints in German history.

At the beginning of the same hundred year period, in 1871, the French, starting with a much older (substantive) national and (procedural) parliamentary tradition than their German neighbors, rebuilt a political system in which the tensions, and the consciousness of them, between substantive and procedural, fundamental and circumstantial concerns always remained closer to the surface. This system, with its increasingly pragmatic bias, endured until the German invasion of 1940, despite the fact that France faced economic and social problems during the 1920s that were not very dissimilar from those Germany was then confronting. Even the four-year interlude of the Vichy regime of Marshal Petain continued, in many ways, the style of the Third Republic, which was then resumed fully in the Fourth Republic. Pragmatism and irresoluteness were incapable of either dealing with or of postponing the novel problems of decolonization in Indochina and Algeria, so that General DeGaulle was asked, in 1958, to return to the presidency and gained assent to his design of a constitution for the Fifth Republic. As the self-styled and generally accepted embodiment of the fundamentals of France's past, he brilliantly designed the framework for his own success in virtually all spheres over the next decade. He was able to do this, because of the existence among the French of a subconscious consensus on the procedures used in situations of extreme conflict, including those bordering upon or actually culminating in civil war, like the "revolution" of May 1968. General DeGaulle evidently sensed the existence of this consensus and consequently won the repeated games of "chicken" that he played with the army in Algeria, the O.A.S., and in 1968 the radical students and trade union organizations. At the same time, he was also able to demonstrate to the French electorate that it was capable of generating much greater resolution than had ever been thought possible or had ever actually been achieved under the Third and Fourth Republics. In the end, this consensus turned against DeGaulle in the constitutional referendum of May 1969 and led to his resignation. He gave a new form and, in a very real sense, a new *telos* to the human and natural material of France, in which the day-to-day political and economic operating procedures of the period before 1958 had been by and large retained.

THE MEANING OF STABILITY

The picture just drawn gives the impression that the style of French politics since 1870 has been more stable than that of German politics. Nevertheless, even the most superficial comparison of these two continental countries with Great Britain permits few doubts as to the relatively extraordinary stability of British government and politics. However, in order to make the comparison something less than superficial, we should clearly understand the meaning of stability. Just what it is that has been stable in Great Britain? A reading of Walter Bagehot's *The English Constitution*, which brilliantly describes and analyzes British politics as of 1867, will provide an answer, if we compare the circumstances prevailing then with those of today.

To test substantive determinist methods like Lipset's, we can begin by comparing economic and social conditions in 1867 and 1967. The changes that have occurred in Britain's domestic economy, and in its position in the international economy, have been enormous. In 1867, Britain was the richest nation in the world, the head of the greatest imperial and colonial system and the undisputed mistress of the seas, with the largest merchant fleet and the most powerful navy. The pound sterling was the most important international currency. By 1967 Britain had fallen behind even the divided, recently defeated West Germany in gross national product and per capita real income. Wealth within the country was much more evenly distributed than had been the case a century before, when the economic pyramid was probably one of the steepest in the world. The empire no longer exists, the colonies have been disposed of, and what is left of the British Navy is dependent upon the financial and technological largesse of the United States. Britain's merchant fleet is of relatively small significance. The dollar has replaced the twice-devalued pound as the principal international currency, and in the late 1960s the central banks of not only the United States but also such previously financially insignificant states as Italy, Japan, or Switzerland have repeatedly had to come to the rescue of the pound sterling.

Social changes have if anything been even more drastic than economic changes during this hundred year period. In 1867 agriculture still played a significant role in the overall economy and in British society. In politics, the conflict between agricultural interests on the one hand and industrial and commercial interests on the other was still of considerable significance. The huge white collar "salariat," probably the single most important segment of the electorate today, simply did not exist in 1867. Then, Bagehot could speak of the English people as a "deferential nation." By this he meant that they naturally deferred to the governing class, whom they regarded as their natural "betters." While one could still detect traces of this type of deference in 1967, it had been much reduced. Tremendous changes have also occurred in the structure and values of the family in Britain. To understand this, one need only read novels about the Victorian family and then compare them with what one knows about the Beatles, Twiggy, or "Swinging London." Again, cultural changes have been of vast scope. In the middle of the nineteenth century, Disraeli could still speak of "two nations" that coexisted within Britain, but whose members could barely communicate with one another. Since then, there have been great improvements in education, and although consciousness of social differences is still much more marked than in the United States, and somewhat more marked than in continental Europe, it has been greatly reduced.

Even Britain's geographical position has changed, paradoxical though this description may sound, since after all "Britain" occupies the same islands as it did two hundred (or two thousand) years ago. But the English Channel and the "silver sea" no longer "serves it in the office of a wall / Or as a moat defensive to a house / Against the envy of less happier lands," in the words of Shakespeare's John of Gaunt. In other words, modern military technology has transformed and generally reduced the advantages that its island position once used to confer upon Britain.

We may conclude that neither the British economy, nor British society, nor British culture, nor even Britain's geography have remained stable, when viewed either from the inside or in relation to the rest of Europe and the world. From this conclusion we may go on to assert that there has not been political or constitutional stability either. In the nineteenth century, when Bagehot was writing, British governments generally pursued an economic policy of laissez faire. There was minimal government interference with or regulation of the economy. In contrast, by 1967 large sectors of industry, including coal mining, steel production, the railways, and the major airlines and telecommunications, were owned by the state, and all the rest of the economy was subject to heavy government regulation and taxation. Until well after World War I, Britain lagged far behind such continental countries as Germany or Sweden in the social benefits it provided for its masses. However, by 1967, the country had been converted into a model welfare state, in which social benefits were provided for each individual, literally from the cradle to the grave. In international politics, Britain had degenerated from being, in the words of 1066 and All That, "top nation," to being a second-rate state. The British party system had been transformed. When Bagehot was writing, politics was being conducted between the Conservative and Liberal parties. A hundred years later, Labor had replaced the Liberals, though the Liberal party continued to play a minor role in national and parliamentary politics.

However, this change had really gone beyond being "merely political." In his analysis of the English constitution, Bagehot never mentioned the system of political parties as such. However, by 1967 —indeed, by 1917—the party system had developed, and the formal and informal constitutions of the political parties became an integral part of the British constitution. Bagehot made the useful distinction between the "efficient" and the "dignified" parts of the British constitution. He considered the Crown, that is, the monarchy and the monarch himself or herself, the dignified part of the constitution, while the two Houses of Parliament, the Commons and the Lords, were among the efficient, that is, the working parts of the constitution. By 1967, and for some decades before that, the House of Lords had been reduced to largely dignified functions, in these terms. In Bagehot's time, the prime minister was still described as "first among equals." Beginning with World War I at the latest, his position in fact became much more important than that within the cabinet, and the cabinet—described by Bagehot as the hyphen or the buckle that joined the government to parliament—had become much more independent of the House of Commons. Some procedures of considerable antiquity in parliamentary politics, whose existence had been only dimly recognized in the nineteenth century, had been formalized a hundred years later. For example, the post of Leader of the Opposition, which certainly existed in an informal way in 1867, was recognized in law only beginning in 1937.

Even more far-reaching constitutional changes occurred in the relations between Britain and her colonial or imperial possessions overseas. In 1867 the Dominion of Canada was constitutionally established as a confederation. It was to take sixty years before Britain's colonies, at least the most advanced ones populated or dominated by white people, were granted independence with respect to their foreign relations and defense by the Statute of Westminster. By 1967, what used to be described as the British Empire had been transformed into the Commonwealth of Nations, a phrase that was usually not even preceded by the word "British." Within this very loose commonwealth, Britain and its other white components, Canada, Australia, and New Zealand, could be outvoted, if votes were ever taken, and were outpopulated by the dark-skinned members from countries including India and Pakistan, Nigeria, Tanzania, and the other African member states, and Caribbean countries like Jamaica, Trinidad and Tobago.

So we must ask once more: What is it that has been stable in British politics? Neither the geographic scope of the political system nor the basic institutions or relations among these institutions have been stable in the period since Bagehot wrote *The English Constitution*. But one thing has retained remarkable stability, and that is the *procedures* by means of which change and adaptation were brought about in all the other political and constitutional, economic and social and cultural realms. Political stability in Britain has been procedural rather than substantive, and this fact, which is the principal achievement of the "genius" of British politics, can be largely explained by the primacy that the British governing class has always accorded to politics over other aspects of human life, including its economic, military, and cultural aspects.

THE CAUSES OF BRITISH STABILITY

The question about the sources of stability can now be rephrased: Why is it that certain procedures of British politics have been able to contain such radical substantive changes over the past century—indeed, over the past three centuries? First, we should dispose of three misleading conventional answers that use *national homogeneity*, *fundamental agreement*, and *monarchy* as explanations.

If the British people were as *homogeneous* as some interpretations let them appear, they would not have had the opportunities to develop their politics and consensus on its procedures to the extent that in fact they have. But Britain has consisted, and consists today, as the Queen phrased it in one of her Christmas addresses, of several countries and nations—England, Wales, Scotland, and Northern Ireland—each with its own nationally conscious population. Northern Ireland even has its own parliament, a counterpart which many Welsh and Scottish nationalists want in their countries. Each of the countries, and many of the counties within them, has its own customs and, more important, its own distinctive modes of speech and unique accents. In addition to this horizontal heterogeneity, there are the vertical divisions between social and economic classes, the members of which are highly conscious of their position and can usually also be identified by their accents. There are other divisions, which crisscross the major horizontal and vertical ones, but usually do not coincide with them. For example, Britain still has a sizable Roman Catholic population of 17 percent, as well as nearly half a million immigrants, Negroes from the Caribbean and Asians from India, Pakistan, and East Africa, who have settled in Britain and whose presence, and the admission of more of them, has been a recurrent political issue during the past decade. To refer to such a mixture of people as homogeneous seems quite inaccurate and will be of little help in explaining constitutional stability.

Lord Balfour once explained the success of British politics by saying that the "British people are so fundamentally at one, that they can safely afford to bicker." But what is the object of this *fundamental agreement*? Certainly not substantive economic and social policy, over which the Conservative and the Liberal, and later the Labor, parties have been fighting for the last hundred years. It also seems peculiar that, if the British people are fundamentally at one, there should be two or three major parties competing with each other. Such an answer to the question about the causes of stability is clearly not a point at which our mind can come to rest.

Monarchy is offered as a source of stability, because the monarch can perform the dignified functions, leaving the efficient functions to the prime minister and his cabinet. As a result, according to this fundamental procedural explanation, the common people can let their potentially irrational emotions be siphoned off onto the stable monarchy with its pomp and circumstance, leaving the government to get on with the job.[2] Actually, however, some aspects of monarchy can exacerbate class animosity and feelings of jealousy among politicians (and their wives as well); consider, for example, awards made in the annual Honors Lists or invitations to entertainments at Buckingham Palace.

Parliamentary procedures and their antiquity at first glance seem to offer a more promising explanation of constitutional stability. They have changed much less in Britain than in France and Germany, and over a much longer period of time. In fact, they were fairly well established in their present mold during the eighteenth century. The growth and transformation of the functions of Parliament has been so slow and gradual, uninterrupted by any real revolutions that few persons active in British politics have ever had occasion to give these procedures a second thought. As a result, there have been few occasions for making a direct attack upon the procedures for purposes of serving one's own immediate, circumstantial political goals. There have been instances, however, including recent

---

[2] See Edward Shils and Michael Young, "The Meaning of the Coronation," *Sociological Review*, vol. 1, December 1953; and N. Birnbaum, "Monarchs and Sociologists: A Reply to Professor Shils and Mr. Young," *Ibid.*, vol. 3, July 1955. Available in Bobbs-Merrill Reprint Series, No. 264.

Also see Harry Eckstein, in *Patterns of Government: The Major Political Systems of Europe*, 2nd ed., S. H. Beer and A. B. Ulam, eds., New York: Random House, 1962, p. 97 f.: "First of all this means that the British, although they probably have as much need for emotional behavior as any other people, can act with sober pragmatism in parliamentary politics because their emotional passions are channeled toward and satisfied by other aspects of their political system: their ceremonial institutions—above all, of course, the monarchy. Party politics, that is to say, are insulated against emotional behavior simply because the political passions of the British have other outlets in a set of generally accepted and politically innocuous (if not irrelevant) institutions. Where the political emotions do not readily find such outlets they tend to fix themselves on other objects, frequently political ideologies. Such ideologies, more often than not, are held for emotional rather than rational reasons and, above all, have the function of enlisting the passions of people who want at least to appear 'reasonable' in their political behavior."

ones, when the Conservative or the Labor party has sought to exploit or abolish certain procedures governing both Houses of Parliament or the relations between them. Moreover, there is always the possibility that procedures that may have been efficient when the country was still largely agricultural, could easily have petrified, so that they would now amount to nothing but empty forms and bottlenecks to the rational conduct of parliamentary business. This procedural determinist explanation is therefore also inadequate.

It does question, however, why the longevity of parliamentary procedure has not degenerated into either procedural routinization or the stagnant mythology of legalism. The brief answer to this question is the continuous centrality of Parliament in British politics. Its two Houses have been regarded as "supreme" only since the Glorious Revolution of 1688. But Parliament, consisting of the Monarch, the Lords Spiritual and Temporal (including the Law Lords), and the Commons, has been central to English government and politics almost since the Norman Conquest, and certainly from the beginnings of the modern British polity in the sixteenth century. This Parliament, regardless of which of its components was the "weightiest," or whether it performed mainly judicial "functions," as it did until the sixteenth century, or mainly legislative ones, as it did in the nineteenth, was always "seized of politics." It always had business to transact. Moreover, it also availed itself from early times of a very useful, efficient, and effective procedure, which was unintentionally transferred to its legislative from its judicial work by parliamentary lawyers. This is the adversary method of the Common Law, which facilitates the clear definition of the issue under debate, rational deliberation in the course of which an optimum of information and participation can be brought to bear upon the issue, its speedy resolution, and the acceptability of this resolution to all parties including the defeated one. Elsewhere I have described the historical origins and political consequences of the adversary method.[3] The point here is that English political style would have developed

---

[3] Spiro, *Government by Constitution: The Political Systems of Democracy,* New York: Random House, 1959, pp. 225-230, and "Privacy and the Adversary Method," in *Privacy,* J. Roland Pennock and John W. Chapman, eds., New York: Atherton Press, in preparation.

differently without the availability of this procedure—an element of procedural determinism or, perhaps better, procedural accidentalism in this method. But this procedure, too, could easily have either lapsed into innocuous desuetude or degenerated into the kind of routine form in which it has survived in some former British colonies, had it not been for the content of the problems that were recognized and processed by means of this procedure, and the sequence in which these substantive problems were taken up by the English (later the British) political system. This is an element of substantive determinism, except that content and sequence were shaped also by intelligent application of the parliamentary procedures.

The religious problem was solved first, in the sixteenth century; the constitutional one next, in the seventeenth; the economic one, during the Industrial Revolution, which lasted on into the nineteenth; and the social problem last, in the twentieth century, by means of the welfare state. Each problem was handled individually and was uncomplicated by the distracting presence of others; in contrast, in France the first three of these major problems came to a head simultaneously during the Revolution and have not been satisfactorily solved to this day. Britain benefitted from this sequence, because the fundamental problems were taken care of first; thus, the potentially most divisive cultural issue of religion had been resolved before the firm establishment of the constitutional framework, within which economic adaptation and the growth and exploitation of British power could later be developed. The constitutional struggles of the sixteenth century were not so fundamental as to revolve around basic procedures, since these had in the main been gradually adapted from the medieval past. Unlike the continental countries, England consequently did not have to face the most troublesome question of how to state questions, how to formulate issues for politics, and how to push them toward resolution. Procedures were simply taken for granted, though they were at the same time always being slowly adapted to changing substantive needs. This was especially true of parliamentary procedures, which served and continue to serve as a model for all other procedures, political, economic, and social, including those used in business-bargaining or child-rearing.

The result of all this was that British politicians (along with students of British politics who were taken seriously by the politicians) never lapsed into the errors of either excessive substantivism or excessive proceduralism, of either excessive fundamentalism or excessive circumstantialism. They kept all these dimensions of politics in sight, and they kept the four basic goals of politics—stability, flexibility, effectiveness, and efficiency—in dynamic tension with one another. Parliament remained central, and politics remained the most important, the most valued, and the most comprehensive and general human activity, truly the master science in the Aristotelian sense. Lord Chesterfield wrote to his son in 1749, "You will be of the House of Commons as soon as you are of age, and you must first make a figure there if you would make a figure in your country." Admiral Sir George Rodney wrote to Lord George Germain from the West Indies in 1780, "To be out of Parliament is to be out of the world, and my heart is set upon my being in."[4] Authority flowed and continues to flow from demonstrated capacity as a politician, especially a parliamentary politician—a House of Commons man, as Winston Churchill described himself most proudly. It does not come from the substantive achievements of the intellectual or the military hero, or from the procedural achievements of the business millionaire or even the great barrister unless he is also a Member of Parliament.

The flexible stability and the effective efficiency of British politics have been explained by methods similar to the one proposed here as long ago as the fifteenth century, by Sir John Fortescue in De Laudibus Legum Anglie, and in the sixteenth century, by Sir Thomas Smith in De Republica Anglorum. Fortescue was a lawyer and judge, Smith a lawyer and civil servant. Both spent time on the continent and were keenly aware of the political differences between England and France, which they sought to explain. Their explanations draw upon both constitutional, procedural differences, and upon economic and social, substantive ones. More recent and more scholarly comparisons have been similarly well balanced. In the twentieth century, however, some political scientists have concentrated upon either the purely legalist or the purely socio-economic

---

[4] Quoted by Sir Lewis Namier, The Structure of Politics at the Accession of George III, 2nd ed., London: Macmillan and Co., 1965, p. 1.

approaches, sometimes oscillating rather wildly from the one to the other. As a result, they have failed to explain the past adequately, to forecast the future accurately, or even to cast light upon the nature of the differences between Europe's three most important political systems.

Selected Bibliography

COMPARISONS

Almond, Gabriel A., and Bingham Powell, *Comparative Politics: A Developmental Approach*, Boston: Little, Brown, 1966.

Almond, Gabriel A., and Sydney Verba, *The Civic Culture*, Boston: Little, Brown, 1963.

Beer, Samuel H., and Adam B. Ulam, eds., *Patterns of Government: The Major Political Systems of Europe*, 2nd ed., New York: Random House, 1962.

Clapham, J. H., *The Economic Development of France and Germany, 1815–1914*, Cambridge: Cambridge University Press, 1936.

Deutsch, Karl W., Lewis J. Edinger, Roy C. Macridis, and Richard L. Merritt, *France, Germany and the Western Alliance: A Study of Elite Attitudes on European Integration and World Politics*, New York: Charles Scribner's Sons, 1967.

Eckstein, Harry, *Division and Cohesion in Democracy: A Study of Norway*, Princeton, N.J.: Princeton University Press, 1966.

Lipset, Seymour Martin, *Political Man: The Social Bases of Politics*, Garden City, N.Y.: Anchor Books, 1960.

Moynihan, Daniel P., *Maximum Feasible Misunderstanding*, New York: Free Press, 1969.

Moynihan, Daniel P., *On Understanding Poverty: Perspectives from the Social Sciences*, New York: Basic Books, 1969.

Moynihan, Daniel P., *The Negro Family: The Case for National Action*, Washington, D.C.: U.S. Department of Labor, March 1965.

Rainwater, Lee and Yancey, William L., eds., *The Moynihan Report and the Politics of Public Controversy*, Cambridge, Mass.: M.I.T. Press, 1967.

Turner, John E., and Robert T. Holt, *The Political Bases of Economic Development*, Princeton, N.J.: Van Nostrand, 1966.

GREAT BRITAIN

Bagehot, Walter, *The English Constitution*, Ithaca, N.Y.: Cornell University Press, 1966.

Beer, Samuel H., *British Politics in the Age of Collectivism*, 2nd ed., New York: Random House, 1969.

Namier, Sir Lewis, *The Structure of Politics at the Accession of George III*, 2nd ed., London: Macmillan, 1965.

Rose, Richard, *Politics in England*, Boston: Little, Brown, 1964.

FRANCE

Ehrmann, Henry, *Politics in France*, Boston: Little, Brown, 1967.

Hoffmann, Stanley *et al.*, *In Search of France: The Society, Economy, and Political System in the Twentieth Century*, New York: Harper & Row, 1963.

MacRae, Duncan, Jr., *Parliament, Parties, and Society in France, 1946–1958*, New York: St. Martin's, 1967.

Macridis, Roy, and Bernard E. Brown, *The DeGaulle Republic: Quest for Unity*, Homewood, Ill.: Dorsey, 1960–1963.

Pierce, Roy, *French Politics and Political Institutions*, New York: Harper & Row, 1968.

Wylie, Laurence, *Village in the Vaucluse*, Cambridge, Mass.: Harvard University Press, 1957.

GERMANY

Dahrendorf, Ralf, *Society and Democracy in Germany*, Garden City, N.Y.: Doubleday, 1967.

Edinger, Lewis J., *Politics in Germany*, Boston: Little, Brown, 1968.

Heidenheimer, Arnold J., *The Government of Germany*, 2nd ed., New York: Crowell, 1966.

Loewenberg, Gerhard, *Parliament in the German Political System*, Ithaca, N.Y.: Cornell University Press, 1966.

There are at the present time two great nations in the world, which started from different points, but seem to tend towards the same end. I allude to the Russians and the Americans. Both of them have grown up unnoticed; and while the attention of mankind was directed elsewhere, they have suddenly placed themselves in the front rank among the nations, and the world learned their existence and their greatness at almost the same time.

All other nations seem to have nearly reached their natural limits, and they have only to maintain their power; but these are still in the act of growth. All the others have stopped, or continue to advance with extreme difficulty; these alone are proceeding with ease and celerity along a path to which no limit can be perceived. . . . The Anglo-American relies upon personal interest to accomplish his ends and gives free scope to the unguided strength and common sense of the people; the Russian centers all the authority of society in a single arm. The principal instrument of the former is freedom; of the latter, servitude. Their starting-point is different and their courses are not the same; yet each of them seems marked out by the will of Heaven to sway the destinies of half the globe.

Alexis de Tocqueville,
Democracy in America (1835), vol. 1,
New York: Knopf, 1945, p. 452.

THE TEST
OF METHODS II:
THE UNITED
STATES
AND THE SOVIET
UNION

6

THE FOCUS OF COMPARISON

The United States of America and the Union of Soviet Socialist Republics are the two superpowers in the world. They are the only ones with space travel capabilities; though France, Great Britain, and China have nuclear weapons, only the two superpowers have been maintaining constant global delivery capabilities. What each does in world politics is of crucial importance for all mankind, because by itself each one could put an end to human life. What the two do in their relations with each other is equally important. For these reasons, and because of the obvious interdependence of external and internal politics of all contemporary states, Soviet and American citizens and policy makers, as well as all politically conscious men and women everywhere, need descriptions, explanations, and forecasts of the political behavior of these two great and powerful countries.

From the time of Alexis de Tocqueville, students of politics have noticed certain similarities between Russia and the United States, and in recent decades, since World War II, more or less systematic comparisons between them have been made. They seem to lend themselves easily as a pair for comparison in terms of their more or less self-evident similarities and differences. Both occupy a large land mass, each had or still has a frontier, both have populations in excess of two hundred million. Each might be thought of as something of a newcomer to the first rank in international politics, though for different reasons. The United States has the world's largest industrial gross national product, and the Soviet Union is in second place (though on a *per capita* basis, a number of European states and Japan are ahead of the Soviet Union). There are some equally evident contrasts between the two. The United States is the oldest political system operating within the framework of a written constitution, which formally commits it to liberal and individualistic values. It has what is now usually described as a mixed economy. It is recognized as the leader of the Free World. The Soviet Union, since its founding in the Russian Revolution, has been explicitly committed to Marxist-Leninist collectivist values. Its economy is based upon state property and is centrally planned. It is the leader of the communist "commonwealth," though its position has recently been challenged by China.

What can we learn from a comparison of these two giants? To begin with, we should be aware of the fact that there is no *need* to compare the United States with the Soviet Union. We can explain and forecast their respective behavior, including their behavior toward each other, by making other kinds of comparisons. For example, we can compare American politics with British politics, since the similarities and differences between these two systems are also fairly obvious. Both are English-speaking, both share the English Common Law, both are relatively prosperous, industrialized, and urbanized, and both have well-educated populations. The United States was founded as a splinter off the old British block, and since 1776 it has followed its own clear pattern of development. American politics can also be compared internally over the course of time—as of 1965, 1945, 1925, and so forth. Similar external or internal comparisons can be made for the Soviet Union.

However, before we make either direct comparisons between these two systems or any other external or internal comparisons involving each of them separately, we must decide precisely what we want to explain in their respective behavior or in their relations with one another. Normally, this focus of comparison is a specific difference. Often the difference for which an explanation is being sought is not clearly defined, and one reason for this vagueness can be found in the inadequate descriptive tools with which the analyst is working. Sometimes the categories used for purposes of description are limited to the statistical materials that provide the basis for only a superficial kind of comparison, as made in the second paragraph of this chapter—for example, gross national product (GNP), structure and distribution of the population, military and police expenditures as a part of the budget, public expenditure as a proportion of GNP, welfare expenditure as a proportion of GNP, and trends in any of these. But these data are really instrumental, that is, they can be used to explain other more basic differences. Why, for example, has the United States experienced urban riots involving considerable violence in the 1960s, whereas nothing similar has been reported from the Soviet Union? Why does the Soviet Union control most of its neighbors in eastern Europe more tightly and by different methods than the United States some of its Caribbean neighbors? Why their different approaches toward developing countries, or their different behavior in the United Nations?

"TOTALITARIANISM": AN ESSENTIALIST METHOD

Some methods do not begin with this approach of making a clear statement of the differences they want to explain, as between two countries, or between two periods in the history of one country. Instead, they are more interested in forecasting the future and perhaps in using a political system like the Soviet Union or the United States as a case study on which to test (or with which to demonstrate the utility of) a particular theory. The concept of "totalitarianism" has frequently been applied in this way.

For example, Professor Adam B. Ulam, in *Patterns of Government*, presents a very comprehensive analysis of the Soviet political system, which is based entirely upon this concept. He begins by assuming that there is an "essence" of totalitarianism. He accepts the anachronistic criticism of Plato, mentioned in Chapter 1 (footnote 2), according to which Plato "anticipates totalitarianism by prescribing what music a well-ordered state should allow. The rulers of Russia followed by prescribing or banning various styles of musical composition. . . ."[1] Ulam asserts that the "*moderate* use of terror can never be abandoned by a totalitarian regime."[2] He comes close to offering a classification of types of totalitarianism, when he distinguishes a "*stable totalitarian* situation" of the kind that prevailed under Mussolini in Italy. He calls the Soviet Union a "police state,"[3] but he fails to mention in this context that France and Prussia, beginning in the eighteenth century, have frequently been described as police states. Professor Ulam writes that "The logic of totalitarianism as well as that of socialism makes the U.S.S.R. a bureaucratic state."[4] But he neglects to mention that the United States, among others that profess to be neither totalitarian nor socialist, is often described as an administrative state.

In other words, Ulam commits an error that no student of Aristotle's theory of causes should commit. Like any analyst of political systems, he begins by asking what "caused" the Soviet political system to have become what it is today, but then he confuses the different types of causes: the material, the efficient, the formal, and the final cause. In the Soviet Union, the material cause consists of the human beings and the nonhuman material. The efficient causes of present conditions in the Soviet Union have to be looked for in history. Aristotle described the formal cause as the essence, as the form or the archetype of a thing, or as its definition. This is what Ulam concentrates on in his assumption that his study of Soviet politics is a case study in totalitarianism. As a result, he confuses what he considers the formal cause with the efficient causes—that is, he confuses what he calls the "logic of totalitarianism" with the "elements" that were needed in order to bring about present conditions. He also confuses what he considers the formal cause with the final cause or *telos*, that is, the purpose or end toward which the

---

[1] Adam B. Ulam, "The Soviet Political System," in *Patterns of Government: The Major Political Systems of Europe*, 2nd rev. ed., Samuel H. Beer and Adam B. Ulam, eds., New York: Random House, 1962, p. 642.

[2] *Ibid.*, p. 693.

[3] *Ibid.*, p. 696.

[4] *Ibid.*, p. 670.

Soviet political system is tending as a result of the intentions of those who make it work.

A political system always tends to some point, in part because at least some of its members want it to move in a certain direction or directions. However, the direction toward which Professor Ulam sees Soviet politics moving is not the one in which Soviet leaders from Lenin through Stalin to Khrushchev have said they *wanted* it to move, but rather the direction in which, according to some definition of the end and essence of totalitarianism, such political systems are said to be *bound* to move. In other words, Ulam assumes at the outset that there is such a general type as "totalitarianism." Then he assumes that the Soviet Union has been and is still such a system. Finally, he reads backwards from these two assumptions in order to confirm them, a relatively easy feat. In this way, and quite unintentionally, Professor Ulam's work provides an excellent illustration of the importance of using sound methods. Had he started with a different method, for example, the one proposed in this book, he might have arrived at quite a different ordering and, therefore, a different understanding of the same set of facts. As a result, his explanation of the peculiarities of Soviet politics, and his forecasts of its future development, would have been different.

Professor Carl J. Friedrich, who has elaborated what is perhaps the most comprehensive and sophisticated theory of totalitarianism, has encountered similar difficulties, somewhat magnified in his case, because he based his theory initially upon a direct analogy between Hitler's Germany and Stalin's Soviet Union as the two prototypical totalitarian regimes. He considers totalitarianism an unprecedented form of government, which could not have arisen before the twentieth century had presented the technological wherewithal. He defines the phenomenon as a syndrome of six mutually related clusters of characteristic features, which include a "technologically conditioned near complete monopoly of control . . . of all means of effective mass communication, such as press, radio, motion pictures, and so on."[5] A similar monopoly of all means of effective armed

---

[5] Carl J. Friedrich, ed., *Totalitarianism*, Cambridge, Mass.: Harvard University Press, 1954, p. 53.

combat and a system of terroristic police control depend upon the same advanced technology. Even the official ideology of the single mass party could hardly have focused on "chiliastic claims as to the 'perfect' final society of mankind," unless modern technology had let the perfection of human society, on a global scale, appear to be feasible. From Friedrich's point of view, then, the crucial difference between earlier forms of tyranny, dictatorship, or absolutism, and totalitarianism is found in the totality of control achieved by the latter, previously unattainable for large societies that lacked the instruments of modern technology.

There are some difficulties in this definitional approach. For example, if each of the six interrelated traits must be present before a system can be labeled totalitarian, how can we classify political systems along a spectrum running from the ideal type of totalitarianism at one extreme to the ideal type of its opposite, presumably constitutional democracy, at the other extreme? And what can we say about developing countries that have not even begun industrialization, but whose governments are accused of the widespread use of coercion and repression? A number of postcolonial regimes in the developing areas have been subject to such charges, Ghana and Egypt among them. They show some traits of the totalitarian syndrome: the single mass party led by its charismatic leader, commitment to some ideology, party control of the economy, mass communications, and means of effective armed combat, and in some instances varying degrees of terror. But they lack the technological base allegedly required to facilitate total control. In fact, the leaders of such regimes often claim to be using aspects of the so-called syndrome to further technological modernization. If they are totalitarian, then it is not because they are industrialized and have the required technology, but because they want to achieve industrialization.

The most promising way to gaining an understanding of the phenomenon called totalitarianism is to compare those systems to which the term is usually applied both with each other and with their nontotalitarian opposites.[6] Nazi Germany under Hitler and the

---

[6] See also Spiro, "Totalitarianism," *International Encyclopedia of the Social Sciences*, vol. 16, New York: Macmillan-Free Press, 1968, pp. 106–113.

Soviet Union under Stalin are usually regarded as prototypical totalitarian regimes, and Communist China under Mao Tse-tung has been added more recently to this category. The Communists themselves naturally reject the label of totalitarianism, which scholars, publicists, and propagandists of the West have pinned on them. But they do not return the charge by calling their opponents totalitarians. Rather, they call them capitalists, imperialists, or colonialists, and their systems of government, minority dictatorships of the bourgeoisie. Since the Marxists conceived of the dictatorship of the proletariat as the first postrevolutionary stage on the road toward socialism and communism, they evidently object not to dictatorship itself, but to minority dictatorship, which they regard as reactionary or nonprogressive. By denying charges of totalitarianism made against their own regimes without calling their critics totalitarian in turn, the Communists remain silent on the issue of totality of control. In this they resemble some non-Marxists who consider the trend toward totality of political control a common feature of all industrial societies, regardless of ideological persuasion.

The most characteristic features of the three major political systems of the twentieth century that have generally been considered totalitarian are listed in descending order of their distinctiveness:

1. Commitment to a single, positively formulated substantive goal, like industrialization, racial mastery, and proletarian unity, and a concomitant lack of commitment to maintenance of procedural stability.
2. Unpredictability and uncertainty, resulting from the condition of procedural flux, under which yesterday's hero is today's traitor, and today's loyal behavior tomorrow's subversion.
3. The large scale use of organized violence by military and paramilitary forces and both uniformed and secret police.
4. Parallel efforts to enforce universal participation in public organizations dedicated to the single goal, and to coordinate or suppress other organizations and associations not geared to the substantive aims of the regime.
5. Universalization of the single goal of remaking all mankind in the image of the totalitarian regime itself.

THE PROBLEM OF DESCRIPTION

The theorists of totalitarianism put the cart of explanation before the horse of description. Their essentialism or definitionalism led them to try to explain phenomena that they had not yet fully grasped in their existential reality. They had failed to grasp them, because they lacked proper concepts. Since we have now described the peculiarities that scholars wanted to single out as common features of Hitler's and Stalin's dictatorships, we can relate our descriptive concepts to the rest of the method proposed in this book.

We have omitted *operational commitment to an ideology* as an integral feature of totalitarianism, because it also characterizes systems not generally classified as totalitarian. Many democratic socialists and some Roman Catholics, among others, seem as firmly committed to their ideologies as the Nazis or Stalinist Communists were to theirs. Ideologism in general may be viewed as a distinctively Western political style, discernible to a greater or lesser extent in all political systems in, or influenced by, the West. The distinctive feature lies not in the commitment to, but in the content of, the ideology. In the course of the Cold War, repeated efforts have been made to fashion an ideology of the Free World with which to combat the Soviet ideology. This has been particularly true in the United States, but such efforts usually met with little success. As we will try to show later in this chapter, the theories of totalitarianism just discussed have sometimes been harnessed to these ideologizing efforts. Their aim has been to marshal popular commitment to the values incorporated in the new ideology, but *not* to further the establishment of totalitarianism in the West. This particular characteristic, therefore, could be used to support the hypothesis of "convergence" between the Soviet Union and the United States, that is, the proposition that in terms of their political behavior they are tending to move toward one another.

Universalization of the single substantive goal of the system toward the reshaping of all mankind in its own image is the least distinctive aspect of typical totalitarianism, because some clearly nontotalitarian regimes have at times displayed a similar outlook. Like the tendency toward ideologizing, this seems related to economic, cultural, and social conditions increasingly prevalent in all modern or modernizing societies, conditions that promise soon to become global. Woodrow Wilson's negative and procedural goal of "making the world safe for democracy" seemed reasonable to many people in the Western world. After World War II, both the United States and the Soviet Union, as well as other modern industrial states, held up to more backward nations the positive substantive goal of modernizing themselves in the image of these highly developed countries. With varying degrees of success, both the Western powers and the Soviet Bloc offered economic and technical aid to the developing countries to promote this transformation. Immediately after World War II, the United States and the Soviet Union both worked more directly toward the goal of reforming in their own image those countries that they ruled by military occupation, especially Germany and Japan.

In any case, the shrinking of distances that advances in the technology of communications and transportation have brought about has been leading to a reduction of substantive economic, social, and cultural differences among political systems. In awareness of this, both the great contenders in the Cold War have naturally exerted themselves toward shaping the anticipated new, more or less homogenized, character of all mankind in their own image.

Enforced general participation in public organizations is more marked under totalitarianism than under nontotalitarianism. This is particularly obvious if voting participation is taken as the only index, since both the Soviet Union under Stalin and Nazi Germany came close to enforcing participation of 100 percent of the electorate in voting, whereas in constitutional democracies only between 40 and 80 percent of the electorate normally vote. Apart from such formal practices as voting, however, advances in the technology of communications have not only facilitated but made inevitable inclusion of the entire population in the political, or at least in the "public," process. In principle, it makes little difference whether radio and television networks and the press are operated by the state and the single party, as in the Soviet Union, by private enterprise under government regulation, as in the United States, or under some mixed arrangement, as in Great Britain.

In both the United States and the Soviet Union these media are used for both commercial advertising and propaganda, though the former predominates in the United States, and the latter in the Soviet Union. But in the United States during the Cold War, privately owned media have urged the population to give financial and moral support to anti-Soviet propaganda organizations like Radio Free Europe, to inform themselves and to practice the American way of life, to buy government bonds, to join the armed forces, and to build fallout shelters. And government agencies, including the Central Intelligence Agency, have subsidized avowedly private organizations, like the National Student Association, in order to use them for anti-Communist Cold War activities.

In all modern societies, the tendency is toward enforcing greater individual attention to public matters and toward eroding the sphere of privacy, though the Soviet Union has moved further in this direction than the United States, and the United States further than Great Britain. The scope of the individual's sphere of privacy, incidentally, seems related less to "totalitarian trends" than to antecedent social patterns. For instance, a Soviet family living in an overcrowded apartment building in Moscow *may* enjoy greater familial privacy than an American family living in its own house in the suburbs of New York City.

The suppression of associations not dedicated to the substantive goal of the regime manifests itself as the concomitant of the enforced coordination, *Gleichschaltung*, of organizations whose existence antedates establishment of the regime. The effort to coordinate, in turn, is an aspect of enforced participation. In constitutional systems coordination and suppression are used mainly in crises and emergencies. In Nazi Germany, Stalinist Russia, and Communist China, they were in constant evidence in varying degrees, depending on the persistence or relative innocuousness, in different periods, of organizations like churches and social groupings like the family.

But even in the United States during the Cold War, efforts have been made to enlist a wide range of organizations in the anti-Communist struggle, from churches and charitable associations to economic interest groups and sports clubs. Communist organizations and their fellow travelers were subjected to legal disabilities. In wartime, coordination and suppression are carried much further, even in constitutional democracies, which then in effect become constitutional dictatorships. In such circumstances, however, suppressed organizations are usually outlawed according to established procedures, which are previously and publicly known. By contrast, in Nazi Germany, the suppression of private associations was achieved by a variety of procedures not previously known to the public, so that the future of these organizations remained permanently unpredictable to their members. This difference suggests that procedural instability, discussed below, is a more distinctive feature of totalitarianism than the suppression of private organizations.

The widespread use of organized violence still more clearly distinguishes the systems most frequently designated totalitarian. In the eyes of the leaders of these systems, military and police violence on a large scale is made necessary, and therefore justified, by the urgency with which they pursue the goal that is the end of the whole system. Nazi extermination camps and the liquidation of the *kulaks* under Stalin illustrate this point. Although violence is in the first instance directed against classes of the internal population, like Jews or remnants of the bourgeoisie, the regime usually identifies these classes with an external enemy in foreign relations.

In constitutional systems during peacetime, violence has not been used against segments of the domestic population on a scale anywhere approaching those in the cited illustrations, with the exception perhaps of racial conflicts. Even in wartime, when constitutional democracies found it necessary to set up concentration camps for population groups identified by race, nationality, or sympathy with the enemy (for example, Japanese-Americans in the United States or German refugees in the United Kingdom), due process was observed to varying degrees, and relatively few acts of brutality were recorded.

While the overall internal use of organized violence may be a function of totalitarian trends, this seems less true of the scope of police functions. Like the sphere of individual privacy, this appears to be more closely related to antecedent traditions of the political system than to the totalitarian orientation of a particular regime. Measured purely in terms of the scope of police functions, including the use of secret police and informers, France and Germany (previously Prussia and other German states) had been "police states" at least since the end of the eighteenth century, and France perhaps more so than Germany. But after Hitler came to power in Germany, the *Geheime Staatspolizei*, Gestapo, which had previously operated as an arm of the constitutional Prussian government, was converted into a dreaded instrument of terror, because it no longer operated according to known procedures, including a system of appeals to higher public authorities. No similar development occurred under the Vichy regime in France.

By contrast, none of the English-speaking countries, probably because of the traditions of the Common Law, could ever have been properly described as a police state. In the United States, even under pressure of the most severe crises the system has confronted so far, the Federal Bureau of Investigation and similar agencies have never become instruments of terror operating outside the channels of due process of law. The police informer's role, often played eagerly on the European continent, is much harder to fill in the English-speaking world. The United States Bureau of Internal Revenue pays secret denouncers of tax delinquents a portion of the amount recovered, but receives relatively few such denunciations. In the United States, large-scale organized violence in times of xenophobic crisis, instead of coming from the police or other government sources, is more often threatened or applied by popular movements, which either operate outside the law, like vigilantes or the Ku Klux Klan, or avail themselves of and try to transform the institutions of government themselves, as did the proponents of McCarthyism in the 1950s.

A less distinctive characteristic of totalitarianism than the scope and style of internal violence is external violence, despite the effort, mentioned above, to link the objects of both. In their foreign relations, totalitarian and nontotalitarian governments alike use similar types of force, since both work with the same technological conditions, and because they have generally expected to fight each other: the Allies against Nazi Germany, the Western powers against the Soviet Bloc. As in the case of Western attempts to forge an ideology, one feels that one must "fight fire with fire." It was the United States that first used the destructive power of the atomic bomb against

Japanese cities. In the Cold War, American and Soviet leaders have professed equal readiness to employ hydrogen bombs against each other, though neither has faced the possibility of nuclear war with as much equanimity as the Chinese Communists apparently have.

The contemplation or the actual use of massive violence against outside enemies tends to deaden sentiments against its internal application. When millions, including one's own fellow citizens, are being slaughtered or kept in foreign prison camps during a war, the liquidation or imprisonment in concentration camps of whole sectors of one's own society loses some of its horror. When the extermination of hundreds of millions and indeed the total end to human life, as the result of a nuclear holocaust, become realistic possibilities, and when government planners think in terms of building shelters to preserve the persons deemed most valuable for the eventual regeneration of society after such a catastrophe, the employment of total internal violence can be tolerated more easily than was the case even during World War II.

Thus there seems to be a clear relation between the quality and quantity of internal violence and worldwide trends toward totalitarianism. Since both totalitarian and nontotalitarian systems exist within the same international environment of potential massive violence, with its ramifications for internal politics, the use of organized violence on a wide scale is listed as a feature less distinctive of totalitarianism than is unpredictability due to procedural instability.

Uncertainty and unpredictability were the rules of life for ordinary men and both high and low members of the dominant party under Hitler and Stalin. Although Hitler never bothered to abrogate or replace the Weimar Constitution, under which he came into office as Chancellor, an act passed by the *Reichstag* in March 1933 made it possible for him, under color of legality, to amend the constitution by decree to the point of its utter transformation. Hitler himself became supreme lawgiver, *oberster Rechtsherr*; his will was "law," and he provided, in effect, whatever constitution Germany had under his rule. Whenever he changed his mind, he could also have changed not only the personnel but the most basic institutions of party and state. And although Stalin, in 1936, elaborately provided the Soviet Union with the constitution named after him, he never allowed it to become the framework of political processes. Stalin not only constantly turned over his personnel and remade institutions, but also kept the interpretation of Marxism–Leninism–Stalinism in a state of continuous flux, controlled only by himself. Mao may have presided over a similar process, by first promulgating and then revoking the doctrine of "letting a hundred flowers bloom and a hundred schools of thought contend" and later during his Great Cultural Revolution, by first encouraging and then restricting popular demonstrations.

In none of these cases was there either a regular publicly known procedure for effecting change or means by which individuals could anticipate which institutions or policies would be changed, and when. Stalin in particular skillfully manipulated and exploited this uncertainty. For instance, by appearing to be moving to the ideological left, he would thereby entice others to go even further in that direction through attempted imitation of the leader. He would then apparently execute an extreme swing to the right, leaving his erstwhile emulators ideologically exposed and ready for liquidation. The feeling of uncertainty created by such maneuvers probably contributed much more to the atmosphere of terror that is generally associated with totalitarianism than did the massive internal use of organized violence. Uncertainty meant that the victims of liquidation might not know the reasons for their fate and, more important, that those who wanted to avoid liquidation in the future had no rational means for doing so. They could not escape from the dilemmas of uncertainty either by withdrawing from politics, because of forced participation, or by mouthing the current party line, because that would expose them to condemnation for merely "mechanical" commitment. Repeated executions of chiefs of secret police can serve as a paradigm for this process. In nontotalitarian police states, by contrast, one chief of secret police often serves in his post for several decades.

Characteristically, in death Stalin became a victim of the very system of manipulated unpredictability that he had perfected during his lifetime, for Khrushchev removed his name from the Marxism-Leninism hyphenation and his body from Lenin's mausoleum. This posthumous de-Stalinization also has no counterpart in nontotalitarian systems where, when yesterday's hero is denounced as today's Public Enemy Number 1, the change can be understood as the result of a major change in the system of government, perhaps even a revolution, as, for example, the change from monarchy to republic. Under Stalin, as under Hitler—for example, in the Nazi Party purge of 1934—loyalty was converted into disloyalty by fiat of the dictator in the absence of other related changes in the system. This is quite different from the relegation to the realms of the powerless, with respect to political patronage, among other things, of the supporters of a displaced government by its successor, often practiced in non-totalitarian systems. Nor does it resemble the falling from favor, and even the prosecution or persecution, of former supporters or agents of a policy that has been discredited and radically reversed as, for example, in the case of public servants associated with the unsuccessful China policy of the United States under McCarthyism. In that case at least the grounds for attempts to brand as subversive previously loyal personnel were understood by all concerned, including the public, because of the link with a parallel effort to change the policy.

While unpredictability and uncertainty are the most distinctive of the totalitarian characteristics discussed so far, they are also the ones most likely to be moderated, or even eliminated, in political systems that retain or develop the other totalitarian traits. And whereas nontotalitarian systems sometimes seem to be developing the other feaures discussed, even long-established totalitarian systems seem to be moving away from unpredictability and toward more nearly constitutional methods. For example, the longest lived of the prototypical regimes, the Soviet Union, has emphasized "socialist legality" in the post-Stalin period, and some students of Soviet affairs have noticed the emergence of more clearly discernible social groups (party bureaucracy, military, management, intelligentsia, and others) that may be trying to stabilize both relations among one another as well as internal operating procedures. This has been explained as a result of the objective demands of efficiency in any modern industrial system. Up to the point of diminishing returns, uncertainty may produce greater productivity out of fear of reprisals; once this point has been passed, however, practices like falsification of statistics and black marketeering interfere with planning for the single substantive goal and, in general, reduce the capacity of the leadership for total control.

Ruthless pursuit of a single, positively formulated goal is the most distinctive common denominator of "totalitarianism." Non-totalitarian systems, to the extent that they articulate their goals at all, are either committed to a plurality of them, like those listed in the Preamble to the Constitution of the United States of America; or concentrate on procedural goals like the settlement of conflicts, as did the founding cantons of the Swiss *Eidgenossenschaft*, literally, "Oath Fellowship," the German title of the Swiss Confederation; or state their substantive goals negatively, like prevention or termination of foreign domination.

Excessive preoccupation with procedural goals can lead to parliamentary routinization, as we have seen. On the other hand, the single-minded pursuit of a positive substantive goal like racial hegemomy, the dictatorship of the proletariat, or the rapid industrialization of a backward economy, in utter disregard of all other possible goals, is likely to lead to what is generally described as totalitarianism. All the resources of the system are ruthlessly geared to attainment of the one great goal. An ideology is constructed in order to explain all reality with reference to this goal and to overcome the obstacles encountered in pursuit of it. Whatever is considered efficient with respect to overcoming these obstacles is done, and whatever is considered distracting from this singlemindedness of purpose is condemned and eliminated. As a result, there are no procedures worked out for the resolution of disagreements. All disagreement within the system is identified as evil. Internal politics is, therefore, banned. But when unanticipated new problems arise, as they must in the ever-changing modern environment, then there is a lack of adaptive procedures by means of which these problems can be tackled and disagreements about them deliberated and resolved. The ruling group as well as ordinary people lack experience with or commitment to such workable procedures. For the same reason, the leadership cannot admit the attainment of its original goal, since the pursuit of this aim is its only reason for existence.

The most distinctive aspect of constitutional systems, by contrast, is the comparatively procedural bias of sources of authority prevailing in them, and the relatively strong procedural commitment of their leaders. These leaders rise to the top more because they are identified with the rules of the political game, than because they have gained fame by bringing their supporters economic, cultural, or social advancement. It follows that those constitutional democracies that are most susceptible to totalitarianism are those in which top leadership is based upon substantive achievement, like military glory, cultural contributions to an ethnic group, great wealth, and the like. Comparisons made from this point of view suggest that the dangers of totalitarianism are greater in Germany than in France, greater in France than in the United States, and greater in the United States than in Great Britain.

Professor Sigmund Neumann aptly described totalitarianism as "permanent revolution."[7] The editors of *Fortune* magazine once applied the same term to the American economy, where products and productive processes are constantly subject to revolutionary change, but where the fundamental procedures of political adaptation remain stable.[8] Under totalitarianism, these procedures are in continuous flux.

SIMILARITIES, ANALOGIES, AND EXPLANATIONS

The preceding description of the peculiarities of so-called totalitarian regimes as contrasted with their constitutionalist opposites should now place us in a position where we can begin to explain the development of Soviet political style since the Revolution. When the Soviet system was founded, Lenin and the other revolutionary leaders had neither much procedural knowhow, nor agreement on the kind of procedures by which to conduct the internal politics of the Bolshevik party and the external politics of the Revolution itself. But they did have knowledge of the techniques of gaining power,

[7] Sigmund Neumann, *Permanent Revolution: The Total State in a World at War*, 2nd ed., New York: Praeger, 1965.

[8] The Editors of *Fortune, U.S.A.: The Permanent Revolution*, New York: Prentice-Hall, 1951.

and they agreed on the desirability of the pursuit of this power. The absence of consensus on the rules of the game at the founding of a political system usually has the long-run consequence of retarding the development of political procedures, of restricting the spread of familiarity with these procedures among the population, and of reducing the depth of commitment to whatever procedures do develop among both politicians and the general public.

The Soviet Union was founded upon an ideology to which the idea of violent class struggle was central. The founders were intent on destroying the existing political system of Russia, with the result that the founding period itself was characterized by intense class hatreds, involving as it did a prolonged period of brutal civil war (which, incidentally, included Western intervention in Russian territory). Largely as a result of these beginnings, for at least three decades thereafter the best if not the only way of gaining authority in Soviet politics was by giving proof of one's full commitment to the current substantive goals of the regime, whatever they might be. In British politics, by contrast, one gains political authority by demonstrating that one has mastered the rules of the game of whichever "club" it is one wants to join. We can illustrate this difference with an analogy to sports. The British, as well as their former colonial charges who learned the game from them, play cricket not so much to win any particular match, as to demonstrate their mastery of the intricate and complex and ever-developing rules of the favorite national sport. The Soviets, on the other hand, play soccer in order to win. (This analogy, of course, is an exaggeration, since soccer happens to be the favorite *mass* sport in Great Britain, and Soviet athletes *have* demonstrated sportsmanship in participating in international tournaments.)

From the Russian Revolution until several years after the death of Stalin in 1953, substantive goals, defined by the pursuit of ideology and power, were predominant in Soviet politics. There was no opportunity to develop procedures to regularize the formulation of issues, to deliberate and resolve these issues, and to solve the problems the recognition of which originally gave rise to the issues. After Stalin had established himself as sole dictator, he alone set the goals to which the Soviet system was dedicated, and these goals were always exclusively substantive. It would have been against his own interest in perpetuating his control to promulgate any set of rules through which disagreements could have been processed. It went counter to his interest, and to his interpretation of Marxist ideology, to admit that disagreement (the generation of issues) might conceivably have beneficent effects. Since, in effect, Stalin claimed to be in possession of the whole truth, based upon his interpretation of Marxism-Leninism, he had to deny the need for any rules by means of which partial truths, or different versions of one and the same truth, could be reconciled. It also clearly went counter to his interest to provide any procedures for the selection of his associates, his subordinates, or, most important, his successors. Stalin therefore concentrated in a very single-minded way upon the forging and the pursuit of certain substantive goals for the Soviet Union, and he did not hesitate to change the content of these goals at irregular intervals, as he saw fit. This erratic, irregular element in Stalin's method of ruling made the development of procedures of politics still more difficult.

The substantive bias in the sources of authority and the substantive nature of whatever consensus exists were the main distinctive features of politics in the Soviet Union from the Revolution until at least some time after the death of Stalin. In terms of the descriptive categories used in this book, the most important change that has occurred in Soviet politics since that period consists of a gradual shift toward a better balance between procedural and substantive concerns. While Soviet political style under Stalin oscillated between ideological violence and pragmatic violence, it approached the politics of purposive compromise much more closely in the 1960s than ever before.

Most of the preceding statements about Soviet politics were based mainly upon internal comparisons between different periods in Soviet history. If we compared Soviet politics with the politics of another system, whether dictatorial or constitutionalist, the emphasis would be different. The point, however, is that this kind of approach can lead to better explanations, for explanations are arrived at by comparing events and situations that are analogous. The fact that at one time or another both Hitler and Stalin conducted themselves as enemies of the West in international politics does not make their methods of internal rule in Germany and the Soviet Union analogous to one another. But the fact that both Hitler and Stalin did try to abolish procedural stability, and largely succeeded in making it impossible for the individual to foresee the consequences of his own actions, does present *analogous* situations, which can be usefully compared. The fact that both Russia and the United States of America are continental countries with large and growing populations and that both had open frontiers made for *similarities* between these two countries that were destined to become the superpowers of the twentieth century. And, as already mentioned, De Tocqueville, the great commentator on American politics of the nineteenth century, noticed these similarities and based certain predictions upon them.

However, *similar* situations and *analogous* situations are not the same thing. Analogies are warranted only where the *relations* among the components of two situations are similar. This means that before we could conclude from the similarities between nineteenth-century America and Russia that analogies between the two countries were warranted, we would have to establish that the similarities went beyond the size of the countries and the existence of frontiers to the relations among the ingredients of those situations in the two countries—for example, the relations between the population and among different segments of it and the land, both settled and open. Or, to return to "totalitarian" Nazi Germany and Stalinist Russia, analogies would be warranted only if the relations among dictator, party, secret police, industry, mass media, and ideology could be shown to have been similar. These relations were in fact quite dissimilar.

Those who use totalitarianism as an explanatory concept often take too seriously the claims made by the dictator himself in his ideological statements. In other words, they accept the "*telos*," or end goal, that the dictator at least professes to have set for himself, his party, and the movement that he claims to be leading. They also tend to accept at face value a regime's statement about the means that it is using in order to achieve the end goal, because they assume from the outset that in a totalitarian state "the end justifies the means." This has led many scholars to credit the operations of

Hitler's secret police, the Gestapo, with much greater efficiency than it actually showed. In any case, the concept of totalitarianism leads to an unbalanced perspective on political systems under study and has contributed very little to our understanding of apparently novel political phenomena of the twentieth century. The best illustration of this is perhaps the almost utter failure to anticipate the cataclysmic changes that occurred in Communist China in the 1960s. China behaved neither the way totalitarian dictatorships nor countries dominated by Marxist-Leninist Communist parties had behaved previously. China certainly did not behave the way China had behaved in the two millennia of its historical existence as an organized political system. The surprising thing was the continuing popularity among both scholars and politicians, especially in the United States, of the concept of totalitarianism and of theories based upon it, despite its failure in helping to interpret reality and to forecast events. This popularity in turn calls for an explanation.

METHOD AS IDEOLOGY

Americans have generally regarded themselves as pragmatists in the way they conduct their politics, both domestic and foreign. Up until World War II their international environment had appeared to them both rational and susceptible to pragmatic manipulation. They had been capable of handling problems of foreign relations quickly, without raising or even becoming aware of problems concerning fundamental values, and the war itself had confirmed this pragmatic attitude. In a short time the United States had put together a great alliance that included the ideologically incompatible Soviet Union; it had defeated the most powerful military coalition ever confronted; and it had brought into being the most destructive weapon ever created and used by man, the atomic bomb, two of which had been dropped on Japan in order to end the war quickly.

Americans consequently expected that they would be able to face their future international relations in a similarly pragmatic, *un*ideological or even *anti*ideological fashion. But their expectations were soon to be disappointed. The wartime alliance fell apart, and the United States saw the Soviet Union as resuming a stance of rigid and often brutal ideologism. The blockade of Berlin, the Korean War, the victory of the Chinese Communists, and other unanticipated events led the United States to "reverse" its alliance and to convert West Germany and Japan, its recently defeated enemies, into its most reliable friends. It also had to consider the possibility of using nuclear weapons, over which it no longer had a monopoly when they were acquired by the Soviet Union as well. Moreover, the last best hope of pragmatic rationalism in world politics, the United Nations, failed to live up to American expectations. The former colonies, whose liberation from European domination had been strongly encouraged by the United States, turned to neutralism or to flirtations, or worse, with the Soviet Bloc in the two-sided politics of the Cold War.

The concatenation of these multiple and interrelated problems pushed Americans away from their previously pragmatic stance in world politics. The Soviets evidently drew much of their obstinacy or commitment from Marxist-Leninist ideology, which purported to explain all history, past, present, and future. The division of the world, in American eyes, resembled an almost Biblical confrontation between the forces of good and evil, which the United States could hardly participate in on the basis of merely circumstantial and pragmatic considerations and motivations. The possibility of actually using nuclear weapons, whose destructiveness was being constantly increased to genuinely global proportions in the "age of overkill," practically foreclosed a pragmatic justification of their employment of the kind advanced by President Truman when he ordered the atomic bombs dropped on Hiroshima and Nagasaki.

In these circumstances, theories of totalitarianism enabled Americans, both policy makers and ordinary citizens, to understand an international environment that appeared increasingly irrational, to tie their present national purpose to an interpretation of their historic past, and to rationalize their current Cold War conduct both to themselves and to their allies. "Totalitarianism" justified the reversal of alliances, since the United States had been fighting this system of rule, not the German and Japanese peoples who were temporarily dominated by it. It was therefore justified in allying itself with its "saved" former enemies and in considering the totalitarian Soviet

Union a danger to itself and to all nontotalitarian nations. Moreover, the theory could explain and predict the behavior of the Communists in terms of the "logic of totalitarianism," to which some scholars and policy makers referred as an inevitable natural law. Soviet totalitarianism also explained the Soviet Union's "wrecking tactics" in the United Nations and, as a response to Communist blandishments, the "irresponsible" conduct of new states both within and outside the United Nations. Finally, the theories of totalitarianism as the institutionalization of the most radical evil threatening mankind were also used to justify American use of nuclear weapons in order to prevent the victory of evil. In its most extreme form, which did *not* become a basis for policy, this attitude is best expressed in the slogan, "Better dead than red."

In the light of this interpretation of the function of theories of totalitarianism, let us consider an interesting and paradoxical transformation of American political style that occurred in the decade or two after World War II. Americans had been pragmatic about international relations and their role in it. Foreign policy was something one could rationally deliberate and arrive at sensible decisions about. When this did not appear to be true any longer, Americans pragmatically looked for an explanation of the change and of the new realities of world politics. They found the explanation in essentialist theories of totalitarianism. Since totalitarian regimes were believed to be thoroughly ideological and therefore fanatically committed to their evil goal of world domination, Americans believed themselves more duty bound to give up pragmatism and adopt a more ideological stance than ever before. They searched for "national goals."[9] At the same time, they also built up the enormous arsenal of nuclear and less unconventional weapons that would be required to turn back totalitarian aggression, in whatever form. After this military machine had been built up to its unprecedented "peacetime" proportions, the old pragmatism began to reassert itself, but in a new way. American foreign policy goals had been set largely in negative terms, congruent with their *anti*totalitarian foundations: to contain or roll

---

[9] President's Commission on National Goals, *Goals for Americans*, Englewood Cliffs, N.J.: Prentice-Hall, 1960.

back communism, to liberate Eastern Europe, to punish aggression, and so forth. The United States still lacked a positively formulated purpose. This enabled those who controlled the military power of the United States to set and reset national goals in a given conflict in terms of particular military capabilities. For example, American goals in Vietnam were repeatedly "escalated," and later "de-escalated," in terms of estimates of what the United States was capable of achieving over any particular short run of time. In other words, the pseudoideologism of antitotalitarianism brought into being vast power, whose immediate potential was used to define pragmatically the purposes of the ideology.

As a concomitant of these changes, and in the face of increasingly visible and almost tangible cleavages within the American polity, political leaders, especially President Lyndon B. Johnson, preached the virtues of consensus perhaps more than ever before, except for periods of open and declared warfare. Moreover, the consensus that they wanted to bring about was on matters of substance, not matters of procedure. It was a consensus on the merits of a specific foreign, racial, or economic policy, not a consensus on the established and formerly highly flexible rules of the game of politics. Sources of authority in American politics were also decreasingly procedural and increasingly substantive. Most significantly, politics itself tended to be denigrated more than before. Americans generally have not accorded it the same primacy among human activities as Britons have usually done (in their less than fully conscious manner). Americans have often been ambivalent about politics, especially in periods of great public corruption. But even at such times, although they disliked the activities of the ward heeler and political boss, they only wanted to clean up politics that had become dirty, not eliminate politics altogether. In the 1960s, however, various efforts were made to transcend or overcome politics by abolishing it as much as possible: through substantive consensus, through the imposition of systematic administration using the administrative method of system analysis, and through other measures. All of these efforts were based more or less on the tacit assumptions that the single truth, providing the best solutions to problems, existed; that a certain type of nonpolitical public figure (often an academic intellectual) had access to this truth; that ordinary people, including elective politicians, could not possibly have this access or even the capacity to understand the problems; and that the definition and solution of problems should therefore be left to the experts.

CHANGE, DESCRIPTION, AND COMPARISON

The preceding discussion shows the dangers of a faulty concept, for both practical politics and its academic analysis. It also points to the causes of the popularity of the concept of totalitarianism in the United States, where it has played a much more important role than in the politics, and especially the foreign policies, of other countries allied with the United States in the Cold War. How can we best identify the causes of this popularity? Once again we face the problem of adequate description. A conventional description of the evolution of politics in the United States would point to the fact that it is a "mixed polity," in the Aristotelian sense, or a constitutional democracy, which for the greater part of the past 175 years has been getting increasingly democratic. Its position in international politics can be described as having moved from relative isolation and powerlessness to increasing involvement and the status as one of the two contemporary superpowers. Recent changes in American domestic politics would probably be attributed to the exigencies of the Cold War, and some observers suggest that opposites in politics are likely to become more and more like one another, that is, to converge. In this sense, and for these reasons, some would say that the United States is becoming more like the Soviet Union and the Soviet Union is becoming more like the United States, because the two superpowers are confronting one another at the lonely summit where both own operational nuclear weaponry. In this same vein it has been seriously suggested, by radical domestic critics, that the United States is beginning to show certain characteristics of totalitarianism. For our purposes, this suggestion again illustrates the vast inadequacies of the concept of totalitarianism.

A description of the evolution of American politics that uses the categories of political style is more likely to lead to understanding. In the period leading up to World War II, American domestic and foreign politics had been comparatively pragmatic—that is, compared both with earlier periods of American history, in which we find the advocacy of "Manifest Destiny" and Woodrow Wilson's "messianism," and with the politics of other major powers during the same period, 1920 to 1939. This predominantly pragmatic style oscillated between a sometimes more legalistic, sometimes more violent emphasis. However, there was relatively little ideologism in American domestic politics or foreign policies during this period. Most Americans active in politics were primarily concerned wth achieving short-term goals, without giving much thought to the long-run consequences of their policies. In promoting these ends, they would alternate between legislation and litigation on the one hand, and the vigorous application of the "power" at their disposal, including the power to use violence, on the other. In domestic politics during the period of the New Deal, for example, a large volume of legislation brought forth an even larger volume of litigation in the courts, including the Supreme Court. At the same time the natural and human resources of the country were marshaled for the solution of various substantive problems, like rural electrification, irrigation, and overcoming the Great Depression, to the accompaniment of a comparatively high volume of political violence, for example, in labor relations. American foreign policies during the period between the two world wars were marked, on the one hand, by participation in a whole series of international conferences designed to reduce the level of armaments, and on the other, by the application of American military force for very short-term pragmatic ends in the area of the Caribbean Sea, where a number of countries were repeatedly occupied by American Marines, sent there partly in order to back up American business interests. American participation in World War II came belatedly and reluctantly, and finally only as a result of the Japanese attack upon Pearl Harbor. Prior to becoming a belligerent, the United States had supported its allies-to-be, because this was believed to be in the "national interest," by supplying them with military and other supplies. It justified these measures in a manner both legalistic and pragmatic, as in the instance of the Lend Lease bill. The United States as an actual belligerent behaved in a similarly legalistic-pragmatic or violent-pragmatic manner. There was certainly less ideologism in the international stance of the United States than in that of any of its allies or opponents. For example, when the condition of "unconditional surrender" was advanced, President Roosevelt gave less consideration to the long-run consequences of this pronouncement than his partner in making it, Prime Minister Churchill of Great Britain. These antecedents help explain why most Americans involved in international politics had expectations of an increasingly rational, manipulatable, and "progressive" international environment for the postwar world.

We have just traced how these anticipations were disappointed, and how this disappointment in turn led to the great receptivity for the concept and the theories of totalitarianism in the years from 1945 to 1968. As happens often, when one extreme form of style does not achieve its ends, people lapse into its extreme opposite—from pragmatism to ideologism, or from legalism to violence. In this case, two points are of methodological significance for the study of politics in general, and of American politics in particular. First, during the years in which this tremendous change in American political style took place, there were no significant changes in the political institutions or procedures of the United States, at least none significant enough to be commented upon by serious students of American politics. And second, the one significant change that did occur in the attitudes toward politics of Americans was *not* commented upon by most serious analysts. This can be described as a change from an optimism about the capacity of achieving one's goals through politics to, at best, a profound ambivalence about the feasibility of gaining one's goals through politics or, at worst, a deep pessimism about this. And it was perhaps in this respect more than in any other that the styles of American and Soviet politics were moving toward one another. In the Soviet Union, at the height of Stalin's rule at least, politics, in the sense in which we are using the term in this book, was denigrated, stifled, and suppressed. In the United States, from the time of the founding, politics was developed almost for its own sake. But in the United States in the period since the end of World War II, skepticism about the capacities of politics has led to its denigration and, especially in periods in which "consensus" was praised for its own sake, to efforts on the part of some politicians to identify "politics as usual" with disloyalty. At the same time that the supreme desirability of consensus is asserted, and even preached, politics itself is identified with power alone, and no longer with the ever tense combination of power and choice, foreknowledge and purpose.

Selected Bibliography

Arendt, Hannah, *The Origins of Totalitarianism*, 2nd ed., New York: Meridian, 1958.

Barghoorn, Frederick C., *Politics in the USSR*, Boston: Little, Brown, 1966.

Fainsod, Merle, *How Russia Is Ruled*, 2nd ed., Cambridge, Mass.: Harvard University Press, 1963.

Friedrich, Carl J., ed., *Totalitarianism*, Cambridge, Mass.: Harvard University Press, 1954.

Friedrich, Carl J., and Zbigniew K. Brzezinski, *Totalitarian Dictatorship and Autocracy*, 2nd ed., rev. by Carl J. Friedrich, New York: Praeger, 1966.

Huntington, Samuel P., and Zbigniew K. Brzezinski, *Political Power: USA/USSR*, New York: Viking, 1963.

Moore, Barrington, Jr., *Political Power and Social Theory: Six Studies*, Cambridge, Mass.: Harvard University Press, 1958.

Moore, Barrington, Jr., *Soviet Politics: The Dilemma of Power*, Cambridge, Mass.: Harvard University Press, 1950.

Moore, Barrington, Jr., *Terror and Progress, USSR: Sources of Stability and Change in the Soviet Dictatorship*, Cambridge, Mass.: Harvard University Press, 1955.

Neumann, Franz, *Behemoth*, New York: Harper & Row, 1966.

President's Commission on National Goals, *Goals for Americans*, New York: American Assembly and Englewood Cliffs, N.J.: Prentice-Hall, 1960.

Spiro, Herbert J., "Foreign Policy and Political Style," *The Annals*, vol. 366 (July 1966), pp. 139–148.

Ulam, Adam B., "The Soviet Political System," in *Patterns of Government*, 2nd ed., Samuel H. Beer and Adam B. Ulam, eds., New York: Random House, 1962.

In one point, however, the history of the development of society proves to be essentially different from that of nature. In nature—in so far as we ignore man's reaction upon nature—there are only blind, unconscious agencies acting upon one another, out of whose interplay the general law comes into operation. Nothing of all that happens—whether in the innumerable apparent accidents observable upon the surface or in the ultimate results which confirm the regularity inherent in these accidents—happens as a consciously desired aim. In the history of society, on the contrary, the actors are all endowed with consciousness, are men acting with deliberation or passion, working towards definite goals; nothing happens without a conscious purpose, without an intended aim. But this distinction, important as it is for historical investigation, particularly of single epochs and events, cannot alter the fact that the course of history is governed by inner general laws. For here, also, on the whole, in spite of the consciously desired aims of all individuals, accident apparently reigns on the surface. That which is willed happens but rarely; in the majority of instances the numerous desired ends cross and conflict with one another, or these ends themselves are from the outset incapable of realization, or the means of attaining them are insufficient. Thus the conflicts of innumerable individual wills and individual actions in the domain of history produce a state of affairs entirely analogous to that prevailing in the realm of unconscious nature. The ends of the actions are intended, but the results which actually follow from these actions are not intended, or when they do seem to correspond to the end intended they ultimately have consequences quite other than those intended. Historical events thus appear on the whole to be likewise governed by chance. But where on the surface accident holds sway, there actually it is always governed by inner, hidden laws, and it is only a matter of discovering these laws.

Friedrich Engels, "Ludwig Feuerbach
and the End of Classical German Philosophy,"
in *Marx and Engels: Basic Writings on Politics and Philosophy*,
Lewis S. Feuer, ed., New York: Anchor Books, 1959, p. 230.

POLITICS AND CONSCIOUSNESS 7

Nowadays, and especially in books like this, the work of Karl Marx and Friedrich Engels is usually studied in order to determine the contribution that they made to subsequent history. For example, the question is often asked: To what extent did Marx and Engels prepare the way for contemporary Communism, "totalitarianism," and/or democratic socialism? Vigorous debates have been raging for decades about the legitimacy of the claims of various political philosophers and ideologues that they are the true interpreters of the work of the founding fathers of Marxism. However, since the general purpose of this book is to introduce politics as the master science, we will be interested mainly in their *approach* to the study of politics and related aspects of human existence. Of course, in connection with our central interest, we will have to consider somewhat the more conventional questions as well.

MORAL VERSUS SCIENTIFIC CRITICISM

Since 1848, when Marx and Engels published their *Communist Manifesto*, the volume of political activity in the world has increased greatly. Marxism itself made major contributions to this tremendous expansion of politics. One could say that everything is different because of, or at least that everything has been affected by the work of, Marx and Engels. Marxism mobilized millions of people into political consciousness and motivated the Russian and the Chinese revolutions, which affected more people than any earlier revolutions.

Today, everyone who is active in politics is, whether he is explicitly aware of it or not, either a Marxist or an anti-Marxist. This is so, regardless of one's position on how the proper lines of legitimate intellectual descent run, that is, for example, whether they run from Marx to Mao or from Marx to Willy Brandt of the German Social Democratic party. The truth of this assertion is not refuted by the fact that many of the people engaged in politics may be utterly ignorant of what Marxism is all about. Its irrefutability may be illustrated by the statement made by Marx himself at a point later in his life, that he himself was not a Marxist. The fact is that no one involved in politics today can be indifferent to these new political issues that were first raised in a clear, dramatic, popularly understandable form by Marx. (For reasons of convenience, we will refer to "Marx and Engels" from now on simply by naming Marx, the acknowledged senior partner in this true marriage of minds.)

At first glance, this Marxist contribution to the expansion of politics may seem paradoxical, since Marx himself asserted the primacy of economic factors in historical causation. Thus, if economic changes, and more specifically changes in the mode of production, are the prime movers of history, then how could it have been possible for Marx, through his sheer intellectual efforts and the impact of his writings upon his contemporaries and his disciples, to have helped bring about tremendous historical changes, including the expansion of politics? This apparent paradox is sometimes explained by pointing to the great moral appeal of the Marxian message, both to the economically oppressed and to their sympathizers in other classes. And in truth, the appeal of the moral criticism that Marx made of the mid-nineteenth-century economy and society in which he lived was very strong. He focused especially upon the terrible conditions under which the working classes in England were living at the time. The accuracy of his accounts can be vouched for by the fact that he took most of his data from the reports of British government factory inspectors. In England, where the Industrial Revolution was in full swing, and in continental European countries, which were trying to emulate British industrial progress, members of the working classes were living without freedom and in conditions of inequality. If there were two basic goals to whose achievement the Marxian moral critique of nineteenth century bourgeois capitalism was addressed, they were freedom and equality. Of course, Marx and his followers were by no means alone in espousing these values. Indeed, freedom and equality were the mainstays of European liberalism in the nineteenth century. To attribute the tremendous impact of Marx's work to his having exposed the conditions of exploitation under which workers lived in his time, and to his advocacy of freedom and equality for these workers, is an insufficient explanation.

A more plausible explanation of the tremendous contribution to the expansion of politics made by Marxism is to be found in the Marxian method rather than the Marxist message and its substantive content and moral appeal. Marx himself would have agreed with this explanation, because he asserted that his socialism was genuinely "scientific socialism." And it was this scientific character of socialism, precisely because it *was* based upon scientific truth, that enabled him to level the most powerful criticism at society (which meant incidentally that the scientific and the moral critiques were identical). Many students of Marxism, however, have disagreed with Marx's self-estimate and have tended to dismiss his claim to being scientific as rubbish. Some have suggested that Marx felt he had to advance this claim because he was a part of the German tradition of intellectualism, in which being scientific was simply one of the requirements of respectability. After all, Marx had earned a Ph.D. in philosophy, awarded him by the University of Jena. Engels called their method "dialectical materialism." Our point here is that this method of political analysis has had and continues to have a strong if delayed impact upon contemporary man's understanding of reality.

Marx himself participated in the Great Conversation in a typically dialectical fashion. The immediate object of his polemic was his great dialectical teacher, Hegel, who has been labeled a "dialectical idealist." This means that Hegel taught that all history is the history of the struggle between ideas opposing one another in dialectical fashion: each thesis brings forth its antithesis and out of the resulting struggle between the two emerges a new synthesis. Marx said that by replacing dialectical idealism with dialectical materialism, he had put Hegel right side up, after Hegel had stood history on its head. Students of dialectical materialism usually emphasize this reversal of emphasis, upon which Marx did indeed insist. However, Marx was also very conscious of another change in emphasis that over the long run has had at least equal importance: Hegel's assertion of the existence of the Absolute, that is, of *the* truth. Many superficial studies of Marx and his influence neglect this aspect of his work, probably as a result of their interest in the question of intellectual pedigrees. Since they assume that certain contemporary Communists are the direct lineal descendants of Marx, and since they classify these contemporaries as totalitarian ideologues, they assume that Marx also believed that the final truth existed and that he himself had access to it. But this was not so. Marx and Engels criticized Hegel not only for his idealism, but also for his assertions about the Absolute. At the same time, Marx did not oppose his own materialist absolute against Hegel's mistaken idealist absolute. On the contrary, he specifically denied that he or anyone else knew *the* truth about anything, including the development of history.[1]

---

[1] "A system of natural and historical knowledge, embracing everything, and final for all time, is a contradiction to the fundamental law of dialectical reasoning. This law, indeed, by no means excludes, but, on the contrary, includes the idea that the systematic knowledge of the external universe can make giant strides from age to age." Friedrich Engels, "Socialism, Utopian and Scientific," in *Marx and Engels: Basic Writings on Politics and Philosophy*, Lewis S. Feuer, ed., New York: Anchor Books, 1959, p. 87.

"That which still survives of all earlier philosophy is the science of thought and its laws—formal logic and dialectics. Everything else is subsumed in the positive science of nature and history." *Ibid.*, p. 88.

"Just as the bourgeoisie by large-scale industry, competition, and the world market dissolves in practice all stable, time-honored institutions, so this dialectical philosophy dissolves all conceptions of final, absolute truth and of absolute states of humanity corresponding to it. For it (dialectical philosophy) nothing is final, absolute, sacred. It reveals the transitory character of everything and in everything; nothing can endure before it except the uninterrupted process of becoming and passing away, of endless ascendancy from the lower to the higher." Engels, "Ludwig Feuerbach and the End of Classical German Philosophy," *ibid.*, p. 199 f.

DEVELOPMENT AND CONSCIOUSNESS

Marx criticized not only what he sometimes called the "metaphysical idealism" of Hegel and his followers but also the mechanistic materialism of certain liberal and other socialist philosophers and economists. He accused them of looking at phenomena in isolation, at rest, as though they were constant, dead, and always harmonious. Marx, on the other hand, looked at phenomena in relation to one another, in movement, as ever-changing, alive, and in conflict.[2] If we put together the two prongs of the Marxian critique of political, economic, and social philosophies, we could summarize Marx's position as follows: he insisted upon the crucial importance of becoming as opposed to being, upon process as opposed to substance, upon development and dynamics as opposed to statics. Quite consistent with this position, Marx made no claim to being able to predict the far distant future, or even the short-run period.[3]

Today, after more than two decades of concentrated discussion about the politics of the "developing areas" and development, it is easy to forget that Marx was the first social scientist to concern

---

[2] "And the metaphysical mode of thought . . . sooner or later reaches a limit beyond which it becomes one-sided, restricted, abstract, lost in insoluble contradictions. In the contemplation of individual things it forgets the connection between them; in the contemplation of their existence it forgets the beginning and end of that existence; of their repose, it forgets their motion. It cannot see the wood for the trees. . . .

None of these processes and modes of thought enters into the framework of metaphysical reasoning. Dialectics, on the other hand, comprehends things and their representations, ideas, in their essential connection, concatenation, motion, origin, and endings." Engels, "Socialism: Utopian and Scientific," *ibid.*, p. 84 f.

[3] "With all philosophers, it is precisely the 'system' which is perishable; and for the simple reason that it springs from an imperishable desire of the human mind—the desire to overcome all contradictions. But if all contradictions are once and for all disposed of, we shall have arrived at so-called absolute truth—world history will be at an end. And yet it has to continue, although there is nothing left for it to do—hence, a new, insoluble contradiction. . . . One leaves alone 'absolute truth,' which is unattainable along this path or by any single individual. . . ." Engels, "Ludwig Feuerbach," *ibid.*, p. 202.

himself in a systematic way with problems of development. The word development, *Entwicklung,* occurs on virtually every page of many of his and Engels' works. What did he mean by "development"? The word itself means unfolding, or unwrapping. When he spoke of development, therefore, he had in mind the unfolding or the unwrapping of something that was already present. Capitalism developed out of feudalism, and socialism will develop out of capitalism, because the core of the new society is wrapped in the old society and needs only development, that is, unwrapping.

But what sets this process of development in motion? According to Marx, it is conflict, which is at the core both of the historical process and of the analytical process, which he himself used. Much of the misunderstanding of Marx is due to a simplistic interpretation of the assertion attributed to him, according to which economic change is the prime mover of history. He did assert that history is kept moving by the contradictions, and especially the irreconcilable contradictions, in the material conditions of human existence. Most important among these is the contradiction between the mode of production, which under the capitalist system had become social (that is, it involved the whole society), and the mode of appropriation and distribution, which under capitalism was still organized on a private, or nonsocial, basis. By insisting upon the inherent contradictions in human existence, especially in its economic aspects, Marx put himself into clear opposition to the prevailing economic philosophers and theorists of his time, because they insisted upon the natural harmony in life. Most liberal economists of the nineteenth century believed that the automatic mechanism of the free market would lead to optimization of the "wealth of the nation." This was just as Adam Smith had put it in his famous book *The Wealth of Nations* (1776): in the free market "each man pursues an end which was no part of his intention," the end being the public welfare, the immediate intention having been private profit. Marx's view of irreconcilable contradictions was closer to that of his contemporary Charles Darwin, in another sphere of science, biology.

Marx saw conflict not only as the core of the historical process itself but also as the best method of thought by which to bring about a more comprehensive grasp of the laws governing reality. It was through dialectical conflict, through the great polemics of the ages that have made up the Great Conversation of political philosophy, that he believed better—that is, more useful and "progressive"—visions and versions of the ever elusive truth could be approached. His familiarity with the great philosophical dialectics, beginning with those between Socrates and his students, may have persuaded Marx that it was only through this kind of vigorous controversy that intellectual and material progress could be brought about. Certainly, few if any of his predecessors were as viciously polemical as he was at times in attacking his forerunners, his adversaries, and, even more, his self-styled disciples.

According to Marx, the primary contradictions are all of an economic nature. Moreover, he viewed politics as the means used by economic interests to promote their goals. For example, he saw political parties as the expression of class interests, and he defined class in terms of the relations between people and the means of production. The capitalist class consisted of those who owned and controlled the means of production, machinery, land, and so forth, and the proletariat consisted of those who owned nothing but their own labor power. In this respect, Marx seems to agree with the conventional wisdom of the nineteenth century. This was the period of the primacy of economics, when many serious thinkers believed that the natural laws governing the economy had been or were about to be discovered, and when industrial and economic progress were viewed as the preconditions for improving the moral welfare of mankind. At this time, what we would now describe as political science was often called "political economy." This raises the question how the Marxian view differed from the conventional view about the primacy of economics.

The answer can best be given by a single sentence, the last of Marx's "Theses on Feuerbach." "The philosophers have only *interpreted* the world; the point however is to *change* it."[4] By definition, to want to change the world means to engage oneself in politics. Marx and Engels themselves, and even more so their successors down to our contemporaries, have certainly tried to change the

---

[4] Marx, "Theses on Feuerbach," *ibid.*, p. 245.

world, and they have succeeded in changing it, though not always in the intended direction. Through their efforts to change the world, the Marxists resolved the alleged contradiction between the apparent economic determinism of their philosophy of history and their actual political activism. Some of Marx's critics have claimed that his insistence on economic change as the prime mover of history was irreconcilable with his advocacy of political action, be it revolutionary or merely reformist. The critics asked, in effect: What is the point of exerting oneself, if socialism will inevitably occur, and if the revolution has to take place in any case? A similar question had been raised earlier about the activism of certain Protestant religious sects, like the Calvinists, who though they believed in rigid predestination, yet exerted themselves greatly, apparently in order to gain the Kingdom of Heaven. The Calvinists may have exerted themselves because they believed that no man predestined for Hell would be allowed to show a capacity for good works while on earth. In the case of Marx, the apparent paradox between economic determinism and political activism is resolved in another way, through the great importance assigned by Marx to consciousness.

In his "Critique of the Hegelian Philosophy of Law," one of his early writings, Marx said:

> The arm of criticism can of course not replace the criticism of arms, and material power must be overthrown by material power; theory, too, however, becomes material power as soon as it pervades the masses, as soon as it argues *ad hominem*; and it argues *ad hominem* as soon as it becomes radical. To be radical means to take things by their roots. The root for man, however, is man himself.[5]

Later on, he might have expanded this to read, "The root for man is man himself and his consciousness of himself." In their later writings, both Marx and Engels placed great emphasis upon the importance of consciousness, to which they believed themselves, after all, to have made a most significant contribution. By discovering the

---

[5] *Aus dem literarischen Nachlass von Karl Marx, Friedrich Engels und Ferdinand Lassalle*, vol. I, Franz Mehring, ed., Stuttgart: J. H. W. Dietz Nachf., 1902, p. 392.

general laws by which history unfolded, they had, so they thought, expanded human knowledge and awareness about human existence. With perhaps unusual modesty, Marx and Engels as a pair did not lay claim to this contribution, though Engels praised Marx in just such terms after the latter's death. The major Marxist philosophers of the next generation, however, singled out precisely the contribution to the expansion and development of proletarian consciousness that Marx had made. The *Communist Manifesto* had stated that, in a certain period of history, some "bourgeois ideologists . . . raised themselves to the level of comprehending theoretically the historical movement as a whole."[6] Undoubtedly, Marx and Engels had themselves in mind in this passage, but undoubtedly they also differentiated between *understanding* the historical movement, and trying to "change the world."

It fell to Karl Kautsky, Lenin's great adversary in the polemics among Marxists of the next generation, to deny that historical consciousness, and especially proletarian class consciousness, would arise spontaneously. On the contrary, Kautsky asserted that consciousness arises out of profound scientific knowledge.[7] By this he presumably meant knowledge of the method of dialectical materialism and of

---

[6] Marx and Engels, *The Communist Manifesto, ibid.*, p. 17.

[7] "To supplement what has been said above we shall quote the following profoundly true and important utterances by Karl Kautsky . . . 'But socialism and the class struggle arise side by side and not one out of the other; each arises under different conditions. Modern socialist consciousness can arise only on the basis of profound scientific knowledge. Indeed, modern economic science is as much a condition for socialist production as, say, modern technology, and the proletariat can create neither the one nor the other, no matter how much it may desire to do so; both arise out of the modern social process. The vehicles of science are not the proletariat, but the *bourgeois intelligentsia* [Kautsky's italics]: it was in the minds of some members of this stratum that modern socialism originated, and it was they who communicated it to the more intellectually developed proletarians who, in their turn, introduced it into the proletarian class struggle where conditions allow that to be done. Thus, socialist consciousness is something introduced into the proletarian class struggle from without (*von Aussen Hineingetragenes*), and not something that arose within it spontaneously (*urwüchsig*). . . .'" V. I. Lenin, *What Is to Be Done?* (1902), New York: International Publishers, 1969, pp. 40–41.

whatever substantive information was needed at the time. The interesting thing is that Lenin, who otherwise agreed with virtually nothing that Kautsky ever said, quotes the passage from Kautsky's work with approval. In his article "What Is to Be Done?" Lenin denies that class consciousness can arise spontaneously among the masses without deliberate organization, agitation, and propaganda. For Marx, the development of consciousness was a good in itself, partly because of its necessity and partly because of the contribution it would make to the forward movement of history, since the emergence of contradictions and their recognition—in our terms, the formulation of new issues for politics—would accelerate and sharpen the dialectical struggle.

Lenin took the concept of consciousness a step further, and in doing so clarified the relations between the economic and political aspects of the dialectical process. He accused Kautsky of detaching economics from politics, by suggesting that advances on the political front could never get ahead of the stage of class consciousness that the proletariat had reached as a result of economic developments.[8] For this reason, Lenin rejected as "merely formal advances" those constitutional political reforms that had taken place in some of the more progressive democracies of Western Europe and North America. In this respect at least, Lenin agreed with the original position of Marx and Engels, who also asserted that the institutions of constitutional democracy served merely as a facade, behind which the state, as the executive committee of the ruling capitalist class, simply facilitated the continuing exploitation of the working class. According to Lenin, there is a dialectic between economics and politics, and this dialectic is kept moving through the development of consciousness.[9] Consciousness is heightened by the convergence, again

---

[8] Lenin, *Imperialism, the Highest Stage of Capitalism* (1917), New York: International Publishers, 1939.

[9] "To develop democracy *to its logical conclusion*, to find the *forms* for this development, to test them by practice, and so forth—all this is one of the constituent tasks of the struggle for the social revolution. Taken separately, no sort of democracy will bring socialism. But in actual life democracy will never be 'taken separately'; it will be 'taken together' with other things, it will exert its influence on economics, will stimulate *its* reformation; and in its turn

dialectical in nature, of scientific socialism and the class struggle itself. This scientific socialism is provided by the bourgeois intellectuals who detach themselves from their own class in order to identify themselves with the working class. In other words, Lenin might have paraphrased Marx, who stated in his "Theses on Feuerbach" that the philosophers had merely tried to interpret the world, while Marx, Lenin, and their working class followers have succeeded in changing it, through struggle guided by expanded consciousness.

POLITICS OR NO POLITICS?

But where would all this lead, after the revolution had overthrown the bourgeois state, and after establishment of the dictatorship of the proletariat? Marx never made any firm predictions beyond the inevitability of the revolution itself, and on this point Engels later admitted the possibility of peaceful evolution, as distinguished from violent revolution, in some of the more advanced countries of Western Europe and North America, including Great Britain, the Netherlands, and the United States. Engels spoke of the "withering away of the state" after socialism and communism had succeeded in establishing the classless society.

Lenin later took the trouble to deny specifically that Marx had ever made any predictions about the classless society,[10] and Mao Tse-tung supports Lenin in this view.[11] However, since Lenin was,

---

it will be influenced by economic development, and so on. Such are the dialectics of living history." Lenin, *State and Revolution* (1917), New York: International Publishers, 1943, p. 65.

[10] "But Marx did not set out to *discover* the political *forms* of this future stage. He limited himself to a precise observation of French history, to analyzing it, and to the conclusion to which the year 1851 had led, *viz.*, that matters were moving towards the *smashing* of the bourgeois state machine." *Ibid.*, p. 48.

[11] "In the capitalist age of free competition, Marx could not know concretely beforehand some of the special laws of the age of imperialism, because this age, the last stage of capitalism, had not yet arrived and there was no practice appropriate to it. Only Lenin and Stalin could shoulder this task. Aside from their genius, the factor that enabled Marx, Engels, Lenin, and Stalin to formulate their theories was their personal participation in the prac-

as it were, "closer to the future," he was more daring than Marx had been in trying to outline the contents of the future. Quoting Engels, he asserted that under communism the government of persons would be replaced by the administration of things.[12] The picture that he draws of the classless society, in rough outline, resembles one that we today can picture still more clearly, because by now many of the fantasies of science fiction, like data processing and the automation of production, have become realities.[13] As a result of the development of nuclear energy and other new sources of energy, of automation, and of other technological advances, it has become conceivable that individuals could rotate freely from one kind of job to another, as Lenin envisaged even before the Russian Revolution.[14] After the hard physical work of production itself has been taken care of almost entirely by machines, and after some of the revolutionary new methods of education and training have been further improved, there will be no reason, at least not in principle, why the increasingly

---

tice of the class struggle and scientific experiments of their time. Without such participation, not even genius can succeed in such a task. . . ." Mao Tse-tung, "On Practice" (1937), in Stuart R. Schram, ed., *The Political Thought of Mao Tse-tung*, New York: Praeger, 1963, p. 126; London: Pall Mall Press, 1964.

[12] Lenin, *State and Revolution, ibid.*, p. 16.

[13] "Capitalist culture has *created* large-scale production, factories, railways, the postal service, telephones, etc., and *on this basis* the great majority of functions of the old 'state power' have become so simplified and can be reduced to such simple operations of registration, filing and checking that they can be easily performed by every literate person, and it will be possible to perform them for 'workmen's wages,' which circumstances can (and must) strip those functions of every shadow of privilege, of every semblance of 'official grandeur.' " *Ibid.*, p. 38.

[14] "Such a beginning, on the basis of large-scale production, will of itself lead to the gradual 'withering away' of all bureaucracy, to the gradual creation of an order, order without quotation marks, which will be different from wage-slavery, an order in which the functions of control and accounting —becoming more and more simple—will be performed by each in turn, will then become a habit and will finally die out as the *special* functions of a special stratum of the population." *Ibid.*, p. 43.

"For, in order to abolish the state, the functions of the Civil Service must be converted into the simple operations of control and accounting that can be performed by the vast majority of the population, and, ultimately, by every single individual." *Ibid.*, p. 65.

specialized division of labor, which characterized the development of industrialism from the beginnings that Marx himself was studying, should not be eliminated.

This possibility is of great importance to Marxists, because Marx and Engels insisted that the worst coercion the workers suffered under capitalism was not the rule of the capitalists, but the division of labor. They argued that because of the division of labor that existed in factories of their time, the worker in effect became a part of the machinery with which he worked but of course did not own. As a result the worker was looked upon, and even looked upon himself, as a thing rather than a human being. This was the essence of "alienation." Neither Marx nor Lenin ever expressed themselves very clearly about the possibility of eliminating this kind of specialization of labor, and it seems reasonable to assume that they believed it would remain even under socialism. This was one reason for their insistence upon revolutionizing the relations between workers and the instruments of production, that is, upon the abolition of private property in the means of production. The fact that Lenin once described communism as that state of affairs in which the whole society would be like a single factory suggests that he expected the productive process with its division of labor to remain basically the same.[15] In this expectation, as in others, Lenin resembled Marx and Engels. Marx once savagely criticized the German Social Democrats of his time for favoring the abolition of child labor after the establishment of socialism, by saying that child labor could never be abolished, the best that could be achieved would be the combination of child labor with education.[16] In general, the great Marxist theorists displayed much less technological imagination than political imagination.

This raises the question: What did they expect to happen to politics after the revolution? Since the class struggle, which was an

---

[15] "The whole of society will have become a single office and a single factory with equality of work and equality of pay. But this factory discipline . . . is but a necessary *step* for the purpose of thoroughly purging society of all the hideousness and foulness of capitalist exploitation, *and for the purpose of advancing further." Ibid.*, p. 84.

[16] Marx, "Critique of the Gotha Program" (1875), *Marx and Engels: Basic Writings on Politics and Philosophy*, L. S. Feuer, ed., p. 131.

intensified form of politics, was to generate and advance consciousness, especially among the working classes, *before* the revolution,
what would be the relation between the expansion of consciousness
and politics *after* the revolution? Lenin never answered this question,
because he died before the Russian Revolution had been fully
secured. Stalin answered it in practice by repressing the development of politics, in favor of the apolitical or antipolitical development
of the industrial and military power of the Soviet Union. Under
Stalin, no new goals were advanced, and the generation of issues,
about either goals or the means by which to reach them, was pro-
hibited, sometimes brutally.

The first Marxist to answer the question about the development
of politics after the revolution was Mao Tse-tung. He is unique in
the history of Marxism, and perhaps in the history of the Great
Conversation of political philosophy, as an original political theorist
who has lived to rule the most populous country in the history of
the world for more than two decades. In the course of this time he
has applied his theories and at the same time constantly revised them
in the light of experience.

Long before the Chinese Communists firmly established their
rule on the mainland, Mao wrote several volumes in which he tried
to adapt Marxism-Leninism to the needs of China. This country
was a vast, underdeveloped, imperially dominated land, whose political system had the oldest continuous existence and traditions on
earth. At the same time he was writing he was constantly and deeply
"engaged" in titanic politico-military struggles. Despite his practical
experience and his constant involvement in practical political fighting, or perhaps because of this experience, throughout his writings
Mao expresses a keen awareness of the great importance of political
theory to political practice.[17] He places great value upon the con-

---

[17] "Thus far our work has not been carried on too badly, but if we do
not study theory more thoroughly, it will be impossible to improve on our
past performance, and it is only such improvement that will make victory
possible. The study of theory is therefore the precondition of victory." Mao
Tse-tung, "On the New Stage" (1939), in Schram, *The Political Thought
of Mao Tse-tung*, p. 113.

tribution made to the promotion of the Communist cause by a certain type of intellectual, in which he includes Marx, Engels, Lenin, Stalin, and himself.[18] Incidentally, in at least two respects Mao's claim to being an intellectual is more convincing than that of his predecessors, because he is both a distinguished poet and a skilled calligrapher.

Mao tried to clarify the distinction between idealism and materialism by asserting that the two stand in a dialectical relation to one another, and that out of this dialectic useful new concepts will grow.[19] He asserts that rational knowledge leads to revolutionary

---

[18] "We need theoreticians who base their thinking on the standpoints, concepts, and methods of Marx, Engels, Lenin, and Stalin, who are able to explain correctly the actual problems issuing from history and revolution, who are able to give a scientific interpretation and theoretical explanation of the various problems of Chinese economics, politics, military affairs, and culture. This is the type of theoretician we need. . . ." Mao Tse-tung, "Reform in Learning, the Party and Literature," ibid., p. 116.

"Thus Marx is to be regarded as a complete intellectual. The difference between him and the half-intellectual is that he participated in an actual revolutionary movement and carried on research and investigation by turning to a reality that was all-inclusive. This type of all-inclusive knowledge is called theory. . . ." Ibid., p. 118.

[19] "The source that enables idealism to develop and deepen and gives it strength to struggle with materialism must be sought in the realm of human knowledge. . . . When men think, they must use concepts. This can easily cause our knowledge to be split into two aspects: reality, which is of an individual and particular character; and concepts, which are of a general character. . . . Originally, the particular and the general are inseparably linked; once separated, they depart from objective truth. . . . To separate the general from the particular, and to view the general as objective reality and the particular merely as the form in which the general exists—this is the method adopted by all idealists. All idealists put consciousness, spirit, or concepts in place of objective reality existing independently from human consciousness. . . . They cannot point out the materialist truth according to which consciousness is limited by matter, but believe that only consciousness is active, whereas matter is only an inert composite entity. Urged on moreover by their own class nature, the idealists then use every method to exaggerate the activity of consciousness, developing this aspect unilaterally. . . . Idealism in economics exaggerates beyond measure a nonessential aspect of exchange, raising the law of supply and demand to the status of the fundamental law

practice and, again dialectically, revolutionary practice will lead to higher forms of rational knowledge.[20] But, and here Mao is more explicit than Marx or Lenin, he denies that men will ever command complete knowledge. He tells us that we will never have access to

---

of capitalism. . . . Idealist historians regard heroes as the makers of history. Idealist politicians regard politics as omnipotent. Idealist military leaders practice the methods of desperate combat [p'ing-ming-chu-i-ti-tso-chan]. Idealist revolutionaries advocate Blanquism. The diehards say that the only way to revive our nation is to restore the old morality. All this results from exaggerating subjective factors beyond measure. . . .

"Pre-Marxist materialism (mechanistic materialism) did not stress the thought process in the development of knowledge, but regarded thought merely as the object of action, as the mirror that reflects nature. . . . Only dialectical materialism correctly shows the role of thought, and at the same time points out the limitation imposed upon thought by matter. It points out that thought arises from social practice and at the same time actively shapes practice. Only this kind of dialectical theory of 'the unity of knowledge and action' can thoroughly vanquish idealism." Mao Tse-tung, "Dialectical Materialism," ibid., p. 122 f.

[20] "Marxist philosophy, dialectical materialism, has two outstanding characteristics. One is its class nature: It openly declares itself to be in the service of the proletariat. The other is its practicality: It emphasizes the dependence of theory on practice, practice being the foundation of theory, which in turn serves practice. . . .

"At first man sees practice only as the external aspect of things, their individual aspects, and their external relations to each other. . . .

"With the continuation of man's social practice, the sensations and images of a thing are repeated innumerable times, and then a sudden change in the cognitive process takes place, resulting in the formation of concepts. Concepts as such no longer represent the external aspect of things, their individual aspects, or their external relations. Through concepts man comes to grasp a thing in its entirety, its essence, and its internal relations. Conception is not only quantitatively but also qualitatively different from perception. . . . This is the second stage of knowledge. . . . In the complete process of knowing a thing, this stage of conception, judgment, and inference is more important than the first stage. It is the stage of rational knowledge. The real task of cognition is to arrive at thought through perception, at a gradual understanding of the internal contradictions of objective things, their laws, the internal relations between this and that process, that is, a rational knowledge. . . ." Mao Tse-tung "On Practice," ibid., p. 125.

"Rational knowledge depends upon perceptual knowledge and perceptual knowledge has to develop into rational knowledge. This is the epistemology of dialectical materialism." Ibid., p. 127.

the whole truth, because the movement that is at the core of dialectical materialism never finishes. Contradictions are ubiquitous, universal, and ever-lasting, in both the real world and in our knowledge
about this world.[21] It is these contradictions that bring about progress
in thought.

Mao introduced a new distinction into Marxist political theory,
between antagonistic and nonantagonistic contradictions. When
contradictions arise, or are raised to the level of consciousness, among
Communists themselves, both before and especially after a successful
revolution, these contradictions are nonantagonistic, that is, they
need not be resolved violently.[22] However, Mao tells us that without
contradictions there would be an end to party life, in other words,
if the members of the Communist Party were to behave as though
there were perfect consensus among themselves, the party would
stagnate and presumably no longer play a progressive role.[23] At one
point, Mao bases himself upon Lenin in asserting that, even under

---

[21] "There is nothing that does not contain contradiction; without contradiction there would be no world. . . .

"Objective contradictions are reflected in subjective thought, constituting
the contradictory movement of concepts, impelling the development of thought,
and ceaselessly solving the problems that arise in man's thinking. . . ." Mao
Tse-tung "On Contradiction" (1937), ibid., p. 130.

[22] "Contradiction is universal, absolute, existing in all processes of the
development of things and running through all processes from beginning to
end.

"As we have pointed out above, the contradiction between correct
ideology and erroneous ideologies within the Communist Party reflects the
class contradictions when the classes exist. In the beginning, or with regard
to certain matters, such a contradiction need not immediately manifest itself
as antagonistic. But with the development of the class struggle, it can also
grow and become antagonistic. The history of the Communist Party of the
Soviet Union shows us that the contradiction between the correct ideology of
Lenin and Stalin and the erroneous ideologies of Trotsky, Bukharin, and
others initially was not manifested in an antagonistic form, but subsequently
developed into antagonism." Ibid., p. 234 f.

[23] ". . . Within the Party, opposition and struggle between different
ideas occur constantly; they reflect the class contradictions and the contradictions between the old and the new things in society. If there were neither
contradictions nor ideological conflicts through which the contradictions are
resolved, the Party's life would come to an end. . . ." Loc. cit., p. 234.

socialism, contradictions can become antagonistic.[24] Statements like this one can help us to understand the Great Cultural Revolution, which was launched on Mao's behalf in 1966. By this time, Mao and his associates had been in control of China for eighteen years, and it would have been consistent with his theoretical statements had he wanted to keep the party alive by bringing to the surface of political consciousness new antagonistic contradictions among the Communists themselves. By generating new issues, conceivably even some "artificial" issues that bore no immediate relevance to the "objective needs" of the society, Mao may have intended to flush out incorrect ideology, and he undoubtedly did intend to fight bureaucratism, the dangers of which he recognized long before the Great Cultural Revolution.[25] In other words, the Cultural Revolution may have been designed to develop new theory out of revolutionary practice; it also, of course, threatened to get out of hand at various times.

There are passages in Mao's political thought that sound almost like John Milton's *Areopagitica*: "Let [truth] and falsehood grapple; whoever knew truth put to the worse, in a free and open en-

---

[24] "Some naïve ideas seem to suggest that contradictions no longer exist in a socialist society. To deny the existence of contradictions is to deny dialectics. . . . One contradiction will lead to another, and when old contradictions are solved new ones will arise." "On the Historical Experience of the Dictatorship of the Proletariat (1956)," Mao Tse-tung, *ibid.*, p. 235 f.

"Lenin said: 'Antagonism and contradiction are utterly different. Under socialism, antagonism disappears, but contradiction subsists.' That is to say, antagonism is only one form of struggle between contradictions, but not its universal form; we cannot apply this formula everywhere." "On Contradiction" (1937), *ibid.*, p. 235.

[25] "Our people's government is a government that truly represents the interests of the people and serves the people, yet certain contradictions do exist between the government and the masses. They include contradictions between the interests of the state, collective interests, and individual interests; between democracy and centralism; between those in positions of leadership and the led; and contradictions arising from the bureaucratic practices of certain state functionaries in their relations with the masses. All these are contradictions among the people. Generally speaking, underlying the contradictions among the people is the basic identity of the interests of the people." Mao Tse-tung, "On the Correct Handling of Contradictions Among the People" (1957), *ibid.*, p. 237 f.

counter."[26] Mao repeatedly returns to emphasizing that "of all the things in the world, people are the most precious," and that it is the political consciousness of the people that must be developed, the people whose development is the primary purpose of revolutionary activity.[27]

Mao invigorated political analysis with a vital method that he applied to both theory and practice and that was, consistent with its own tenets, full of its own contradictions. For example, at one point he denied the omnicompetence of politics and labeled those who held to this position "idealists."[28] At other times he asserted the primacy of politics as vigorously as any Marxist—or any Aristotelian, for that matter—ever has. Moreover, Mao's own historical role contributed more than anything else to the revival of theorizing within international Communism. This occurred because of the great dialectical struggle in which Mao engaged the leadership of the Soviet Union.

Communist political theory had been stagnating before Mao began to challenge the previously undisputed primacy of the Kremlin as the interpreter of Marxism-Leninism. Stalin himself had made only indifferent contributions to Communist political theory, and his most significant writings in this field dealt with basically "non-political" topics, such as the development of languages. Stalin himself, as already mentioned, preferred to repress politics within the Soviet Union. Under his rule, the processes of depoliticization and bureaucratization paralleled one another. Only after Stalin's death

---

[26] "Marxism must therefore still develop through struggle. . . . That which is correct always develops in the course of struggling against that which is wrong. . . . As mankind in general rejects an untruth and accepts a truth, a new truth will begin struggling with new erroneous ideas. Such struggles will never end. This is the law of the development of truth and it is certainly also the law of the development of Marxism. . . ." *Ibid.*, p. 241.

[27] Mao Tse-tung, "Revolution Can Change Everything" (1949), *ibid.*, p. 251, and Mao Tse-tung, "China Is Poor and Blank" (1958), *ibid.*, p. 252.

[28] "Idealist historians regard heroes as the makers of history. Idealist politicians regard politics as omnipotent. Idealist military leaders practice the methods of desperate combat." Mao Tse-tung, "Dialectical Materialism" (1940), *ibid.*, p. 123.

in 1953 did politics slowly begin to develop once more. This was true both of the Soviet Union and of what used to be known as the "Communist Bloc." Under Stalin, ideologically couched statements would justify the use of Soviet power on behalf of goals set by the dictator. There was never any admission of disagreement within the Soviet Communist party. Disagreement was used only as "deviationism," exposed after some leaders had been or were about to be liquidated. In other words, disagreement, the beginning of all politics, was denigrated, and this was as true of internal Soviet affairs as of relations between the Soviet Union and its Communist allies.

This appearance of monolithic unity was destroyed when China began to challenge the policies and the interpretations of Marxism-Leninism of the Soviet leadership. Mao and those purporting to speak for him have insisted upon the primacy of politics in all spheres—even to the point of denying the importance of nuclear weapons. They have called both the superpowers, the United States and the Soviet Union, "Paper Tigers," but they have developed their own hydrogen bombs at the same time. On the other hand, and in what non-Marxists would call an "inconsistency," and Marxists a "dialectical contradiction," Mao was quoted as saying that "Power grows out of the barrel of a gun."

The Chinese challenge to Soviet leadership of "International Communism" was bound to have a strong impact, especially in the other so-called developing areas. This was so not only because China itself, by reason of population, was the most important of the developing countries, but also because the leaders in the "Third World" were looking for practical models and theoretical guidelines from which to draw lessons for themselves. Until the late 1950s, especially if they were under the influence of the propaganda of the Cold War, they had two basic competing models to choose between, the Western and the Communist. A simplified view would contrast the two as follows: the Western countries, of which the United States was the outstanding example, were richer, more advanced industrially, more "political," and less egalitarian than the Communist countries, of which the Soviet Union was the prototype. The Western powers urged the developing countries of Asia, Africa, the Middle East, and Latin America to concentrate on economic progress before political advancement. The Soviet Union, on the other hand, advocated complete political independence, especially for colonial territories, to be achieved, if need be, by violent means, and to be followed by parallel economic and political advances. When Communist China presented itself as a third and in its own view superior model for the developing countries, the opportunities apparently available became more confused. The fact that most of the developing countries have nonwhite populations, and that China's population is nonwhite, whereas most of the peoples of the Soviet Union are white, added to this confusion. In any case, the new explosion, and it almost amounted to that after years of political dormancy, necessarily meant a new awakening of political activity and thought within both the Communist countries and the developing world. As a result of the emergence of new disagreements within the Communist camp, Communists, their opponents, and those who tried to be "unaligned" bystanders were virtually forced to clarify, both to themselves and for others, the expectations they held of modernization and development, and the roads they considered best suited for moving toward those goals. In this way, some theories advanced by two "obscure German intellectuals" working in England in the middle of the nineteenth century had, more than a century later, helped to stimulate the political consciousness *and* participation of hundreds of millions of people all over the globe.

The development of the objective process is full of contradictions and conflicts, and so is the development of the process of man's cognition. All the dialectical movements of the external world can sooner or later find their reflection in man's knowledge. The process of coming into being, development, and elimination in social practice as well as in human knowledge is infinite. As the practice of changing objective existing conditions based upon certain ideas, theories, plans, or programs moves forward step by step, man's knowledge of objective reality also *deepens step by step. The movement or change of the world of objective realities is never finished, hence man's recognition of truth through practice is also never complete. Marxism-Leninism has in no way put an end to the discovery of truths, but continually [pu tuan ti] blazes the path toward the recognition of truths through practice. Our conclusion is that we stand for the concrete and historical unity of the subjective and the objective, of theory and practice, of knowledge and action. . . .*

The discovery of truths through practice, the verification and the development of them through practice, the active development of perceptual knowledge into rational knowledge and, by means of rational knowledge, the active direction of revolutionary practice and the reconstruction of the subjective and the external world—practice, knowledge, more practice, more knowledge, and the repetition ad infinitum *of this cyclic pattern, and with each cycle, the elevation of the content of practice and knowledge to a higher level—such is the epistemology of dialectical materialism, such is its theory of the unity of knowledge and action.*

Mao Tse-tung, "On Practice,"
in Stuart R. Schram, ed.,
The Political Thought of Mao Tse-tung,
New York: Praeger, 1963, p. 128;
London: Pall Mall Press, 1964.

Selected Bibliography

Berlin, Isaiah, *Karl Marx: His Life and Environment,* New York: Galaxy, 1963.

Jacob, Philip E., and James V. Toscano, *The Integration of Political Communities,* Philadelphia: J. B. Lippincott, 1964.

Lenin, V. I., *Essential Works of Lenin*, Henry M. Christman, ed., New York: Bantam, 1966.

Marx, Karl, *Writings of the Young Marx on Philosophy and Society*, Loyd D. Easton and Kurt H. Guddat, trans. and eds., Garden City, N.Y.: Anchor, 1967.

Marx, Karl, and Friedrich Engels, *Basic Writings on Politics and Philosophy*, Lewis S. Feuer, ed., Garden City, N.Y.: Anchor, 1959.

Popper, K. R., *The Open Society and Its Enemies*, vol. 2, *The High Tide of Prophecy: Hegel, Marx, and the Aftermath*, New York: Harper & Row, 1962.

Schram, Stuart R., *The Political Thought of Mao Tse-tung*, New York: Praeger, 1963.

Schwartz, Benjamin I., *Chinese Communism and the Rise of Mao*, 2nd ed., New York: Harper & Row, 1967.

Tucker, Robert C., *The Marxian Revolutionary Idea*, New York: W. W. Norton, 1969.

Tucker, Robert, *Philosophy and Myth in Karl Marx*, Cambridge: Cambridge University Press, 1961.

Weber, Max, *The Protestant Ethic and the Spirit of Capitalism*, Talcott Parsons, trans., New York: Charles Scribner's Sons, 1958.

Probably the most useful thing we can do at present is to take note of all the possibilities for change; they are less fixed than one might suppose, and nothing is absolutely inevitable. The real obstacles, however, are still those which Shakespeare indicated in the minds of Caliban and Prospero, and it may be that they are so much a part of human nature as we know it that there is no point in our studying them. In that case the only genuinely collective psychotherapy is what is known as politics.

[Footnote:] Certain it is, in any case, that a good political training could make up for the lack of a psychological training, for political development can alter the whole structure of the personality. Indeed, it is hardly necessary to stress so obvious a point, since this has always up to now been the way in which personalities have been transformed. In presenting a psychological against the political point of view, I am not in any way suggesting that the one should be substituted for the other!

O. Mannoni, *Prospero and Caliban:
The Psychology of Colonization,*
New York: Praeger, 1956, p. 171.

POLITICAL
DEVELOPMENT

8

Until about 1960, the so-called developing areas were studied either by institutionalists, who looked at formal institutions, laws, and constitutions, and expected or advocated the transfer of western or communist institutions to developing political systems; or by determinists, who studied the effects *on* politics of economic, social, and cultural changes. Events soon proved both approaches to be mistaken. The failure of these conventional approaches, even when applied to conventional Western political systems like Germany, France, Great Britain, or the United States, should have been a warning to those who used them in a non-Western context.

INSTITUTIONALISM

Institutionalist students of the politics of the developing regions committed the error of holding excessively high expectations of politics in these areas. To use the words of Mao Tse-tung, this is the error of "idealism." And according to the categories of this book, the institutionalists paid too much attention to the quadrants of law and power, and not enough to the factors of culture and economy. They expected that when the British or the French or the Belgians, or any colonial power, imposed its own type of constitutional and legal system upon the population of a colonial possession, this system would soon begin to operate as intended, that is, as in the home country. They thought of law-making as the principal activity of politics, and believed that laws were always, or almost always, "executed" as intended by the legislator. This assumption is, of course, erroneous even when applied to the most mature, most stable political systems in the West. And, indeed, the unsatisfactory yields of institutionalist studies of Western political systems, for example, the Weimar Republic in Germany between the wars, should have warned those who applied the institutionalist approach to developing countries of their likely failure.

Excessively preoccupied with the basic goals of bringing about stability and efficiency, the institutionalists neglected the importance of gaining effectiveness and providing for flexibility. After the end of World War II, few of these scholars, now newly interested in vast continents that had previously been of concern mainly to the anthropologist, the colonial administrator, and the planter or merchant in tropical raw materials, foresaw the great popular movements against colonialism and imperialism that were soon to sweep out almost all the alien rulers. Most of them took the view that the great masses of the "native" population were completely uninterested in politics, ignorant even of the possibility of getting along without the colonial administration, and easily controllable by whatever method, be it benevolent or malevolent, the government of the home country favored.

Those eager to "advance dependent peoples to independence and self-government" as speedily as possible—as all signers of the United Nations Charter had formally proclaimed themselves to be—did not realize that their constitutions and their legal systems would not be readily accepted by the leaders of independence movements or that, even if they were accepted, the fact that the cultural background of these "non-Western" peoples was very different would make it difficult, if not impossible, for these institutions to operate as they had in Europe. For example, considering that the various French constitutions usually did not work well in their own French context, this particular nearsightedness comes as a surprise.

But there were more profound reasons why constitutional forms transplanted from the West, with its heritage of Greek logic and Roman law, were very unlikely to grow roots in the quite different cultures of Africa and Asia. For example, the two-camp pattern of politics that most of the English-speaking peoples are used to, under which *the* government is pitted against *the* opposition, is related to at least two historical factors that are not found in the non-Western world: the "oppositeness" of Aristotelean logic (also reflected in the old dialectical tradition of Western politics and philosophy) and the adversary method of the Common Law, whose origins lie in the judicial procedures of the English Middle Ages. The so-called two-party systems of the United States and Great Britain are possible because, in an unconscious way, people in these two countries simply assume that debate can be conducted most efficiently, and is most likely to lead to a realistic outcome, when a problem is treated as though it had only two different solutions, and when these two solutions are stated by two political parties and their leaders in the form of competing and opposing policies. In the Orient, on the other hand, the non-Aristotelian background and the complete absence of anything resembling the adversary tradition of the Common Law may lead people to expect that there can be only one solution to any problem or, on the other hand, that there may be a hundred different solutions, one of which "blends" into the next, and that one in turn into the next, and so on. Thus, a clear statement of competing solutions is impossible; in addition, such a statement may be considered lacking in piety or destructive of harmony and consensus, which are valued more highly than flexibility and efficiency.

Students applying the institutionalist approach to the study of the developing areas also failed to foresee the great scope and the extreme rapidity with which change occurred in these countries. This is surprising since the very term *development* implies growth, change, and unfolding. They should, therefore, have anticipated that it was not likely that constitutional forms introduced from Europe or America would be capable of containing the tremendous economic and cultural changes that were then already beginning to take place in the Third World. The result was that many institutionalist studies not only turned out to be wrong over the long run, but were out of date even before their publication. Such studies would describe in detail the constitution of some colonial territory or of a colony that had reached independence a year ago, while at the same time the new leadership was in fact intent either upon experimenting with its own constitutional forms or upon discarding constitutionalism as a whole because of its Western and therefore "neocolonialist" origins and purposes.

DETERMINISM

By contrast with the institutionalists, the determinists held expectations of politics that were much too low. To use Mao's words, they committed the error of mechanistic or non-dialectical materialism. In our terms, the determinists seemed to expect that the almost automatic pursuit of efficiency and flexibility made more deliberately fashioned aspects of law and the ancient habits of culture totally irrelevant. Their basic assumption was that the causal sequence of development ran from the economy to the society to the culture and finally to politics and government. Politics was basically only a secondary reflection of underlying economic processes seen in a "vulgar Marxist" way. In this view, given the economic resources of a country, economic change somehow results from "natural" processes or from causes external to the country itself; deliberate human action, that is, politics, is incapable of influencing subsequent "development" in any significant way. Moreover, change is necessary and inevitable, so that no attempt to channel it through even the most cleverly designed constitutional structure could succeed in giving a relatively stable framework to this process of substantive transformation.

The institutionalists held excessive expectations of something that the determinists almost completely neglected, and that was constitutional and legal forms. It did make a difference, after all, whether two neighboring countries with similar populations approached independence with a French-made or a British-made or a Belgian-made constitution. It made a difference, partly because leaders of independence movements either had to learn the political procedures of the constitution imposed upon them by the colonial power, or, where the latter denied all political participation to native leaders, they had to forge a vocabulary of political protest that was heavily influenced by the object of their protest. Again, after independence had been achieved, constitutions and systems of laws, even if they succeeded one another very rapidly, at least had the negative significance of defining what it was that the leaders, however cynically, wanted to avoid being called by their opponents.

Many of those who used the determinist approach, especially when they emphasized the importance of economic factors, neglected the independent influence of such factors as nationalist or internationalist ideologies, religions, and the "charisma" of leaders who identified themselves with goals that might be quite unrelated to economic change or economic development. For example, the very commitment to granting independence to their possessions by the signers of the United Nations Charter in 1945 became an important factor in undermining the willingness of colonial powers like France and Belgium to maintain their rule by force alone, although it might have appeared to them to be in their economic interest to remain in control, especially after the discovery of newly valuable raw materials like uranium in the Congo. Again, an ideology like that of Gandhi, with its antiindustrialist, antimodern bent (his symbol was the spinning wheel) was able to attract millions of Indian followers, because it was congruent with traditional religious values and presented by the saintlike figure of Gandhi.

Many students of the determinist persuasion have ranked colonies on the verge of independence on the basis of their "viability" for independence. By this they mean that one country, because of its adequate economic resources and the prospects for their development, is more likely to be successful at independence than another, which lacks the raw materials or the outside aid needed to exploit them. On this basis, for example, the Belgian Congo was judged viable before independence, whereas the French Sudan, later the Republic of Mali, was judged nonviable. In fact, however, politics in the independent Congo has been a dismal failure, whereas politics in Mali has been somewhat more successful, when compared with the Congo. What this kind of comparison, based upon "viability ratings," overlooked was the political framework and training, or the lack of it, provided in the terminal stage of colonialist tutelage.

STRUCTURAL FUNCTIONALISM

Both the institutionalist and the determinist approaches had been found wanting when applied to highly developed Western political systems, and they were now even more inadequate when applied to the developing countries of the Third World. As a result of their dissatisfaction, political scientists began to devise new methods, some of which were designed specifically to deal with the novel and apparently unprecedented problems presented by politics in the developing areas. The most influential of these new methods has been the structural-functional approach, which was adapted from sociology and more especially from the work of Professor Talcott Parsons. As the term implies, this approach studies the *structures* in a society in relation to the *functions* that they perform.

Professor Gabriel Almond worked out this approach and applied it in *The Politics of the Developing Areas*.[1] Because the structures in the developing political systems were likely to be in a state of flux and, therefore, inaccessible to analysis, Almond concentrated on political functions. He distinguished between input functions and output functions. The input functions are: (1) political socialization and recruitment, (2) interest articulation, (3) interest aggregation, and (4) political communication. The output functions are: (1) rule making, (2) rule application, and (3) rule adjudication. These output functions are clearly a reformulation, in jargon, of the functions of the conventional separation of powers—legislation, execution, and adjudication—upon which the Constitution of the United States is based. This suggests the first major shortcoming of Professor Almond's approach. It assumes that the work, that is, the "output," of government is identical and coterminous with the functions that are supposed to be performed, in constitutional theory, by the three coordinate branches of the American Federal Government. The approach does recognize that, especially in developing political systems, neither constitutional theory nor political practice will actually

---

[1] Gabriel A. Almond and James S. Coleman, eds., *The Politics of the Developing Areas*, Princeton, N.J.: Princeton University Press, 1960.

allow clear structures like the tangible, visible Congress, Presidency, and Supreme Court, and the very buildings they occupy, to develop. However, it asserts, in effect, that the functions that are supposed to be performed by the three branches have to be performed by someone, somewhere, in every political system, no matter how underdeveloped. It also assumes that with the performance of these three output functions *all* the work of government is comprised. In fact, however, in many non-Western societies, not heirs to the Greek tradition of logic and the Roman tradition of law, the main work of government does not revolve around "rules," at least not in the explicit sense that it does in most Western societies. And even in Western political systems, governments do a great deal more than rule-making, rule application, and rule adjudication.

The concentration upon ruling and rules of the structural-functional approach is due to its acceptance of the definition of the state, provided by Max Weber: that institution in society that has a monopoly of legitimate physical violence. Moreover, as Professor Almond himself phrases it, "The political system is the legitimate, order-maintaining or transforming system in the society."[2] This view tends to restrict the state, and therefore government and politics, to the quadrants dealing with power and constitutional problems (in our diagram), thereby ignoring the quadrants of economic and cultural problems. It also imparts a strong bias in favor of stability to this perspective upon politics and fails to suggest any method for systematically relating the various dimensions of the political process to each other.

One rebuttal of this criticism would point to Almond's input functions. These, the answer could state, focus on the more informal aspects of politics. Political socialization and recruitment take place not only in schools but also in the family and in many kinds of very informal situations. Interests are articulated by pressure groups, minority ethnic associations, and many other kinds of organizations. They are then aggregated by more comprehensive organizations, and in countries like the United States and Great Britain by political parties. Finally, the input function of political communication is

---

[2] *Ibid.*, p. 7.

performed by the press, radio, television, and other media as well as by properly "political" communications within political structures, like interest groups and political parties.

One objection to this approach is again that it is too closely tied to the particular institutions existing in a very few mature Western political systems. In the United States and in Great Britain, but in very few other countries, it *may* be a main function of interest organizations to articulate interests and of political parties to aggregate them, but elsewhere these functions may actually be reversed or performed in a much more diffuse way by any number of different structures. Moreover, there does not seem to be any good reason why political socialization and recruitment and political communication should be considered input rather than output functions. (In a later book Professor Almond has only six functions, instead of the seven of the original approach, but he seems to have merely compounded the confusion of the earlier work.[3])

The major difficulty with structural-functionalism is that it starts out with false analogies to a few institutions that exist in a few mature Western political systems. It then proceeds to universalize these Western political systems by claiming that the four input and three output functions are "universal political functions," that is, functions that have to be performed in *all* political systems in *all* periods of time. As a result, the utility of this approach turns out to be almost as restricted as that of the institutionalism, in rebellion against which the structural-functionalists began. This, in turn, has led some adherents of structural-functionalism to end up with the old-fashioned determinists, who would proclaim the primacy of economic change. Professor James Coleman, in his conclusion to *The Politics of the Developing Areas*, writes that the book has been trying to study "the impact *on* politics of various factors making for change."[4] In other words, the book treats politics as a dependent variable, not an independent variable capable of generating change at the primary level.

---

[3] Gabriel A. Almond and Bingham Powell, *Comparative Politics: A Developmental Approach*, Boston: Little, Brown, 1966.

[4] Almond and Coleman, p. 576. Italics supplied.

THE IMPLICATIONS FOR POLICY

The shortcomings of these three approaches to the study of politics in developing countries are not restricted to academic analysis but also affect concrete policies that politicians and governments are likely to recommend and pursue. For example, the problems raised for the United States by the war in South Vietnam could be, and in fact were, looked at from each of these points of view and from various combinations of the three. Extreme institutionalists said that all South Vietnam needed was constitutional reform, along whatever lines the particular observer or policy maker favored, from a presidential system to a parliamentary one. Various efforts by American administrations to reform the South Vietnamese constitution bear witness to the fact that the institutionalist approach had its proponents within the government. This was also true of the determinist approach, whose adherents asked whether South Vietnam had the prerequisites, and especially the economic and urbanization prerequisites, for viability and political independence. The answer was usually negative, and the solution offered to the problem therefore consisted of massive economic and technological assistance designed to raise the standard of living and to enlarge the proportion of the population that could be described as urban or "middle class." This economic help was to be provided, and was provided, regardless of the current regime in Saigon. Structural-Functionalism also had its advocates among those responsible for advising American policy toward Vietnam. One argument based on this approach held that the input functions were too highly developed in South Vietnam for the relatively underdeveloped output structures. In other words, too many interests were being articulated, though they were probably not being sufficiently well aggregated, in order to be converted into acceptable outputs on the side of rule-making, rule application, and rule adjudication. The solution to the problem consisted of throttling the input, that is, reducing what Professor Samuel P. Huntington has called "social mobilization," while at the same time strengthening the structures or the institutions of government.[5]

---

[5] Samuel P. Huntington, "Political Development and Decay," *World Politics*, vol. 52, no. 3 (April 1965), pp. 386–430.

Each of these approaches had its adherents among policy makers and their advisers within the government of the United States, and actual policies were often a more or less haphazard blend of proposals based on all three approaches—which is not to say that the proponents of specific lines were always aware of their methodological assumptions. Unfortunately, from both an academic and a political point of view, each of the three approaches was not only inadequate by itself but the three together did not complement one another in a balanced way. The same was true of American policies toward most other developing countries, for example, Ghana. Just before the Gold Coast achieved independence from Great Britain in 1957, and for several years thereafter, many American students of its politics assumed that prospects for "political institutional transfer," a phrase of Professor David Apter, were excellent on the Gold Coast.[6] Because Ghanaian politicians had been trained in British parliamentary ways, chances were that they would continue to behave rather like British politicians after independence. However, when President Nkrumah introduced a new, supposedly authentically African constitution in 1960, and when he began to behave in a somewhat dictatorial way, the determinists among American interpreters of Ghanaian politics began to gain the upper hand. They said that Ghana lacked the economic and social prerequisites for stable democracy, and that therefore the dangers of totalitarian development loomed large. In terms of American policy this meant either that aid be provided to enable Ghana to catch up on these economic prerequisites, or that President Nkrumah's regime be overthrown in order to be replaced by one more congruent with Ghanaian realities and more responsive to American wishes—or both. In fact, the United States under President Kennedy advanced massive loans to President Nkrumah for construction of the giant Volta River dam. Shortly after completion of the dam, Nkrumah was overthrown by a military junta, which in fact turned out to be friendlier toward the United States and more hostile toward the Soviet Union and Communist China. But while Nkrumah was still

---

[6] David E. Apter, The Gold Coast in Transition, Princeton, N.J.: Princeton University Press, 1955.

in office, presiding over his single-party system of the Convention Peoples Party, some advisers, who were apparently adherents of the structural-functional approach and who shared Professor Huntington's skepticism about excessive social mobilization, urged the United States government to support one-party states rather than the other two most frequent alternative regimes in developing countries, that is, military juntas and so-called charismatic leaders without the backing of a single party. Throughout the period between 1957 and 1967, American policy was usually an inept mixture of policies based upon the three approaches we have discussed, with the result that neither Ghana nor the United States benefited as much from relations between the two countries as might have been possible.

VULGAR TELEOLOGISM

Another approach to the study of developing countries, which bears many affinities to both determinism and structural-functionalism, is exemplified by Professor Walt W. Rostow's book *The Stages of Economic Growth*.[7] As an economic historian, Rostow traced the stages through which now-mature economies, like those of Great Britain and the United States, passed on their way from underdevelopment, through the Industrial Revolution, to present maturity. He assumes that presently underdeveloped economies will have to pass through the same stages in the same sequence toward the same goal as their predecessors. This approach is teleological in that it posits an end, goal or *telos*, to the process of growth. We call it "vulgar teleologism" because of its wholly erroneous assumption that the leaders of underdeveloped countries want to achieve, as the be-all and end-all of their present activities, the kind of economies that exist in the United States or Great Britain today. Moreover, it tends to ignore that these economies are also still engaged in a process of either growth or decay. Vulgar also is its assumption that, even if this were the end goal, the road traveled toward it today has to be, or indeed can be, the same as that over which Britons and Americans

---

[7] Walt W. Rostow, *The Stages of Economic Growth*, Cambridge: Cambridge University Press, 1960.

traveled during the past two centuries. In fact, contemporaries always at least *think* that they have learned something from the "lessons of the past," or from the mistakes that they believe their forerunners in their own or other countries have committed. This knowledge, which may be profoundly misleading *mis*knowledge, always becomes a factor in the present situation and inevitably makes the present different from, and usually nonanalogous to, the past.

VULGAR REALISM

There is, finally, the approach to the politics, and especially to the international politics, of the developing countries of the self-styled "realists." They focus upon the importance in politics of power, by which they usually understand force, especially military and police force. Students and policy makers influenced by this approach tended to assert that the relative powerlessness of independence movements implied the permanence of colonial rule. It was on the basis of such assumptions that some predictions were made about the permanence of Belgian rule in the Congo, since Belgium controlled a police force of twenty thousand troops, the strongest in black Africa. This turned out to be quite irrelevant to actual events when the Belgian government lost its will to govern the Congo—for whatever reasons—in the face of not very resolute demands for independence from Congolese leaders. Thereupon, the realists, without learning from their past mistakes, shifted their ground and predicted that the Congo would be one of the most stable of the newly independent African states precisely because its government would be able to rely upon the *Force Publique* to put down any rebellions and to maintain "law and order." In fact, however, the *Force Publique* itself rebelled and then disintegrated a few days after independence, June 30, 1960.

The whole history of the movement from colonial domination to independence in the developing areas testifies to the inadequacies of the realist approach. In almost every case, nationalist leaders that had no power at all in the sense of force, were able to gain independence from a colonial administration that exercised a complete monopoly of physical violence that was initially perfectly legitimate.

On the other hand, after independence was achieved, neither within newly independent states nor in relations between them did the control of greater means of military or police force always go with the retention of political control. Yet, "realistic" assumptions often informed the foreign policies of the United States toward developing countries, for example, when it provided massive military aid to countries all the way from Cuba before the rise of Fidel Castro, to Pakistan before the Pakistani-Indian war. Military aid was based upon the assumption that the governments to which it was supplied would be helped in staying in control and would, moreover, be more amenable to American pressures in conducting their own foreign policy. Nevertheless, to restrict ourselves to the cases of Cuba and Pakistan here, Fidel Castro, who began with some twenty-five comrades and no weapons to speak of, was able to overthrow the militarily very strong dictatorship of Batista, and President Ayub Khan of Pakistan did not hesitate to use military armaments supplied to him as a member of the CENTO pact, which was originally directed against the Soviet Union, in the war over Kashmir against India, and then even to dissociate himself from CENTO's policies and to establish relatively friendly relations with Communist China.

THE DEVELOPMENT OF POLITICS

The preceding critique of prevailing approaches to the study of politics in the developing areas shows the distorting consequences of excessive preoccupation with any one of the four basic goals that political systems pursue. Exclusive focus upon the goal of effectiveness leads to a vulgar teleologism, which assumes, expects, or advocates that all developing systems will move toward that condition in which the United States or other mature systems find themselves today. Excessive concern with the goal of flexibility leads to a vulgar undialectical materialism and determinism, according to which underlying changes in economy, society, or culture will have inevitable consequences in politics, consequences that are quite unaffected by deliberate political action. Exclusive focus upon the goal of efficiency leads to the vulgar realism of power, which assumes that the only thing that matters in politics is possession of the organized means of force. And excessive preoccupation with the goal of stability leads to the vulgar idealism of institutions, according to which any goals can be achieved and all crises can be averted through the design and construction of appropriate constitutional frameworks. The dangers inherent in these vulgarizations are by no means confined to the study of the developing countries, but are just as much present in applications to mature Western political systems, like France, Germany, or Great Britain.

In view of these deficiencies of the prevailing, mutually non-complementary approaches to the study of politics, we should try to work our way forward toward a notion of politics that is genuinely realistic, in the sense that it takes account of human consciousness of the human condition. This notion of politics would have to be teleological, dialectical, "materialist," and epistemological. Each of these four aspects of our understanding of politics is related to one of the four basic goals of political systems. The teleological aspect is related to effectiveness, the dialectical to flexibility, the materialist to efficiency, and the epistemological to stability.

By a teleological understanding of politics we mean an awareness of *becoming* in the Aristotelian sense. All things and all beings, and especially politics the master science, change as a result of the contradictions between goals, the achievement of goals, and the invention of new goals. This is becoming in the Aristotelian and not the Platonic sense, since for Plato the goals were essentially static.

Our understanding of politics must be dialectical in the sense that all politics moves. Without motion there is no politics, but because motion is everywhere, politics is everywhere. Politics moves as a result of the inescapable inherent tensions or contradictions between the various basic goals pursued by human beings and their political systems, which are an existential part of the human condition.

This understanding of politics is "materialist," perhaps "phenomenal" would be a more suitable term, in its awareness of the substantive problems the recognition of which triggers the political process, which then arises out of disagreements about their solution.

Finally, this notion of politics is epistemological in its focus upon the integral relation between politics and human consciousness.

Unless people know something about the real world, and unless they believe that this knowledge—no matter how mistaken it may "objectively" turn out to be—enables them to change the conditions of their existence, there will be no politics. For politics to begin, there must be disagreement, there must be issues. Issues arise in part because people have different understandings of the "real world"; they therefore forge different goals for the future and advance different means by which to move toward those different goals.

Just as there are the inherent conflicts between the basic goals of stability and efficiency, of flexibility and effectiveness, so there are inherent tensions between the dialectical and the teleological, between the epistemological and the materialist aspects of our *understanding* of politics.

This kind of approach to the study of the politics of the developing areas suggests that what has been studied as the "politics of development" should be studied as the "development of politics." The phrase "politics of development" implies that because of changes in the underlying substance of the economy, culture, and society, a peculiar type of politics arises in "developing areas." What has actually been happening, however, is that economic and other substantive changes are the *result* of the development of politics, that is, of the growth, expansion, proliferation, and multiplication of politics itself. In virtually all the developing countries, the leadership sets new goals, sometimes literally invented out of their new interpretation of international and local realities, and popularizes these goals. The new goals, like national independence, industrial modernization, free and comprehensive public education, revitalization of an ancient and forgotten language and culture, come into conflict with one another and with the material conditions of the society. As a result of this conflict a dialectic of ends and means is set in motion. This is accompanied by, and mutually interacts with, a heightened and expanded awareness, and changing interpretations, of the material realities with which people are living. As a result of this heightened awareness, more people than before participate in politics, new issues are generated, and politics itself grows, expands, and develops.

In order to understand the politics of development as the development of politics, three new distinctions will be of value. First, we should distinguish between different *levels* of the development of politics. This is a *quantitative* measure. For example, there is "more" politics in the United States than in the Soviet Union, more in the Soviet Union than in East Germany, and probably more in Sweden than in Zambia. We can expect, generally, that the higher the level of development attained, the lower the rate of the development of politics. For example, the volume of politics in the United States did not grow appreciably during the 1950s, indeed, it may have declined. On the other hand, in most African countries, which until ten years ago were colonial possessions of the great European powers that denied their native populations the opportunities to participate in politics, the growth of politics is likely to continue at a high rate until some time in the future, when it reaches a level of development similar to that in the United States today or fifty years ago.

Second, there is the distinction between *quantity* of the development of politics just discussed and *quality* of its development. The volume of politics has been growing in most of the so-called developing countries, but the quality of this new politics varies a great deal. It is this quality which Professor Huntington evidently had in mind when he complained about the decay of politics in the passage referred to above. In many developing countries, politics has been growing in relatively pathological styles. However, simply because politics in Latin America has tended to be violent; in the Middle East it has tended to be both ideological and violent; in Africa it has often been pragmatically corrupt; and in international relations among developing states and between them and the West it has tended toward the legalistic, does not mean that politics in and among these states has not been growing, that is, developing. What most American students of political development mean when they say that we are witnessing the decay instead of the development of politics is that they do not like the kinds of new politics that are developing. The proposed distinction between the quantity and the quality of developing politics is meant to avert this kind of confusion.

Third, we should make the rather basic distinction between *politics* and *government*. By politics we mean the processes of dealing with issues, whereas by government we mean the institutions used for solving problems. This distinction is again useful for purposes of making comparisons. For example, in some Latin American countries, some institutions of government are being developed, in the sense of being strengthened. Thus, poor people in certain cities are benefiting from the provisions of social security administrations, but—and this is the significant factor—these same people are not "politicized" as a result of the new government benefits. They simply accept what an institution of government is doing *for* them, without in any way participating in its activities or wishing to do something for themselves through politics. In fact, often as a result of this kind of more or less paternalistic "handout" by government, ordinary people are made *less* political than they were before. They let their goals be presented to them by the government, instead of following their own leadership, actual or potential, which would forge new goals. These new goals might then be in opposition to those of the government, thereby creating new issues and newly recognizable problems for the proliferation of politics. In most new states of black Africa, on the other hand, government started from a much lower level of development than that which had been reached in most Latin American countries half a century earlier, but politics has generally been developing at a much faster rate in Africa than in Latin America. Indigenous politics, that is, politics to the extent that it is unaffected by outside, non-African interference, has been developing more rapidly in Africa than in Latin America partly because of a greater awareness of greater needs and of the possibility of satisfying these needs through politics. Politics in Africa has also generally been developing in less pathological styles than in Latin America, for a variety of "historical" reasons.

These distinctions of level, of quantity *versus* quality and of politics *versus* government, should of course also be applied in making comparisons between neighboring countries in the same developing area, or indeed between different parts of one and the same political system. For example, politics among the members of the American Negro community has recently been developing at a much faster rate than among their white fellow citizens. It would be interesting and rewarding to make studies of the growth of political institutions within the Negro community, as well as comparisons over time in the style of Negro politics, say, in respect to civil rights. Such a comparison would probably show that the legalistic pragmatism of the period up to 1954 has slowly been changing into an increasingly ideological and occasionally violent style. The case of the Negroes of the United States illustrates again, incidentally, the strong bias in favor of stability that pervades conventional political science. Many of the Negro's self-styled erstwhile friends, latter-day critics of Negro efforts to gain equal rights, were sorely dismayed by phrases such as "Black Power," and by the frequent involvement of Negro leaders in violence, regardless of whether they initiated it or responded to it. They would have preferred to see progress made within the stable institutions and procedures that had been generally accepted by everyone, including the Negro leadership, until the Supreme Court decisions of 1954 failed to be put into effect. What these critics failed to realize was that Negroes themselves, as well as certain other groups within the American political system, were at least as interested in flexibility, effectiveness, and efficiency, as in stability, and that their awareness of the possible was constantly expanding.

This case of the newly expanding political consciousness and participation of American Negroes raises the question: Where do new goals, values, needs, and the recognition of new problems come from? How are these new goals popularized? What concepts, what words, can grasp the reality of the condition of flux, which is one of the central characteristics of the process of development? The question is difficult to answer, because, as we have tried to show in this chapter, the political science vocabulary that may have been adequate for gaining an understanding of the realities of politics in developed countries is quite inadequate when applied to the developing areas.

The problems recognized by the peoples of these regions are qualitatively unprecedented, precisely because of these peoples' awareness of their quantitative precedents: They *know* that Britain, Germany, the Soviet Union, and the United States passed through a period of industrialization and modernization similar to the period they have recently entered. But as a result of their awareness of these precedents, they not only want to avoid the errors apparently committed by their "Western" predecessors, they also want to set themselves a *telos* different from the ones achieved by their forerunners. Moreover, since some of these earlier modernizers had also been their own colonial rulers or imperialist "exploiters," our contemporary self-developers have radically questioned the moral, conceptual, and methodological assumptions underlying all politics and therefore also political science.

As a result, political science today finds itself in a position somewhat analogous to that in the period following the Protestant Reformation. Then as now a whole political and moral order is being transformed. Then as now matters formerly sacrosanct are being subjected to more or less objective critical analysis. Then as now previously dormant population groups have awakened to participation in politics in order to realize novel goals. Then as now optimism about the feasibility of achieving these goals through politics is dampened by pessimism about the survival of mankind. In the post-Reformation period, the refounders of political science were able to create new values and new concepts capable of generating sufficient support for a fresh understanding of a transformed reality, and for its further, deliberate transformation toward the newly fashioned goals. We are turning to these new founders of the discipline now in order to inquire into the conditions that might facilitate another refounding of political science in today's analogously revolutionary situation.

Selected Bibliography

Adams, Richard N., *et al.*, *Social Change in Latin America Today: Its Implications for United States Policy*, New York: Vintage, 1961.

Almond, Gabriel A., and James S. Coleman, eds., *The Politics of the Developing Areas*, Princeton, N.J.: Princeton University Press, 1960.

Apter, David E., *The Gold Coast in Transition*, Princeton, N.J.: Princeton University Press, 1955.

Apter, David E., *The Politics of Modernization*, Chicago: University of Chicago Press, 1965.

Black, C. E., *The Dynamics of Modernization: A Study in Comparative History*, New York: Harper & Row, 1966.

Fagen, Richard R., *Politics and Communication*, Boston: Little, Brown, 1966.

Hagen, Everett E., *On the Theory of Social Change: How Economic Growth Begins*, Homewood, Ill.: Dorsey, 1962.

Horowitz, Irving Louis, *Three Worlds of Development: The Theory and Practice of International Stratification*, New York: Oxford University Press, 1966.

Kautsky, John H., *Political Change in Underdeveloped Countries: Nationalism and Communism*, New York: Wiley, 1962.

Organski, A. F. K., *The Stages of Political Development*, New York: Knopf, 1965.

Mannoni, O., *Prospero and Caliban: The Psychology of Colonization*, New York: Praeger, 1956, p. 171.

Plank, John N., ed., *The Theory and Practice of Political Development*, Washington, D.C.: Brookings, 1970.

Pye, Lucian W., *Aspects of Political Development*, Boston: Little, Brown, 1966.

Rostow, Walt W., *The Stages of Economic Growth*, Cambridge: Cambridge University Press, 1960.

Rudolph, Lloyd I., and Susanne Hoeber Rudolph, *The Modernity of Tradition: Political Development in India*, Chicago: University of Chicago Press, 1967.

Silvert, K. H., ed., *Expectant Peoples: Nationalism and Development*, New York: Random House, 1963.

Spiro, Herbert J., *Africa: The Primacy of Politics*, New York: Random House, 1966.

Spiro, Herbert J., *Patterns of African Development*, Englewood Cliffs, N.J.: Prentice-Hall, 1967.

Spiro, Herbert J., *Politics in Africa: Prospects South of the Sahara*, Englewood Cliffs, N.J.: Prentice-Hall, 1962.

Staley, Eugene, *The Future of Underdeveloped Countries: Political*

Implications of Economic Development, New York: Praeger, rev. ed., 1961.

Ulam, Adam B., *The Unfinished Revolution: An Essay on the Sources and Influence of Marxism*, New York: Random House, 1960.

Whatsoever therefore is consequent to a time of war, where every man is enemy to every man; the same is consequent to the time, wherein men live without other security, than what their own strength, and their own invention shall furnish them withal. In such condition, there is no place for industry; because the fruit thereof is uncertain: and consequently no culture of the earth; no navigation, nor use of the commodities that may be imported by sea; no commodious buildings; no instruments of moving, and removing, such things as require much force; no knowledge of the face of the earth; no account of time; no arts; no letters; no society; and which is worst of all, continual fear, and danger of violent death; and the life of man, solitary, poor, nasty, brutish, and short.

Thomas Hobbes, "Of the Natural
Condition of Mankind as concerning
their Felicity and Misery,"
in *Leviathan* (1651), chap. 13.

THE MODERN
REDISCOVERY
OF POLITICS

9

THEOLOGY VERSUS POLITICS

Politics was the master science when man made his first great leap into self-awareness, and Socrates, Plato, and Aristotle founded political science. Today it is once more becoming the "queen of the sciences," simply because the most awesome problems facing mankind can be solved, if they can be solved at all, only through politics. But politics has not always occupied this preeminent position. For example, during the European Middle Ages, theology occupied the position of primacy. For Christians, the most important problem was the salvation of their souls, that is, how to go to heaven and avoid going to hell. Until the Reformation, it was generally believed that this problem could be solved only by the intervention of the Church. The Church was possessor, guardian, and elaborator of theology, the science of relations between God and man. In these circumstances, politics was denigrated. In the *res publica Christiana*, the Christian community that covered Europe, an essentially substantive consensus prevailed on the goals prescribed by the Roman Catholic Church for life in this world and the next. Both spiritual and temporal rulers agreed on the propriety of these goals, and there was, therefore, little reason to place a high value upon politics, which depends upon disagreement for its very existence.

This is not to say that there was no politics during the Middle Ages, or that all parts of Europe were equally antipolitical. In fact, a very active kind of politics was going on both within the Church itself and between it and the Holy Roman Empire. During the prolonged struggle between Pope and Emperor, a set of "rules of the political game" slowly emerged, just as the Church's internal conflicts led to the building of layer upon layer of procedural consensus and to a very respectable body of literature on constitutional problems. After the Reformation, the modernizers of political thought and practice were to draw upon this work. Nevertheless, compared with classical Greece and Rome, and compared with the centuries since their end, the Middle Ages were apolitical. The One Church regarded itself, and was generally regarded by all those who mattered, as the guardian of *the* single truth. But only after the Reformation had destroyed this sense and reality of unity did a consciousness of the need for politics revive, and only then was politics in the classic sense of the word rediscovered.

The Reformation itself contributed most heavily to this sudden rediscovery. Until Luther successfully challenged the Church's previously unquestioned monopoly to saving souls, few genuinely novel problems had been recognized that invited novel solutions. The most influential philosopher of the Middle Ages, St. Thomas Aquinas, relied almost entirely upon Aristotle—whom he always referred to as "The Philosopher"—for his conceptual vocabulary, his typology, and even the general content of his philosophy of politics, which he effectively integrated into the overall framework of Christianity. Luther's work regenerated politics in a number of ways. To begin with, he raised the basic issue, which was in fact the single most important disagreement of the time, of whether he was right or the Church was right. On this issue, all Christians (at any rate, all rulers in Christendom) *had* to take a stand. The immediate result was the wars of the Reformation. These, in turn, led to raising an unprecedented problem of loyalties for millions of people in Europe. To whom did a man owe obedience? To his traditional ruler, regardless of his religion? If the subject was a Catholic and his prince a Protestant, did he owe him allegiance? If the subject was a Protestant and his king a Catholic, did he owe him loyalty? Was the ruler still under obligation to protect those of his subjects who professed the other religion? According to what procedures, what set of rules, should such conflicts be resolved? Where Catholics and Protestants lived intermingled, as neighbors or in neighboring communities, how could they get along with one another? As the Pope's ultimate authority to excommunicate became ineffective—because this sentence no longer frightened Protestants to whom it was applied—what could be substituted for it, that is, what power short of death on earth could be used to enforce agreements among rulers?

THE FOUNDING
OF MODERN
POLITICAL THEORY

All of these questions were unprecedented and radically new. Just how novel the problems generated by the Reformation were is shown by a comparison of the writings of Machiavelli and Hobbes. Niccolò Machiavelli wrote before the Reformation, in Italy; Thomas Hobbes after the Reformation, in England. Some students of the history of political thought consider Machiavelli the founder of modern political science probably because his work has a much more secular tone than that of any of his predecessors or contemporaries. Indeed, very soon after he published *The Prince*, it became fashionable to label anyone whose political behavior evinced disregard for conventional moral and religious standards as a "Machiavellian." In *The Prince*, Machiavelli gives advice to rulers on how to stay in power and how to enlarge their power. Some of his advice seems to be quite cynical, although it really does not go very far beyond Aristotle's discussion of the causes of sedition in *The Politics*. As his other writings show, Machiavelli was in fact very much in the tradition of classical Greek and Roman writings on politics. Some students have claimed him as the founder of modern political science, because he is said to have described man as "half lion and half fox," and this is supposed to illustrate that his approach was totally amoral, perhaps what our contemporaries would call "behavioralist." In the passage from which this phrase is taken, however, Machiavelli in fact said that princes should use both the human and the bestial way to achieve ends, and that the bestial way in turn is sometimes copied from the lion and sometimes from the fox.[1] This may be an interesting intuitive insight, but hardly a "behaviorally scientific statement."

Machiavelli lived in Italy one hundred years before the Reformation, during the Renaissance, perhaps the period of the greatest artistic creativity in the history of mankind. Jacob Burckhardt, the historian of the Renaissance, entitled a chapter on Renaissance politics, "The State as a Work of Art."[2] In this phrase we can find the greatest difference between Machiavelli and Hobbes and the two periods of history in which they lived. Machiavelli seems more like a belletristic essayist; Hobbes, on the other hand, tries to be the rigorous scientist. This difference may be only one of degree, for example, as implied by the title: "Faculty of Arts and Sciences." A comparison of Machiavelli and Hobbes, however, shows the difference between them to be one of kind.

Hobbes lived and worked after the Reformation, during the English Civil War of the seventeenth century. Although this was a relatively unsettled period in English history, the English polity was then on much firmer and older foundations than Italy in the fifteenth

---

[1] "You should understand, therefore, that there are two ways of fighting: by law or by force. The first way is natural to men, and the second to beasts. But as the first way often proves inadequate one must needs have recourse to the second. So a prince must understand how to make a nice use of the beast and the man. The ancient writers taught princes about this by an allegory, when they described how Achilles and many other princes of the ancient world were sent to be brought up by Chiron, the centaur, so that he might train them his way. All the allegory means, in making the teacher half beast and half man, is that a prince must know how to act according to the nature of both, and that he cannot survive otherwise.

"So, as a prince is forced to know how to act like a beast, he should learn from the fox and the lion; because the lion is defenceless against traps and a fox is defenceless against wolves. . . ." Niccolò Machiavelli, *The Prince*, George Bull, trans., Baltimore, Md.: Penguin, 1961, p. 99.

[2] Jacob Burckhardt, *The Civilization of the Renaissance in Italy*, vol. 1, New York: Harper & Row, 1958, chap. 1.

century, or, one is almost tempted to say, at any time until the present. In Italy, which was not unified as a nation until 1869, many principalities, including the Papacy in its secular aspects, were forever warring with one another as well as internally. However, since the Reformation did not penetrate to Italy and Rome, the seat of the Church itself, these wars and "revolutions" rarely involved any questions of loyalties to ultimate values. On the other hand, by Hobbes's time England had behind it five hundred years of national history since the Norman Conquest of 1066. It had passed through the loyalty-churning period of the Reformation, Henry VIII's separation from Rome and establishment of the Church of England, Elizabeth I's long, stabilizing, and glorious reign, in order, in Hobbes's own day, to settle some basic constitutional issues by force of arms. Perhaps one can compare the difference between the ages of Machiavelli and Hobbes to the difference between the 1920s and the 1960s. In the aftermath of World War I, the 1920s were a period of troubles, accompanied by artistic creativity, but marked by very little radical innovation in political science. On the other hand, in the aftermath of World War II, the 1960s—the third decade of the nuclear age, during which virtually all the remaining colonies gained their independence, and in which drugs like the contraceptive pill and LSD were raising wholly unprecedented questions about man, his potential, his relations to his fellows, and his destiny—were a decade of considerable normative, methodological, and conceptual ferment in political science.

This was similar to Hobbes's time. He had his predecessors, of course—all the participants in the Great Conversation except Socrates, who began it, did. Few of the concepts that he used were entirely original with him. For example, the notion of sovereignty was introduced into political philosophy by Jean Bodin, who used it to demonstrate that the French king, for whom he worked, was *legibus solutus*, that is, unbound by the laws of his kingdom, though bound to obey the laws of nature, including the laws governing succession to the throne. But Thomas Hobbes was the first to attempt, in modern times, a comprehensive and systematic *science of politics* (he used this phrase) that includes, as such an attempt always must, a complete philosophy.

SOVEREIGNTY

Hobbes and his contemporaries faced new realities, and they were not yet equipped with the conceptual tools needed to grasp this reality. His age has been described as the "age of power," because both technological advances and man's new consciousness of his own potential had created means of power of a strength never before conceived of. The question was less what to do with this power than how to describe it, just as in the twentieth century, after the explosion of the first two atomic bombs over Japan and the subsequent development of peaceful uses of nuclear energy, the problem of understanding these vast new forces that have been tapped is at least as important as, and logically prior to, the problem of using the new power. The problem of loyalties, or of obedience, which Hobbes's contemporaries faced, was similarly difficult to describe, because it was radically new. In the medieval past, subjects had obeyed their rulers simply because each man and each piece of land had its ruler; there was an unbroken chain of mutual obligations reaching from the lowest serf up to the Holy Roman Emperor. Wars were occasionally fought between competing claimants to the succession of a throne, and of course between claimants to the same territory. This was so because it was believed always to have been so. One of Hobbes's Royalist contemporaries, Sir Robert Filmer, whom John Locke was to attack in the next generation, tried to establish the legitimacy of the English kings by tracing their descent back, through the succession of eldest males, literally to Adam. (As Locke showed, this was not a very safe way of defending absolute monarchy, since all other men were believed also to be descendants of Adam.)

Now, as a result of both the Reformation and men's novel faith in the powers of their own reason, simple tradition proved to be an inadequate foundation for stability in loyalties. In the previous century, there had been a large body of pamphlet literature by the so-called Monarchomachs that dealt with the question: When is one justified in killing an unlawful ruler? Some answered the question by saying that anyone could kill a usurper, others by leaving such a weighty decision to certain lawfully constituted bodies, and still others by denying the right of killing even the most outrageously tyrannical usurper. But most of this literature, as indeed even Machiavelli's writings, had an *ad hoc* character, that is, it was written on the spur of the moment to grind someone's axe, or to curry favor with a particular ruler. None of it tried to delve into the universals of politics, or at any rate none of it succeeded in such an effort.

Hobbes saw the problem in universal terms and solved it, at least for his time. His solution consisted of the concept and the institution of sovereignty. The sovereign, who could be one man, an assembly of men, or all men in a commonwealth, was the representative of all, because all had made themselves authors of his power. They had done this through the device of the covenant, or contract. It is through the covenant that men lift themselves out of the anarchical "state of nature," which Hobbes describes as a condition in which man's life is "solitary, poor, nasty, brutish, and short."[3] Hobbes provides the formulas that men are supposed to pronounce when they establish the commonwealth and its sovereign, but these are less important than the idea of the social compact. By making the sovereign the representative, Hobbes began to cut through the problem of conflicting claims to loyalty. Now you obeyed your ruler not because your father had obeyed the ruler's father, and so on back to Adam, but because you were the coauthor of the sovereign's actions. He had power because all the members of the commonwealth had surrendered their small portions of power to him. This was a radically rationalist argument and opposed to the traditionalist arguments that had previously been used to justify obedience. In criticism of Hobbes, as well as of later social contract theorists, including Locke and Rousseau, the question has often been raised whether such a covenant ever actually occurred, as an historical or anthropological fact. One could cite precedents from coronation ceremonies and the oaths sworn by subjects to their new king and by the king to uphold the customs of the realm; the Mayflower Compact; the Fundamental Orders of Connecticut; Oliver Cromwell's Instrument of Government, England's first, shortlived, and only written constitution; or even the Biblical covenant between Abraham and God. But this historical argument misses the main point of Hobbes's innovative contribution to political theory, which was pre-

---

[3] Thomas Hobbes, *Leviathan* (1651), Michael Oakeshott, ed., New York: Collier, 1962, chap. 3.

cisely his attempt to substitute the reason of individuals for the tradition of communities in providing firm and stable foundations of loyalty.

THE INDIVIDUAL

The sovereign is the end product of Hobbes's theory of politics. The initial building blocks of his theory are individuals. Some scholars who accept the concept of totalitarianism have called Hobbes a forerunner of modern totalitarianism because of the apparently unlimited power that he invests in his sovereign. The best answer to this (in any case anachronistic) charge would be the extreme and quite unprecedented individualism of Hobbes's philosophy. (His radical individualism and rationalism may have been the cause of a prohibition placed upon his books by the Nazi government in Germany.) It is individual human beings who come together, moved by reason, to form the commonwealth by a majority of their votes. It is to protect these individuals, above all against the eventuality of a return to the disastrous state of nature, that the sovereign exists. The sovereign does not function in order to protect the lives of groups, communities, or other collectivities, but to protect individuals. Previously, and for some centuries to come, political philosophy had been more concerned with groups than with the individual. Hobbes, however, looked upon such groups as "worms in the entrails of a natural man,"[4] which no sovereign in its right mind would tolerate. Group theorists of politics often assign different values, or at least different importance, to different groups, with the result that they value individuals hierarchically, depending upon their group membership. Hobbes, on the other hand, was led by his radical individualism and his opposition to groups to an equally radical egalitarianism. All individuals were equals in the state of nature, because of their equal powerlessness to prevent sudden and violent death; and in the commonwealth, because of their equal acceptance of its "constitution" through the covenant. Only the sovereign—which, to emphasize this point again, could be

---

[4] *Ibid.*, chap. 29, p. 245.

either one man, an assembly, or the whole body of citizens—stood above this equality, since it was the sum of all the equalities. (This is illustrated beautifully by the famous frontispiece to the first edition of Hobbes's *Leviathan*.)

Those who have accused Hobbes of totalitarian tendencies have also asked what good all this equality did the individuals who were subjects of the sovereign, since they had surrendered all their powers unto it and were therefore wholly at its mercy. Here again, Hobbes, basing himself upon natural law, which is accessible to all rational beings, sounds surprisingly modern in his individualism. For example, he provides a clear forerunner of the right against self-incrimination, which is guaranteed to citizens of the United States by the Fifth Amendment to the Constitution.[5] He denounced the sovereign's effort to force anyone to do something that would lead to his own injury or destruction, as contrary to natural law. He even urged that men who were of a "timorous nature," that is, physical cowards, be allowed to provide a substitute when called upon to perform military service.[6] (This was actually possible in the

---

[5] "A covenant not to defend myself from force, by force, is always void. For, as I have showed before, no man can transfer, or lay down his right to save himself from death, wounds, and imprisonment, the avoiding whereof is the only end of laying down any right; nor is obliging.

"A covenant to accuse oneself, without assurance of pardon, is likewise invalid. For in the condition of nature, where every man is judge, there is no place for accusation: and in the civil state, the accusation is followed by punishment; which being force, a man is not obliged not to resist. The same is also true, of the accusation of those, by whose condemnation a man falls into misery; as of a father, wife, or benefactor. For the testimony of such an accuser, if it be not willingly given, is presumed to be corrupted by nature; and therefore not to be received: and where a man's testimony is not to be credited, he is not bound to give it. Also accusations upon torture, are not to be reputed as testimonies. . . ." *Ibid.*, chap. 14, p. 110 f.; also chap. 21.

[6] "Upon this ground, a man that is commanded as a soldier to fight against the enemy, though his sovereign have right enough to punish his refusal with death, may nevertheless in many cases refuse, without injustice; as when he substituteth a sufficient soldier in his place: for in this case he deserteth not the service of the commonwealth. And there is allowance to be made for natural timorousness; not only to women, of whom no such danger-ous duty is expected, but also to men of feminine courage." *Ibid.*, chap. 21, p. 165.

Union during the American Civil War.) Most important, Hobbes would always have relied upon the individual's capacity to recognize, through the use of his reason, what was in his own interest, and upon the capacity of thousands or millions of individuals, upon such a foundation, to establish and maintain political systems. Reason, not authority or tradition, was to be the foundation of the polity. Similarly, in his own writings, Hobbes always rejected arguments that were based only upon the authority of what others had said or written, no matter how exalted, famous, or saintly they were. When accused of not citing sufficient scholarly or Biblical authority for his own writings, Hobbes once said, "If I had read as much as others, I should know no more than they know." This although he was himself an enormously learned man.

Hobbes, like his most important predecessors and successors among the great political philosophers of the ages, made his most enduring contribution in the field of method. He also resembles many of his peers in that he turned out to be a poor prophet in his own country. The concept of sovereignty, of which he gave the clearest exposition, was never accepted in English constitutional theory or institutional practice, whereas in the continental European countries it found and continues to find wide acceptance. The same is true of an explicit covenant, or social compact, which Great Britain does not have to this day, whereas most other countries, of whatever political leanings, including the United States, do have a formal covenant in the form of their written constitutions and requirements that citizens and officials take an oath upon this constitution.

THE NEW METHOD

But what was so novel about Hobbes's approach to the study of politics? His most important innovation was his conviction that politics could be studied as a science like mathematics, but unlike tennis-playing, which he described as an art. (Hobbes liked to play tennis.) We know today that the analogy between mathematics and political science has its shortcomings. Hobbes's contemporaries realized that his expectations of the capabilities of mathematics were also somewhat excessive: he thought that he had discovered the formula for squaring the circle and never forgave the Royal Society for failing to elect him to membership. He did, however, make a strong beginning toward clearly distinguishing between prescriptive and descriptive natural law. In an earlier chapter, we traced the slow evolution of the notion of the law of nature, from its Greek beginnings, when the law of the *polis* was projected upon the gods and nature, through its universalization and regularization by the Stoics, to its conversion into entirely prescriptive law in the hands of Christian theologians. This was the evolutionary view of natural law that Hobbes inherited and that he completely rejected. He clearly distinguished between things that all men do (descriptive law) and things that men ought to do, for whatever reasons (prescriptive natural law). Descriptive law is a fair generalization about human behavior, though it may admit of a few exceptions; e.g., all men seek to preserve themselves, or each man seeks power after power until his death.[7] But it would not be an accurate description to say that all men keep their promises—even though they ought to, because it would probably be in their own long-run interest. Hobbes clearly saw this distinction, which is central to his political writings.

POWER

Hobbes's distinction between what men "naturally" do and what they ought to do would have sufficed to win him an honored place among the contributors to the Great Conversation. His systematic elaboration of the concept of sovereignty would have been enough to earn him fame as one of the great theoretical innovators, who forged a word by means of which it became possible to grasp

---

[7] "So that, in the first place, I put for a general inclination of all mankind a perpetual and restless desire of power after power, that ceaseth only in death. And the cause of this, is not always that a man hopes for more intensive delight, than he has already attained to; or that he cannot be content with a moderate power: but because he cannot assure the power and means to live well, which he hath present, without the acquisition of more." *Ibid.*, chap. 11, p. 80.

new realities and to build institutions that were to bring order into an otherwise chaotic politics. He heightened the impact of his contribution—Marx once said, "Hobbes is the father of us all"—by linking these two with his most general and elegant definition of power: "The power *of a man*, to take it universally, is his present means, to obtain some future apparent good; and is either original or instrumental."[8] This enabled those who accepted the definition to give some intellectual order to political reality, that is, to understand the novel facts of power with which they were living. Using the word in this sense, it was true to say, descriptively: man seeks power after power unto death. This simply means that man seeks to improve his present means to obtain whatever at a particular time appears to him to be his future good, until he dies. It does not mean, as has sometimes been suggested by Hobbes's critics, that all men are power mad in the sense of pursuing increasing dominion over other men. Hobbes's approach was sufficiently dialectical for him to realize that, especially in an age as dynamic and ever-changing as his own, men's vision of their apparent future good frequently changed. Hobbes's political science was sufficiently "materialist" and dialectical to be acceptable to Marx. It was also sufficiently teleological[9] and epistemological to pass the standards set up in the previous chapter. At the same time, however, these last two qualifications created a dilemma for Hobbes that he was unable to solve entirely.

CONSENSUS OVER TIME

The problem of constitutional stability over generations did not seriously arise until after the Reformation. Until then, the constitution was accepted because it was believed to have existed for a long

---

[8] *Ibid.*, chap. 10, p. 72.

[9] Although Hobbes's radical opposition to Scholasticism and its patron St. Thomas Aquinas made him criticize Aristotle in numerous passages, he had not entirely emancipated himself from Aristotle's teleological method: "The *final cause*, end, or design of men, who naturally love liberty, and dominion over others, in the introduction of that restraint upon themselves, in which we see them live in commonwealths, is the foresight of their own preservation, and of a more contented life thereby. . . ." *Ibid.*, chap. 17, p. 129. Italics supplied.

time. Especially in England, even when fairly important changes in the constitution were in fact brought about, the fiction was always maintained that these changes consisted only of a reaffirmation of old practices, or of a return to very old practices that had fallen into neglect, or at worst of an adaptation of old practices to modern realities. Throughout the Middle Ages, in the strict meaning of the word *consensus*, constitutional consensus between generations was not only relatively unimportant, but could not exist. Consensus means "thinking with," and during the Middle Ages relatively little thinking of any kind was done about the constitution, since it was not an issue. All this had changed by the seventeenth century. Jacob Burckhardt wrote of Renaissance Italy, that its politics was dominated by the "great modern fallacy that a constitution can be *made*, can be manufactured by a combination of existing forces and tendencies."[10] The moment one no longer accepts a constitution simply because it is believed to have existed for all times, the moment constitutions are rationally manufactured, one person or party is likely to assert that it can make a better constitution, or a constitution more to its own advantage, than the last one. At this point, people begin to *think* about the constitution, and the problem of constitutional consensus and stability from one generation to the next arises. Indeed, the problem may arise several times within the life of one generation of men, as Hobbes knew from his own experience during Oliver Cromwell's Commonwealth.

Suppose all men come together, out of a civil war, which is the state of nature ("the war of all against all"), and through mutual covenants establish a commonwealth with its sovereign. The sovereign performs its functions well for a time, enabling the subjects to improve the conditions of their life, and leaving to their own pursuits where "the laws are silent."[11] But then, for whatever reasons internal or external to the commonwealth, the sovereign no longer

---

[10] Jacob Burckhardt, *The Civilization of the Renaissance in Italy*, New York: Harper & Row, 1958, p. 68. Italics supplied.

[11] "The greatest liberty of subjects, dependenth on the silence of the law. . . . In cases where the sovereign has prescribed no rule, there the subject hath the liberty to do, or forbear, according to his own discretion." Hobbes, *Leviathan*, chap. 21, p. 165 f.

fulfills its functions and, among other things, denies citizens some of their basic rights, for example, the right against self-incrimination or the right to substitution for military-service. Or the sovereign is no longer able to protect its subjects against incursions from outside enemies, so that they in fact find themselves back in the state of nature. What can they do, since they surrendered all their power to the common power of the sovereign? Hobbes clearly said that they would be "absolved of their obedience," and the moment they did rebel successfully, in the sense that the sovereign was unable to put down the rebellion, the sovereign ceased to exist and no one was bound by his promises to it.[12] Everyone was then in fact back in a state of nature, to which only the successful establishment of a new commonwealth with its sovereign would put an end. In other words, rebellion was "legitimized" by its success, whereas an existing sovereign that managed to suppress an incipient rebellion was "relegitimized" by its success. And this is Hobbes's dilemma: as men approach the goals they considered important yesterday, some of

---

[12] "*In what cases subjects are absolved of their obedience to their sovereign.* The obligation of subjects to the sovereign, is understood to last as long, and no longer, than the power lasteth, by which he is able to protect them. For the right men have by nature to protect themselves, when none else can protect them, can by no covenant be relinquished. The sovereignty is the soul of the commonwealth; which once departed from the body, the members do no more receive their motion from it. The end of obedience is protection, which, wheresoever a man seeth it, either in his own, or in another's sword, nature applieth his obedience to it, and his endeavour to maintain it. And though sovereignty, in the intention of them that make it, be immortal; yet is it in its own nature, not only subject to violent death, by foreign war; but also through the ignorance, and passions of men, it hath in it, from the very institution, many seeds of natural mortality, by intestine discord." *Ibid.*, chap. 21, p. 166 f.

"To resist the sword of the commonwealth, in defence of another man, guilty, or innocent, no man hath liberty; because such liberty, takes away from the sovereign, the means of protecting us; and is therefore destructive of the very essence of government. But in case a great many men together, have already resisted the sovereign power unjustly, or committed some capital crime, for which every one of them expecteth death, whether have they not the liberty then to join together, and assist, and defend one another? Certainly they have . . . ." p. 165.

them, the leaders, will invent and forge new goals for the day after tomorrow. These new goals will include not only matters of policy, which could be contained within one and the same constitution over many generations, but also changes in the constitution itself, or even its complete replacement. As men's awareness of the possibilities of change through politics are expanded, and as they place more emphasis upon flexibility and efficiency, the effectiveness of present values is weakened and the stability of the constitution itself may be undermined. The more you cut yourself off from tradition, and the more you rely upon reason for the construction of your constitution, the more you must anticipate, and, indeed, logically, the more you must *advocate*, change (progress), since the free play of reason is likely to bring forth better policies and better constitutional devices in the future.

This was the dilemma that Hobbes faced but failed to resolve. But through his other radical methodological innovations he contributed the tools of understanding by means of which in the next century and in an unexpected place, in a "new nation" with a burgeoning, expanding, developing new politics, other English-speaking men were able to solve it through brilliant political invention. However, the invention of the authors of the Constitution of the United States, which was patented in Philadelphia in 1787, is not adequate to the needs of the new states of the 1960s, as they face the current equivalent of Hobbes's dilemma. In Indonesia, Nigeria, Vietnam, and Pakistan, the covenant of the independence Constitution was rejected after passage of less than the life of one generation. Problems of intergenerational conflict, of competing claims to loyalty, and of warring notions of the good man, the good citizen, and the good constitution, change their content from time to time and therefore call for novel substantive solutions. The only things that *may* be constant and universal about politics are the methods of political science.

Selected Bibliography

Augustine, St., *The Political Writings of St. Augustine*, Henry Paolucci, ed., Chicago: Gateway, 1962.

Bodin, Jean, *Six Books of the Commonwealth*, M. J. Colley, trans., New York: Macmillan, 1955.

Brown, K. C., ed., *Hobbes Studies*, Cambridge, Mass.: Harvard University Press, 1965.

Burckhardt, Jacob, *The Civilization of the Renaissance in Italy*, 2 vols., New York: Harper & Row, 1958.

Butterfield, Herbert, *The Statecraft of Machiavelli*, New York: Collier, 1962.

Cassirer, Ernst, *The Myth of the State*, Garden City, N.Y.: Doubleday, 1955.

d'Entrèves, Alexander Passerin, *The Notion of the State: An Introduction to Political Theory*, Oxford: Clarendon Press, 1967.

Friedrich, Carl J., *The Age of the Baroque, 1610–1660*, New York: Harper & Brothers, 1952.

Hobbes, Thomas, *Body, Mind, and Citizen*, Richard S. Peters, ed., New York: Collier, 1962.

Hobbes, Thomas, *Leviathan*, parts 1 and 2, New York: Liberal Arts Press, 1958.

Hobbes, Thomas, *Leviathan*, Michael Oakeshott, ed., New York: Collier, 1962.

Levy, Leonard W., *Origins of the Fifth Amendment: The Right against Self-Incrimination*, New York: Oxford University Press, 1968.

Lindsay, A. D., *The Modern Democratic State*, New York: Oxford University Press, 1947.

Machiavelli, Niccolò, *The Prince*, George Bull, trans., Baltimore, Md.: Penguin Books, 1961.

Machiavelli, Niccolò, *The Prince and The Discourses*, New York: Modern Library, 1950.

Machiavelli, Niccolò, *The Prince and Selected Discourses*, Daniel Donno, ed., New York: Bantam, 1966.

Morrall, John B., *Political Thought in Medieval Times*, New York: Harper & Row, 1958.

Stephen, Sir Leslie, *Hobbes*, Ann Arbor, Mich.: University of Michigan Press, 1961.

Ullmann, Walter, *A History of Political Thought: The Middle Ages*, Baltimore: Penguin, 1965.

Walzer, Michael, *The Revolution of the Saints*, Cambridge, Mass.: Harvard University Press, 1967.

Thus in the beginning all the World was America, *and more so than that is now....*

John Locke,
Second Treatise on Civil Government,
no. 49, chap. 5.

AMERICAN LEGALISM AND ENGLISH PHILOSOPHY

10

Between the age of the Founding Fathers and the age of the atom bomb, American politics was remarkably pragmatic and unphilosophical, if not downright antiphilosophical. The Founding Fathers themselves were unoriginal as political philosophers, though they were highly original as constitutional engineers. Except for a brief period before the Civil War, the functions performed in other Western countries by political philosophers, theorists, and ideologues have either not been performed at all in the United States, or they have been taken care of by litigation in the courts, especially the Supreme Court of the United States. The major American political parties have been unideological or antiideological, again with few and brief exceptions. Consistent with this background, American politics remained unphilosophical and unideological even when it confronted the gravest problems ever faced by any political system in history, those involving the survival of mankind.

THE GREAT MR. LOCKE

There are many reasons for this unphilosophical character of American politics, among them the uninterrupted continuity of the English Common Law, the relatively low status accorded, at least until recently, to American intellectuals, or the "intelligentsia," and the great opportunities for achievement on both the geographical and the technological frontiers. In addition, one of the most important historical reasons is that the Founders had their philosophy ready, almost "packaged," and waiting for them in the work of John Locke. For at least fifty years after the founding of the United States, hardly a Fourth of July oration was given that did not contain reference to the "great Mr. Locke."[1] Professor Louis Hartz has gone so far as to assert that, ever since the founding, American political thought has been dominated by an irrational Lockean consensus, especially on his trinity of basic values: life, liberty, and property. These are of course enshrined in the Constitution, as rights which the citizen may not be deprived of without due process of law.[2]

How can Locke's great influence upon the Founding Fathers and their heirs be explained? The first reason is that he brought together into a fairly well integrated whole several of the great traditions of the Western political heritage. For example, throughout the *Second Treatise on Civil Government*, his most influential political work, the strong influence of Aristotle's method is clearly evident. We can tell from the titles of Chapters 7, 8, 9, and 10 of that book, that they deal respectively with the material, the efficient, the final, and the formal causes of civil society.[3] Locke's work is permeated by the natural law tradition, which can be traced from Aristotle through the Stoics to St. Thomas Aquinas, who heavily influenced the "judicious Hooker," to whose book, *Ecclesiastical*

---

[1] Merle Curti, "The Great Mr. Locke—America's Philosopher, 1783–1861," *Huntington Library Bulletin*, no. 11 (1937), pp. 107–151.

[2] Louis Hartz, *The Liberal Tradition in America*, New York: Harcourt Brace, 1955.

[3] Chapter 7, "Of Political or Civil Society," deals in part with the material, that is, the human beings that make up society. Chapter 8, "Of the Beginning of Political Societies," describes, *inter alia*, their founding. Chapter 9 is "Of the Ends of Political Society and Government." And chapter 10 is "Of the Forms of a Commonwealth." The subtitle of the *Second Treatise* is *An Essay Concerning the True Original, Extent, and End of Civil Government*.

Polity, Locke refers frequently throughout the *Second Treatise.* According to this tradition, natural law is embedded in nature and can be perceived by every man who has been endowed with the spark of reason by the Creator. Locke happily blended this natural law rationalism with the more modern, radical rationalism of Hobbes, according to which man's instrumental reason will tell him what to do in his own interest. This is different from the position of those adherents of natural law who believe that a beneficent deity is moving mankind and the world toward good ends through natural law. Locke remained in the Stoic-Christian tradition when he seemed to be describing the state of nature as a peaceful condition (though he contradicted this in other passages). For Hobbes, on the other hand, the state of nature was a state of war. But Locke changed to a Hobbesian rationalism when in his psychology he asserts that man's mind at birth is a *tabula rasa,* that is, a blank slate, on which experience writes. As a result, in Locke's work a prescriptive view of natural law seems sometimes to be in conflict with a descriptive view, although both Locke (in his *Treatises on Civil Government,* at least) and his American disciples seemed unaware of this difficulty. The Declaration of Independence repeats the contradiction in its very first paragraph: "We hold these truths to be self-evident,"—presumably Thomas Jefferson and his associates were about to describe the obvious facts here—"that all men are endowed by their Creator with certain unalienable Rights, and that among these are Life, Liberty and the pursuit of Happiness." But the rights to life, liberty, and certainly the pursuit of happiness were not in fact being enjoyed by all men of Jefferson's time or, for that matter, of our own. Nor did many contemporaries of Jefferson consider even the prescription of such rights as a "self-evident" matter. Perhaps Locke included the mutually exclusive prescriptive and descriptive views of natural law in his political philosophy because he was also very much a part of the dialectical-critical tradition of Western political thought, as for example, in his attack on Sir Robert Filmer, who based the authority of the kings of England on their descent from Adam. This may help explain why Locke took contradictory positions in different intellectual battles.

The second reason why Locke exerted such great influence

upon the generation of the American Founding Fathers was that he wrote in knowledge of the earlier American colonial experience, and therefore he spoke in an idiom that could appeal to Americans. Indeed, it is likely that Locke, even more than Hobbes before him, modeled his concept of the social compact upon actual contemporary historical American experiences, like the Mayflower Compact and the Fundamental Orders of Connecticut.[4] He himself wrote a constitution intended for the colony of Carolina. We can conceive of the adoption of formal constitutions by English settlers in the American colonies as a movement from a peaceful state of nature into a civil society. The mutual exchange of promises to accept the terms of their homemade constitutions signifies this. According to Locke, this compact for the establishment of civil society was then followed by the establishment of a "fiduciary" government. Whereas for Hobbes the sovereign itself was not formally bound by the terms of the covenant, according to Locke the government—and especially the umpire-like legislature—was so bound and performed a fiduciary function. This meant that when the government violated its part of the bargain, the subjects were no longer bound to obey it. The overthrow of a government did not lead to dissolution of civil society, as was the case in Hobbes's scheme. This theory was bound to appeal to the makers of the American Revolution, since they wanted only to get rid of British rule, but not to dissolve their own civil society.

The third reason, related to the second, for the Founding Fathers' receptivity to Locke can be found in the analogous positions in which he in 1688 and they in 1776 found themselves. Locke's *Second Treatise* provided a rationale for the Glorious Revolution of 1688. (This is not meant to suggest that the *Second Treatise* was written for *ad hoc* purposes, like Machiavelli's *Prince*. Recent research has demonstrated that Locke started work on this

---

[4] Edward S. Corwin, "The 'Higher Law' Background of American Constitutional Law," *Harvard Law Review*, vol. 42 (1928), pp. 386 ff. Also available in Bobbs-Merrill Reprint in History, H-45.

book several years before 1688, and in general his political writings were intended to be as universal as Hobbes's.)[5] The most important end result of the Glorious Revolution was that it settled once and for all the supremacy of Parliament over the king. Both in Hobbes's theory and in British constitutional practice of the time, the "sovereign"—if one man, then the monarch—was looked upon as the *representative* of the nation. However, after the decapitation of Charles I, after Oliver Cromwell's shortlived Protectorate, and after the troubles of the Restoration period, the emphasis in the phrase "The King in Parliament" changed from the first word to the last, and Parliament was thought of as more representative of the nation than the monarch alone. This theory was again useful for the American revolutionaries, who addressed King George III, not the British Parliament, as the usurper who had gone beyond his constitutional powers and had, therefore, violated the trust implicit in the British Constitution. When the Founding Fathers adopted the Constitution, they remained faithful to John Locke by devoting its first chapter to the legislative power, which was the Congress, and not to the executive or the judiciary. In other words, Locke's theoretical justification of parliamentary supremacy provided the Americans with a rationale for their claims to independence and, at the same time, with a theory for their own successful experiment in constitutional architecture.

PROPERTY AND CONSENSUS

Since Locke built his commonwealth on as rationalist a foundation as Hobbes did, he confronted the same dilemma: If you reject tradition as a source of legitimacy, how do you provide for constitutional stability from one generation to the next? When Cromwell, who had had the king's head cut off, faced this problem, it led him

---

[5] See Peter Laslett, ed., *John Locke: Two Treatises of Government— A Critical Edition with an Introduction and Apparatus Criticus*, Cambridge: Cambridge University Press, 1960.

to make the distinction between fundamentals and circumstantials, which is a part of the method used in this book. However, the things that Cromwell considered fundamental survived him by only a few years. Locke recognized this difficulty, to which Hobbes had found no "permanent" solution. In Locke's theory, as in English constitutional practice until at least the sixteenth century, the most important function of Parliament was a judicial one, "umpirage," or the settlement of disputes.[6] This meant that whenever a major dispute arose between a part of the civil society and the government, the government could not act as judge, since no one can be the judge in his own cause. In such a case the only appeal lies in a rebellion.[7]

---

[6] "89. Wherever therefore any number of men are so united into one society as to quit everyone his executive power of the law of nature, and to resign it to the public, there and there only is a political or civil society. And this is done wherever any number of men, in the state of nature, enter into society to make one people, one body politic under one supreme government: or else when anyone joins himself to and incorporates with any government already made. For hereby he authorizes the society, or which is all one, the legislative thereof, to make laws for him as the public good of the society shall require, to the execution whereof his own assistance (as to his own decrees) is due. And this puts men out of a state of nature into that of a commonwealth, by setting up a judge on earth with authority to determine all the controversies and redress the injuries that may happen to any member of the commonwealth; which judge is the legislative or magistrates appointed by it. And wherever there are any number of men, however associated, that have no such decisive power to appeal to, there they are still in the state of nature." John Locke, *Second Treatise on Civil Government*, chap. 7.

[7] "240. Here 'tis like the common question will be made, Who shall be judge whether the prince or legislative act contrary to their trust? This, perhaps, ill-affected and factious men may spread amongst the people, when the prince only makes use of his due prerogative. To this I reply, The people shall be judge; for who shall be judge whether his trustee or deputy acts well and according to the trust reposed in him, but he who deputes him and must, by having deputed him, have still a power to discard him when he fails in his trust? If this be reasonable in particular cases of private men, why should it be otherwise in that of the greatest moment, where the welfare of millions is concerned and also where the evil, if not prevented, is greater, and the redress very difficult, dear, and dangerous?

"241. But, farther, this question, (Who shall be judge?) cannot mean that there is no judge at all. For where there is no judicature on earth to

Now, as Locke pointed out, the word rebellion comes from the Latin *rebellare*, which means to go back to war. In this respect then, there is little difference between Locke and Hobbes. For both of them, a government that cannot settle disputes to which it is itself a party can be overthrown by its own subjects by force. This puts everyone back into a state of war, which is also the state of nature.

However, Locke tried to find a roundabout solution to this problem, through the inheritance of private property, mainly land. In dealing with whether any societies have ever actually been established as a result of a social compact, he suggests the irrelevancy of this question by asserting that those who accept the inheritance of property also implicitly accept the conditions under which this property was granted, and is held and protected, by the government. In this way, everyone who owns property gives his tacit consent to the terms of the social contract. Those about to inherit land from their father, who do not like the terms of the social contract, that is, of the constitution, should not accept their inheritance but instead go in *vacuis locis*, into the open spaces.[8] Locke obviously had in

---

decide controversies amongst men, God in heaven is judge. He alone, 'tis true, is judge of the right. But every man is judge for himself, as in all other cases so in this, whether another hath put himself into a state of war with him, and whether he should appeal to the supreme Judge, as *Jephtha* did.

"242. If a controversy arise betwixt a prince and some of the people in a matter where the law is silent or doubtful, and the thing be of great consequence, I should think the proper umpire, in such a case, should be the body of the people. For in such cases where the prince hath a trust reposed in him, and is dispensed from the common, ordinary rules of the law; there, if any men find themselves aggrieved, and think the prince acts contrary to, or beyond that trust, who so proper to judge as the body of the people (who at first lodged that trust in him) how far they meant it should extend? But if the prince, or whoever they be in the administration, decline that way of determination, the appeal then lies nowhere but to Heaven. Force between either persons, who have no known superior on earth, or which permits no appeal to a judge on earth, being properly a state of war, wherein the appeal lies only to Heaven; and in that state the injured party must judge for himself when he will think fit to make use of that appeal and put himself upon it." *Ibid.*, chap. 19, "Of the Dissolution of Government."

[8] "119. . . . [E]very man that hath any possession or enjoyment of any

mind the possibility, which existed in his own time, of going to the North American colonies. This, incidentally, may have been another reason for his great appeal to the American colonists, because in America, too, one could always go into the open spaces on the frontier—as long as that possibility lasted—and there either live in a more or less peaceful state of nature or enter into new social compacts. But this affinity at the same time also points to a major difference between the Founding Fathers and Locke. Although Jefferson and many other members of the Continental Congress, especially from the southern colonies, were members of what in England would have been described as the "landed gentry," their outlook was much more democratic and egalitarian than that of Locke. Neither Locke's theory nor the constitutional practice of Britain after the Glorious Revolution could be described as democratic. Members of Parliament were still elected on the basis of a highly restricted franchise, and Parliament in fact represented little more than the landowners and the richer merchants of the cities.

---

part of the dominions of any government doth thereby give his tacit consent, and is as far forth obliged to obedience to the laws of that government, during such enjoyment, as any one under it, whether this his possession be of land to him and his heirs forever, or a lodging only for a week; or whether it be barely travelling freely on the highway; and, in effect, it reaches as far as the very being of anyone within the territories of that government. . . .

"121. But since the government has a direct jurisdiction only over the land and reaches the possessor of it (before he has actually incorporated himself in the society) only as he dwells upon and enjoys that, the obligation anyone is under by virtue of such enjoyment to submit to the government begins and ends with the enjoyment; so that whenever the owner, who has given nothing but such a tacit consent to the government, will, by donation, sale or otherwise, quit the said possession, he is at liberty to go and incorporate himself into any other commonwealth, or agree with others to begin a new one *in vacuis locis*, in any part of the world they can find free and unpossessed; whereas he that has once, by actual agreement and any express declaration, given his consent to be of any commonweal, is perpetually and indispensably obliged to be, and remain unalterably a subject to it, and can never be again in the liberty of the state of nature, unless by any calamity the government he was under comes to be dissolved; or else by some public act cuts him off from being any longer a member of it." *Ibid.*, chap. 8.

Moreover, and more importantly, in America property in the form of land could not be used for purposes of stabilizing the constitution between generations, as it had in England. The reason was very simply the availability of unclaimed virgin lands, both within the colonies on the east coast and beyond them to the west.

It is clear from the Declaration of Independence that Jefferson recognized this difference between himself and the great Mr. Locke. The Declaration changes Locke's phrase "life, liberty, and property" to "Life, Liberty, and the pursuit of Happiness." It was, incidentally, also Thomas Jefferson who, as Governor of Virginia, abolished the old English institutions of primogeniture and entail, under which the eldest son of a landowner inherited the whole estate of his father. Since in America land could no longer be used as the cement between generations and to provide constitutional stability, how did the Founding Fathers solve the problem of stability that they had created through their rejection of the traditions of British rule?

A CONSTITUTIONAL PATENT

They provided the answer to the question of stability in their written constitution. The first answer is in their version of the separation of powers, which differed from Locke's. Locke distinguished three powers: the legislative, the executive, and the federative. His legislature really performed many basically "judicial" functions, as already mentioned, while the federative power was in charge of foreign relations. The American constitutional founders separated the judiciary from the legislature and took from the executive one very important power that Locke would have lodged in it: the power to convene and dismiss sessions of the legislature. In Great Britain to this day, this power is part of the royal prerogative, one of Bagehot's dignified functions, though it is in fact exercised as one of Bagehot's "efficient functions," by the Prime Minister. Under the American Constitution, the terms of the two Houses of

the Congress and the times of their elections and sessions are provided for, in basic outline, by the constitutional document itself.

The most brilliant constitutional invention of the Founding
Fathers, however, one that went as far as constitutional engineering
could toward solving Hobbes's dilemma and Locke's problem, was
the procedure for amending the constitution itself. This insured the
stability of those fundamental procedures of politics that were acceptable to successive generations, while it at the same time facilitated the flexibility of those procedures that successive generations
found it convenient or necessary to change. Combined with their
invention of the judicial review of legislation for its constitutionality,
the amending process helped to make the Constitution acceptable
(with the one major exception of the Civil War) to a population
and electorate whose makeup and goals have changed many times
over the past one hundred and eighty years. Incidentally, the amending procedure also solved another dilemma inherent in Locke's
theory. According to his theory the slightest majority, 50 percent
plus one, would always be in a position to make changes, even in the
most fundamental provisions of the constitution itself. Through the
amending process and judicial review, extraordinary changes would
require extraordinary majorities.

In the ever-continuing dialectic of the political process, the
solution of one problem creates another problem. Sometimes the current of heated political passions makes it easy to marshal for a brief
period of time the extraordinary majorities required for extraordinary, and even constitutional, changes. And almost always, public
opinion changes so profoundly in the twenty-five years that are
arbitrarily assigned to the life of a single generation, that it can
become extremely difficult to protect the stability of the constitution
itself against this kind of generational change. Partisan contests,
fanned by the peculiarities of the adversary method of the Common
Law, lead to exaggerated statements of political positions, which in
turn can give the appearance, at least superficially, of great fickle-
ness. Only one American president so far has served in office for
more than eight years, Franklin Delano Roosevelt, and even as
respected and well liked a president as Dwight Eisenhower met with

difficulties when he claimed to be the repository of the national interest in times of crisis. After all, he was also the head of the Republican party. In other words, the problem, created by the limited majoritarianism invented by the Founding Fathers, was how to define the permanent, general, public, national interest. Even to the extent that the permanency of the basic rules of the political game, as defined by the largely procedural provisions of the Constitution, is accepted, there still remains the problem of the standards by which to judge whether particular substantive policies are in keeping with the general interest.

Some political analysts have tried to solve this problem by returning, somewhat pathetically, to the older Stoic and Christian traditions of natural law. Walter Lippmann, for example, in his book *The Public Philosophy* has argued that questions about the propriety of specific policies can be answered on the basis of standards derived from a natural law philosophy.[9] However, this "solution" continues the confusion between prescriptive and descriptive natural law by returning to the rights that Thomas Jefferson, in the Declaration of Independence, considered self-evident. But what appears self-evident to one group or one generation of men may appear very controversial to other groups and later generations, and in fact may be at the very heart of controversy itself.

Other Americans have thought it expedient to ignore the problem of a definition of the public, or general, interest by asserting, or at least hoping, that the natural play of pressures in the market place of public opinion would lead to an outcome that would be best, simply because it would work pragmatically. Adherents of the philosophy of Rousseau would, as we shall see in the next chapter, condemn this attitude as a confusion of the "will of all" with the "general will."

In any case, American politics has not squarely confronted this problem of a possible definition of the general interest. Although Americans were facing, in the 1960s, more awesome and more clearly

---

[9] Walter Lippmann, *The Public Philosophy*, Boston: Little, Brown, 1955.

definable crucial problems than anyone else at any other place or time of history, they were not able to generate a philosophy that could articulate these problems for them in manageable terms. It seemed as though the practices of constitutional litigation had emasculated philosophical-theoretical capacities. Because Locke's synchretistic blandness had triumphed over Hobbes's systematic brilliance, Americans were thereby trapped into the habit of making false analogies, like the one implied by the concept "totalitarianism," in a domestic institutional setting that had performed creditably as long as politics could afford to refuse to recognize fundamental and radically divisive problems.

Selected Bibliography

Barker, Sir Ernest, ed., *Social Contract: Locke, Hume, Rousseau*, New York: Oxford University Press, 1947.

Corwin, Edward S., "The 'Higher Law' Background of American Constitutional Law," *Harvard Law Review*, vol. 42 (1928), pp. 386 ff. Also, Ithaca, N.Y.: Cornell University Press, 1955.

Curti, Merle, "The Great Mr. Locke—America's Philosopher, 1783–1861," *Huntington Library Bulletin*, no. 11 (1937), pp. 107–151.

Hartz, Louis, *The Liberal Tradition in America*, New York: Harcourt, Brace, 1955.

Locke, John, *An Essay Concerning Human Understanding*, Maurice Cranston, ed., New York: Collier, 1965.

Locke, John, *The Second Treatise on Government*, Thomas P. Peardon, ed., New York: Liberal Arts Press, 1952.

Locke, John, *Two Treatises of Government*, Thomas I. Cook, ed., New York: Hafner, 1947.

Locke, John, *Two Treatises of Government: A Critical Edition with an Introduction and Apparatus Criticus*, Peter Laslett, ed., Cambridge: Cambridge University Press, 1960.

Lippmann, Walter, *The Public Philosophy*, New York: Mentor, 1955.

It is my wish to inquire whether it be possible, within the civil order, to discover a legitimate and stable basis of Government. This I shall do by considering human beings as they are and laws as they might be. I shall attempt, throughout my investigations, to maintain a constant connexion between what right permits and interest demands, in order that no separation may be made between justice and utility. I intend to begin without first proving the importance of my subject. Am I, it will be asked, either prince or legislator that I take it upon me to write of politics? My answer is—No; and it is for that very reason that I have chosen politics as the matter of my book. Were I either the one or the other I should not waste my time in laying down what has to be done. I should do it, or else hold my peace.

I was born into a free state and am a member of its sovereign body. My influence on public affairs may be small, but because I have a right to exercise my vote, it is my duty to learn their nature, and it has been for me a matter of constant delight, while meditating on problems of Government in general, to find ever fresh reasons for regarding with true affection the way in which these things are ordered in my native land.

Jean Jacques Rousseau,
The Social Contract (1762).

MAJORITY AND GENERALITY

11

The United States was the first political system to new-model its constitution with great success, except for the disaster of the Civil War. The Founding Fathers solved the problem of generational instability by giving a procedural bias to the sources of authority and consensus in American politics. Nevertheless, the United States has experienced persistent difficulties in its search for consensus on a definition of "general welfare" or "public interest." This difficulty is much more marked in the United States than in Europe, where interests are defined by tradition, but where *the* national interest is defined by such imperceptibly changing existential realities as the geography or the demography of a country, which do not seem to change in their relations to one another or to the outside environment except very, very slowly. Of course, in Europe too after a great feat of constitutional engineering, the need has arisen to find a new cement between generations. This has been particularly true after major revolutions on the continent, and after the two world wars of the twentieth century.

In a sense the continental Europeans are still suffering from the aftermath of the breakup of medieval unity. It was at the end of the Middle Ages, during first the Renaissance and then the Reformation, that "the great modern fallacy," as Burckhardt called it, that one could give oneself a new constitution on a rational basis first became fashionable. The continental Europeans never provided as efficient a solution to this problem as did the English, partly because their problem was more severe, and partly because they found themselves forced to analyze it in much more explicit terms. The consequences are reflected in Jean Jacques Rousseau's denunciations of feudalism in his *Social Contract*. These are much stronger explicit criticisms of the feudal system than those of John Locke or Thomas Hobbes, despite the fact that Rousseau was writing two centuries after Hobbes and almost one century after Locke.[1]

WHAT CAN MAKE IT LEGITIMATE?

Because he was living in France, which had not experienced its equivalent of the nationalization of the church undertaken by Henry VIII in England, Rousseau's denunciations of the priestly hierarchy of the Roman Catholic Church sound much more vehement than those of Locke, though less ferocious than Hobbes's in Books 3 and 4 of the *Leviathan*.[2] Because he was brought up in the universalist tradition of the Roman law, as well as for other reasons, Rousseau

---

[1] "As to those private wars which were authorized by the Ordinances of King Louis IX and suspended by the Peace of God, they were merely an abuse of Feudalism—that most absurd of all systems of government, so contrary was it to principles of Natural Right and of all good polity." Jean Jacques Rousseau, *The Social Contract*, book 1, chap. 4.

[2] "Wherever the Clergy constitute a corporate body they are the masters and the legislators within their sphere of influence. [Footnote:] It should be noted that what knits the clergy together into a corporate body is not so much the existence of formal assemblies, as in France, but the communion of churches. Communion and excommunication from the social pact of the clergy, and armed with this, they will for ever be masters both of the kings and of the People. All priests who are in communion with the Church, no matter whether they come from the ends of the earth, are fellow citizens. This invention is a political triumph. There never was anything at all resembling it in the pagan priesthood, where a corporate body of clergy was unknown." *Ibid.*, book 3, chap. 8. For Hobbes's attack on the Church, see *Leviathan*, part 3, "Of a Christian Commonwealth," and part 4, "Of the Kingdom of Darkness."

reformulated the basic questions raised by Locke and Hobbes in still more general terms. Instead of trying to find an historical or anthropological social contract, he simply started off with the fact, as it seemed to him, that man everywhere is in chains. By this he meant that man was everywhere subject to conventions—living in communities that restricted his "natural freedom" and subjected him to the power of other men. "Man is born free, yet everywhere he is in chains. . . . How this change came about, I cannot explain."[3] Some contemporary political scientists of the behavioral persuasion would stop reading Rousseau's *Social Contract* at this point, because they are interested only in explanations of human behavior. But Rousseau went on to ask the only question that mattered to him and to many others who consider normative, prescriptive questions more important than behavioral, descriptive ones: "What can make it legitimate? That question I think I can answer."

The only thing that can make legitimate the condition that one man owes obedience to others is his obligation to some acceptable definition of the public, or general, interest and welfare. The whole of *The Social Contract* is a search for such a definition. In the course of this search, Rousseau attempted to distinguish between descriptive and prescriptive rights. He tells us that might, that is, superior physical force, cannot by itself be converted into right. In other words, the *fact* that one man has more power at his command than another, does not by itself create a *norm* according to which the weaker should and will obey the stronger.[4] The solution that

---

[3] *The Social Contract*, book 1, chap. 1.

[4] "However strong a man, he is never strong enough to remain master always, unless he transform his Might into Right, and Obedience into Duty. . . . The mighty man who defeats his rival becomes heir to his Right. So soon as we can disobey with impunity, disobedience becomes legitimate. And, since the Mightiest is always right, it merely remains for us to become possessed of Might. But what validity can there be in a Right which ceases to exist when Might changes hands? If a man be constrained by Might to obey, what need has he to obey by Duty? And if he is not constrained to obey, there is no further obligation on him to do so. It follows, therefore, that the word Right adds nothing to the idea of Might. It becomes, in this connection completely meaningless." *Ibid.*, book 1, chap. 3.

Rousseau advances for the problem stated by both Hobbes and
Locke before him is an extremely consensual solution initially:
Rousseau insists that there must be complete unanimity at least once,
and that this occurs at the formation of the society through the first
contract.[5] When individuals enter into society they surrender their
individual wills to the general will, which is expressed by the sovereign. Rousseau's sovereign differs from Hobbes's in that it always
consists of the whole body of citizens, whereas Hobbes's sovereign
could consist of the whole body of citizens, or of an assembly of men,
or of a single man. The sovereign expresses the general will in
response to the "right questions." When it does that, and it *is* the
general will only when it does answer the right questions, it is by
definition always right.[6] Rousseau ingeniously arrives at this solution
to the problem of the definition of the general interest by distinguishing between the general will and the will of all. The general
will acts for the whole society, whereas the will of all acts only for
the sum of separate special interests. This means that the sovereign
has to address itself to problems that, in our terms, are mainly
procedural, whereas more substantive problems, if they are dealt
with by legislation, are more likely to be exposed to pressures from

---

[5] "The institution of the franchise is, in itself, a form of compact, and
assumes that, at least once in its operation, complete unanimity existed."
Ibid., book 1, chap. 5.

"There is one law which, by its very nature, demands unanimous
consent, and that is the social pact. For civil association is, of all acts, the
most deliberately willed. Since every man is born free and his own master,
none, under any pretext whatsoever, can enslave him without his consent. . . .

"If, then, when the social pact is made, voices are raised in opposition,
such opposition does not invalidate the contract, but merely excludes from it
those who voice it, so that they become foreigners among the general body
of citizens. When the State is formed, residence implies consent. To live in a
country means to submit to its sovereignty." *Ibid.*, book 4, chap. 2.

[6] "Now, the Sovereign People, having no existence outside that of the
individuals who compose it, has, and can have, no interest at variance with
theirs. Consequently, the sovereign power need give no guarantee to its subjects, since the body is incapable of injuring its members; nor, as we shall see
later, can it injure any single individual. The Sovereign, by merely existing,
is always what it should be." *Ibid.*, book 1, chap. 7.

the will of all.[7] In order to make practical this distinction between the general will and the will of all, Rousseau provided that, depending on the importance of particular issues to be resolved by the sovereign, different kinds of majorities should be required.[8] However, significantly, he opts in favor of graduated majorities without at the same time asserting—indeed, while denying—any natural harmony of interests of the kind that the Utilitarians were to base their philosophy upon.

NEW COMMUNITIES

Rousseau's solution of the problem of the general interest is not a happy one, and it has caused a great deal of confusion among both his disciples and his interpreters. It is important for our purposes, however, because he addressed himself to a series of problems that are very similar to those being faced today by the emerging and developing new states. Without being in any way prophetic about the emergence of scores of new states two centuries after his own

---

[7] "But when the whole body of the people makes an enactment valid for all alike, it has in mind only itself. . . . When that is so, then the matter about which the enactment is concerned is as much general as the will which produces the enactment. It is an action of this kind to which I give the name 'law.'

"When I say that the matter of law is general, I mean that the law is concerned with the subjects of a State taken as a whole, and with actions considered as purely abstract. It never treats a man as an individual, nor an act as special or exceptional." Ibid., book 2, chap. 6.

[8] "In fact, as soon as issue is joined on some *particular* point, on some *specific* right arising out of a situation which has not previously been regulated by some form of general agreement, we are in the realm of debate. The matter becomes a trial in which certain interested individuals are ranged against the public, but where there is no certainty about what law is applicable nor about who can rightly act as judge. It would be absurd in such a case to demand an *ad hoc* decision of the general will, since the general will would then be the decision of one of the parties only. . . . Thus, just as the will of the individual cannot represent the general will, so, too, the general will changes its nature when called upon to pronounce upon a particular subject. In so far as it is general, it cannot judge of an individual person or an isolated fact." Ibid., book 1, chap. 4.

time, Rousseau recognized the weakness of any society that has just been founded or undergone some kind of revolution.[9] The makers of the French Revolution, many of whom were heavily influenced by the writings of Rousseau, soon after his death experienced that weakness that results when one attempts to cut himself off from the effectiveness of an old ruling class. Something similar happened in former colonies, after the colonial administration had removed itself, or the traditional elite had been overthrown. At this point, as in the course of the French Revolution, ambivalent feelings about the society's own traditions come into conflict with one another and generate new issues, for the processing of which the political system may not be fully prepared.

During the independence struggle itself, for example, in most of the African colonies, there was virtual unanimity on the desirability of independence from foreign rule. This could be looked upon as the equivalent of the unanimity that Rousseau required for the social contract itself. But after independence is achieved, how is this unanimity, this consensus on a single substantive goal, to be carried forward? Or if, as in most cases, it is in fact soon dissipated, how can a new sense of community be created? Who belongs and who does not belong to the new community? And who is to decide the procedures by which the last question can be answered? Rousseau himself suggested the possibility of the Great Legislator, who would provide the first constitution, and who would, in contemporary terms, be endowed with the charisma necessary to tie his own and future generations together, but who would remove himself from the scene after his great task of initial nation-building had been accomplished. To varying degrees, men like Nehru, Nkrumah, and Sukarno played the role of Rousseau's Great Legislator, though none of these three

---

[9] "It is with a State in its infancy as with a newly formed regiment: it is weaker at its inception than at any other time, and more vulnerable. Resistance could be more successfully staged when all is chaos than in the early days of fermentation, when every man is busy with his duties within the community, and no one has a thought to spare for perils threatening from without. Should war, famine, or sedition occur at such a time, it will mean the inevitable overturning of the State." *Ibid.*, book 2, chap. 10.

removed himself voluntarily from the scene after the first constitution had been designed. But in an instance closer to Rousseau's home
and to our own time, President DeGaulle did remove himself after
having acted as France's great legislator for eleven years. At any
rate, the trouble with both Nkrumah and Sukarno, and several other
leaders of new nations, was that they were unable to maintain the
momentum that had first propelled their countries into independence, after this goal had been reached. They were unable to prevent
rebellions against their own governments, in the sense in which
Locke used the term.

The question therefore arises: How can one keep a new political system going? How can the leadership prevent rebellions, revolutions, or the disintegration of their polity? There has been a great
deal of recent literature on this question, some of it under the
heading of "national integration." Much of this literature emphasizes the need for sound representative institutions. Generally, the
function of representation is assigned to the national legislature, but
this location is based upon a misleading analogy. Simply because in
most developed Western political systems the legislature has often
been thought of as performing the representative function alone,
there is no reason to assume that this is the only or the best possible
way of getting the job of representation done. Even in the United
States, where the lower chamber of the Congress is called the House
of Representatives, many other institutions in the Federal Government, including the President, the Senate, and the Supreme Court,
perform representative functions. Rousseau himself contributed,
quite against his own intentions, to this conventional identification
of representation with the legislature. He insisted that "will" had to
be coupled with power in order to convert might into right and
therefore considered legislation legitimate only if it emanated from
the general will. Since legislation amounted to an expression of will,
Rousseau denied that a representative assembly, like the British
Parliament, was capable of legitimate legislation. This led him to
the conclusion that the British people were profoundly mistaken in
their belief that they were free. They were free only on election day,
he held, and overtaken by slavery thereafter, because they permitted
representatives to make laws for them. Since will is either mine or

someone else's, without an intermediate possibility, no representative, someone who is there on my behalf, can make legitimate laws on my behalf.[10] Only a sovereign expressing the general will, especially in a new nation, can hope to create the feeling of community without which no notion of the public interest will take hold and neither stability over time nor integration over space will be achieved.

Nevertheless, contemporary students of "new nations" often urge the improvement of these nations' representative institutions, and by this they usually mean their legislative assemblies, in order to assure their survival. This recommendation overlooks the connection between will and the problem of creating a new community. Where this will to togetherness, to community, is lacking, even the most representative of legislative assemblies will not solve the problem. In established nations this problem of will does not exist, because it has been solved long ago, and representative assemblies function less as community integrators than as issue generators, that is, as the stimulators of politics. Rousseau wanted to stimulate politics not through representation, but through the direct participation of all citizens in the deliberations of the sovereign. At the same time, he was aware of the dangers of overstimulation and the inherent dialectical conflict between the general will and the will of all individual citizens. In order to guide this conflict into constructive directions, he advocated, in addition to his procedural solutions to the questions about the general interest and generational stability, a secular substitute for Christianity in the form of the "civil reli-

---

[10] "Sovereignty cannot be represented, for the same reason that it cannot be alienated. It consists essentially of the general will, and will cannot be represented. Either it is itself or it is different. There is no middle term. The Deputies of the People are not, nor can they be, its representatives. They can be only its Commissioners. They can make no definite decisions. Laws which the People have not ratified in their own person are null and void. That is to say, they are not laws at all. The English people think that they are free, but in this belief they are profoundly wrong. They are free only when they are electing members of Parliament. Once the election has been completed, they revert to a condition of slavery: they are nothing. Making such use of it in the few short moments of their freedom, they deserve to lose it." *Ibid.*, book 3, chap. 15.

gion."[11] There have been many conscious and some unconscious attempts in the nineteenth and twentieth centuries to accept this recommendation of Rousseau. These attempts have included various forms of nationalism, communism, socialism, African socialism, and many efforts to harness religious commitments to the pursuit of secular goals. In the new states of the postwar world, such efforts usually failed if the new civil religion had an antipolitical intent, because it then failed to contribute to the development of politics and the expansion of the awareness of the population.

Selected Bibliography

Barker, Sir Ernest, ed., *Social Contract: Essays by Locke, Hume, Rousseau*, New York: Oxford University Press, 1962.

Rousseau, Jean Jacques, *The First and Second Discourses*, Roger D. Masters, ed., New York: St. Martin's Press, 1964.

Rousseau, Jean Jacques, *Political Writings,* C. E. Vaughan, ed., New York: Wiley, 1962.

Rousseau, Jean Jacques, *The Social Contract*, Lester G. Crocker, ed., New York: Washington Square Press, 1956.

Rousseau, Jean Jacques, *The Social Contract*, Charles Frankel, ed., New York: Hafner, 1947.

Rousseau, Jean Jacques, *The Social Contract*, Willmoore Kendall, trans. and ed., Chicago: Gateway, 1954.

Shklar, Judith, *Men and Citizens: A Study of Rousseau's Social Theory*, New York: Cambridge University Press, 1969.

---

[11] *Ibid.*, book 4, chap. 8.

We have now recognized the necessity to the mental well-being of mankind (on which all their other well-being depends) of freedom of opinion, and freedom of the expression of opinion, on four distinct grounds, which we will now briefly recapitulate:

First, if any opinion is compelled to silence, that opinion may, for aught we can certainly know, be true. To deny this is to assume our own infallibility.

Secondly, though the silenced opinion be an error, it may, and very commonly does, contain a portion of truth; and since the general or prevailing opinion on any subject is rarely or never the whole truth, it is only by the collision of adverse opinions that the remainder of the truth has any chance of being supplied.

Thirdly, even if the received opinion be not only true, but the whole truth; unless it is suffered to be, and actually is, vigorously and earnestly contested, it will, by most of those who receive it, be held in the manner of a prejudice, with little comprehension or feeling of its rational grounds. And not only this, but, fourthly, the meaning of the doctrine itself will be in danger of being lost or enfeebled, and deprived of its vital effect on the character and conduct: the dogma becoming a mere formal profession, inefficacious for good, but cumbering the ground and preventing the growth of any real and heartfelt conviction from reason or personal experience.

John Stuart Mill,
On Liberty, Currin V. Shields, ed.,
New York: Liberal Arts Press,
1956, p. 64.

INDIVIDUALS AND GROUPS

12

The founding of new political systems always calls for new statements of the content of the general welfare. This was the one problem that the founders of the American Constitution did not satisfactorily solve. The spectrum of answers to the question—How do we find the general welfare?—ranges between two extremes. One extreme is exemplified by Rousseau, for whom the general will is always right, and for whom, conversely, the right answers must be expressions of the general will. The other extreme is illustrated by Jeremy Bentham, the founder of the British school of Utilitarian philosophy, who simply stated that the general interest of a society is the same as the sum of the interests of all its members.[1] In other words, Bentham opted in favor of the will of all, which Rousseau had specifically condemned. Bentham went beyond this in denouncing a concept like the general will as a foolish or vicious myth. For

---

[1] "The interest of the community is one of the most general expressions that can occur in the phraseology of morals: no wonder that the meaning of it is often lost. When it has a meaning, it is this. The community is a fictitious *body*, composed of individual persons who are considered as constituting as it were its *members*. The interest of the community then is, what?—the sum of the interests of the several members who compose it." Jeremy Bentham, *An Introduction to the Principles of Morals and Legislation*, chap. 1, iv.

Bentham the purpose of government was to secure the greatest happiness for the greatest number. This view carried the individualism and the rationalism of Thomas Hobbes to its logical conclusion. But it still did not solve the problem of generational stability, which both Hobbes and Locke had faced. However, this problem did not bother the Utilitarians, because rather than wanting to insure the stability of the political system that they knew from one generation to the next, they wanted to unsettle the system in order to reconstruct it on a more rationalistic and individualistic foundation. Like Hobbes, Bentham did not accept institutions merely because they were in existence and had a long history. On the contrary, the antiquity of institutions and practices was rather to be held against them. While they intentionally tried to overlook the past, the Utilitarians unintentionally tended to ignore the future. This occurred because they believed that the best future could be provided by thousands and millions of individuals rationally pursuing their respective self-interests. The procedures for doing this would presumably be dictated by the workings of the human mind, that is, by reason.

LIBERTY

However, even Jeremy Bentham himself did not leave all the separate individuals entirely to their own devices, but rather provided for them, in many of his works, models of constitutional, civil, and criminal laws, which were to provide the framework within which the pursuit of individual happiness would redound to the general welfare. Bentham's disciple John Stuart Mill further refined the Utilitarian position by taking up the problem of the relations between majority and minority, not within the context of the stability of procedures, but rather in terms of the protection of minority and individual "rights" against majority "power." Bentham's *Fragment on Government* was published in 1776, the year of the Declaration of Independence. This was also the year of the publication of Adam Smith's *The Wealth of Nations*. Smith gave the classic statement of the economic doctrine of laissez faire, according to which the wealth of the nation would be maximized by letting each "economic man" seek to promote his own profit. According to Adam Smith, each man, in pursuing his own profit, is guided by an "invisible hand" to promote an end that is not a part of his intention, that is, the wealth of the nation.[2] Smith wanted and helped to destroy traditional economic restrictions, just as Bentham wanted and helped to destroy traditional legal and constitutional restrictions. Bentham succeeded more outside than inside Great Britain.

By 1859, when John Stuart Mill wrote his famous essay *On Liberty*, some of the goals of both political and economic Utilitarianism had been achieved, and, as always, new problems had been recognized in the course of their achievement. For example, Mill was very much impressed by the fears of De Tocqueville, presented in his book *Democracy in America*, concerning the dangers of majority tyranny in that new democracy.[3] A strict majoritarianism of the kind implied by Bentham would not provide any protection for a small, intelligent, and progressive minority against a large, ignorant, and reactionary majority. Especially during periods of democratic growth, when suffrage was being extended to previously subject people, the absence of such protection seemed a great defect to Mill. In his essay *On Liberty*, he lays the foundations for a set of criteria by means of which procedures designed to operate in both individuals' interest and the general interest can be designed. In doing so, Mill entirely retains the individualistic bias of his great teacher, Bentham. He begins by distinguishing between self-regarding acts and other-regarding acts. The individual should be left entirely to his own devices when it comes to acts that are self-regarding. His liberty may be circumscribed only with respect to acts whose consequences affect others. But even here, there are to be virtually no restrictions upon freedom of speech or opinion. Mill argues that a false opinion, widely held, can only be improved by one that is more nearly correct. On the other hand, even a true

---

[2] Adam Smith, *An Inquiry into the Nature and the Causes of the Wealth of Nations*, Edwin Canaan, ed., New York: Modern Library, 1937, book 4, chap. 2.

[3] John Stuart Mill, *On Liberty*, New York: Liberal Arts Press, 1956, p. 6 f.

opinion, if challenged by a false one in public debate, will be adhered to more rationally after than before such a debate by those who hold it. Mill's intellectual liberalism is, in a way, the counterpart of Adam Smith's economic liberalism, and both intellectual and economic Utilitarianism carry John Milton's statement on freedom of speech, in the *Areopagitica*, to its logical conclusion. Mill advocates debate because it will improve man's rational faculty, partly by leading to the expansion of consciousness through the development of politics.[4]

At the same time, however, Mill, like Bentham and Milton before him, did believe in the existence of a single truth, or at least he believed in its eventual emergence through the use of correct method.[5] The more intelligent members of society were more likely to perceive this truth, and should therefore be allowed to govern. In fact, the constitution was to be constructed in such a way as to encourage government by the intelligent elite, who would at the same time see it as one of their principal tasks to educate the rest of the population to their own level of intelligence. In this respect Mill

---

[4] See, e.g., *ibid.*, p. 77: ". . . [I]ndividuality is the same thing with development. . . ."

[5] Like most of the other participants in the "Great Conversation," Mill was keenly aware of the importance of method to the substance of political debate. His first major work was *A System of Logic, Ratiocinative and Inductive, Being a Connected View of the Principles of Evidence and the Methods of Scientific Investigation* (1843). Mill wrote this largely in order to prepare the methodological ground for his attack upon the "German, or *a priori* view of human knowledge. . . . The notion that truths external to the mind may be known by intuition or consciousness, independently of observation and experience, is, I am persuaded in these times, the great intellectual support of false doctrines and bad institutions. By the aid of this theory, every inveterate belief and every intense feeling, of which the origin is not remembered, is enabled to dispense with the obligation of justifying itself by reason, and is erected into its own all-sufficient voucher and justification. There never was such an instrument devised for consecrating deep-seated prejudices. And the chief strength of this philosophy in morals, politics, and religion, lies in the appeal which it is accustomed to make to the evidence of mathematics and of the cognate branches of physical science." John Stuart Mill, *Autobiography*, cited by Ernest Nagel, ed., *John Stuart Mill's Philosophy of Scientific Method*, New York: Hafner, 1950, p. xxviii.

was, consistent with his belief in the existence of a single truth, an intellectual elitist. His view of politics tended to be mechanistic rather than dialectical, and his faith in progress generally was a faith in the capacity of others, both individuals and nations, to raise themselves to the level of intelligence at which British intellectuals of his own circle had already arrived. In other words, Mill's historical perspective and vision was rather more limited and ethnocentric than that of Karl Marx, whose life in England overlapped that of Mill. A more important difference between the two is, however, Marx's insistence upon viewing history as the outcome of struggle among *collectivities* and Mill's consistent individualism.

THE GROUP

The individualism of liberal Utilitarians originated in their attack upon the ancient and parochial collectivities that still remained from the Middle Ages. The individualism of twentieth century liberalism, on the other hand, has been more importantly directed against the new collectivity of class or nation, which has threatened to gobble up both the older feeling of identification with a manageable, comprehensible community and the recently discovered feeling of individual autonomy, in a situation of forced belonging to the capitalist or the working class, or to the nation. In the effort to mediate between the extremes of individualism and the general will, a whole new school of political theory, both normative and analytical, arose. *Pluralism* focused upon the role of groups in politics and, more especially, upon the great variety of groups that operate within any political system. Some pluralists were particularly interested in older and more "natural" groupings, like churches, localities, and the surviving remnants of medieval guilds, universities or other chartered corporations. Other pluralists were more concerned with modern, more or less rationally founded groups like business corporations, labor unions, professional associations, and, above all, political parties. Those who preferred more traditional groupings generally did so because they bemoaned the collectivization and standardization that modern industrialism was bringing in mass societies. But the ancients and the moderns in this argument generally agreed that groups provide the best if not the only medium through which individuals can assume some responsibility, however limited, for the decisions that have to be made in the huge political systems to which they belong. This agreement follows from the assumption that all men in fact belong to a whole series of social groups, beginning with the family and ending with the nation or race or mankind itself. Membership in social groups increases with increasing social differentiation. Developed industrial societies are, virtually by sociological definition, also the most highly differentiated societies. Therefore they offer the greatest opportunities for group membership, while at the same time they have the greatest need to offer channels of responsibility to counteract the dangers of "massification."

PARTIES

Although John Stuart Mill was very much interested in electoral law, and offered a system of preferential voting, which his political heirs, the British Liberal party, were still advocating in recent years, he does not discuss political parties in his major works. We have already noticed the same oversight on the part of Walter Bagehot in *The English Constitution*. The main reason for this neglect of political parties was the fact that, although already of importance within Parliament, they had not yet begun to play the role in popular politics that they were to assume during the last third of the nineteenth century. It seems characteristic of the conflict between the "ancient pluralists" and the "modern pluralists" that one of the first, and perhaps the most influential, definitions of a political party was given by Edmund Burke. Burke was a member of Parliament, who achieved his most lasting fame as a critic of the French Revolution.[6] He would have to be classified with the "ancient pluralists," because he argued in favor of prescriptive rights and urged each man to stay in "his little platoon" in life. In Burke's view a political party was a body of men agreed "upon some particular

---

[6] Edmund Burke, *Reflections on the Revolution in France* (1790), New York: Doubleday, 1961.

principle" in pursuit of which they united, presumably over a fairly long period of time.

The rationalistic and individualistic thinkers, whose political philosophy Burke opposed, did not discover political parties for more than another century. When they did discover parties, they looked upon them primarily as the means through which individual citizens could contribute to central decisions and make choices between alternatives. This view of political parties seemed particularly plausible in the major English-speaking countries, especially the United Kingdom and the United States, because there control of the government usually alternated between the two major parties. Voters in general elections could, therefore, presumably choose rationally between two major, practicable alternative programs. This model gained further plausibility in the 1920s, when the British Labor party began to replace the Liberal party as the major opposition to the Conservative party and occasionally even put up a minority government. This enabled some Marxists to identify the three major parties schematically with the three major classes in British society: the Conservative party with the ruling, capitalist class; the Labor party with the exploited, working class; and the Liberal party with the middle class, which was being decimated as the result of class struggle, with most of its members being proletarianized, and only a few joining the party of the upper class. Though popular, this interpretation was in fact quite mistaken. But it was no more mistaken than the anti-Marxist view, according to which the British two-party system simply gave voters a choice between two competing groups within the governing class, so that the choice was phony and the electorate was really being manipulated by the elite.[7]

Here we have mentioned only three of the many different competing models of party systems, taken only from literature that deals with countries in which two major parties are competing most of the time. Other models in the literature have been drawn from countries with multiparty systems. But wherever they came from or whatever purpose they were supposed to serve, the models were most

---

[7] See, e.g., Seymour Martin Lipset, *Political Man*, p. 27.

frequently used to test the argument that parties can serve to transmit citizens' responsibility for government and governments' accountability to citizens.[8] Especially after the full extension of suffrage, and in countries where accurate statistics of elections were kept, these models could be used to check, at least to some extent, the realism of some of the basic democratic theories.

IRRATIONALISM AND MANIPULATION

Democratic party politicians are in the public eye much of the time, and voting statistics in constitutional democracies are readily accessible to the public and, even more so, to political scientists. Elections are among the most dramatic events that take place in democratic countries. The average individual—the "common man" or the "man in the street"—can obviously do very little by himself to affect the course of public policy. Yet government is supposed to "rest on the consent of the governed," and citizens are supposed to have equal opportunities to participate in the political process. There is no better place to check these democratic suppositions than in the study of political parties and elections. Much, probably too much, of political science has concentrated upon these two phenomena during the past twenty-five years. Most of the findings have contradicted the simple democratic assumptions.[9] For one thing, the voters did not behave in the rational manner that had been attributed to at least the intelligent elite by philosophers like Mill. In some democracies, especially the United States, a very large proportion of the voters rarely if ever exercised their democratic rights. Of those who do participate in elections, an even higher proportion, often a majority, have little accurate information about either the issues or the candidates about whom they are to decide. A high percentage of voters do not even know the names of their own representatives in parliament or congress, and a surprising proportion of voters in

---

[8] Spiro, *Responsibility in Government: Theory and Practice*, New York: Van Nostrand Reinhold, 1969.

[9] See, e.g., James D. Barber, *Citizen Politics: An Introduction to Political Behavior*, Chicago: Markham, 1969.

many countries cannot name the chief of government. Moreover, studies of the organization of political parties, beginning with Ostrogorski's classic study of the German Social Democratic party before World War I, have shown that there is little internal democracy within parties, which are more often tightly controlled by a small elite and/or a self-perpetuating bureaucracy.[10] Each large party can thus, according to some interpretations of such findings, manipulate its own membership and following, though there is but little evidence of any collusion between the leaderships of two or more parties to manipulate the total electorate.

There is another reason why students of politics have become skeptical about the role of parties as instruments for the realization of citizen responsibility, and that is the commercial and political success of advertising and propaganda during the past half century. Abraham Lincoln once said: "You can fool all of the people some of the time, and you can fool some of the people all of the time, but you can't fool all of the people all of the time." Modern techniques of public relations may have disproved Lincoln. Occasionally programs or candidates have been packaged so effectively that whole populations have been "fooled" over long periods of time. However, few critical studies of political behavior that focus upon the quantitative side of electoral behavior are likely to yield adequate answers to the basic questions about the validity of the democratic assumptions made by the classical, rationalist, individualist theorists of the nineteenth century. This is so because such studies tend to take a static view of parties, whose role is in fact most significant during periods of great change within political systems. When parties are genuine "movements," as, for example, during the last years of colonialism in Africa, they contribute importantly to the dissolution or formation of consensus and to setting the political style of the newly independent country. On the other hand, after a political system has matured and gained stability, political parties more often operate at what C. Wright Mills called the "middle levels of power." He made this suggestion in a book entitled *The Power Elite*, which,

---

[10] M. I. Ostrogorski, *Democracy and the Organization of Political Parties*, 2 vols., S. M. Lipset, ed., Chicago: Quadrangle, 1964.

as its title indicates, advanced the thesis that the most important decisions in the United States were not made as a result of the democratic process, but by a small elite.[11] From this point of view, even in constitutional democracies, policies are made neither by millions of rational individuals acting autonomously nor as the outcome of the interaction of democratically controlled groups. Nor does the competition among private groups, or between private and public organizations, present individual citizens with meaningful choices. Quite the contrary, a small elite manipulates that small proportion of the population that has any active political concerns and interests through its manipulation of groups, including political parties. The general interest is what the power elite decides it should be, and neither the rational individual, nor the democratic group, nor, finally, the political party whose members are agreed upon some common principle, contributes to the definition of the general interest. Representation is a mockery, popular politics consists of empty and meaningless motions, and the only politics that matters is the politics—or mere intrigue—that takes place *within* the small circle of the ruling elite. We have returned to a Platonic kind of politics, only it is a vulgarized form of Platonism, because it is no longer dedicated to the truth. Unlike Plato's Guardians, this new power elite does not believe in the true, the good, the beautiful. It believes only in the enhancement of its own power and will do anything that seems to serve that goal.

Selected Bibliography

Bachrach, Peter, *The Theory of Democratic Elitism: A Critique*, Boston: Little, Brown, 1967.

Barber, James D., *Citizen Politics: An Introduction to Political Behavior*, Chicago: Markham, 1969.

---

[11] C. Wright Mills, *The Power Elite*, New York: Oxford University Press, 1956.

Bentham, Jeremy, *A Bentham Reader*, Mary Peter Mack, ed., New York: Pegasus, 1969.

Bentham, Jeremy, *The Handbook of Political Fallacies*, New York: Harper & Brothers, 1952.

Bentham, Jeremy, *An Introduction to the Principles of Morals and Legislation*, Laurence J. Lafleur, ed., New York: Hafner, 1948.

Bentham, Jeremy, and John Stuart Mill, *The Utilitarians*, Garden City: Dolphin, 1961.

Burke, Edmund, *Reflections on the Revolution in France*, New York: Doubleday, 1961.

Kariel, Henry S., *The Decline of American Pluralism*, Stanford, Cal.: Stanford University Press, 1961.

Mill, John Stuart, *Essays, on Politics and Culture*, Gertrude Himmelfarb, ed., Garden City: Doubleday, 1962.

Mill, John Stuart, *Mill's Ethical Writings*, J. B. Schneewind, ed., New York: Collier, 1965.

Mill, John Stuart, *On Liberty*, Chicago: Gateway, 1955.

Mill, John Stuart, *On Liberty*, New York: Liberal Arts Press, 1956.

Nagel, Ernest, ed., *John Stuart Mill's Philosophy of Scientific Method*, New York: Hafner, 1950.

Ostrogorski, M. I., *Democracy and the Organization of Political Parties*, S. M. Lipset, ed., 2 vols., Chicago: Quadrangle, 1954.

Smith, Adam, *An Inquiry into the Nature and the Causes of the Wealth of Nations*, Edwin Canaan, ed., with an Introduction by Max Lerner, New York: Modern Library, 1937.

Smith, Adam, *Moral and Political Philosophy*, Herbert W. Schneider, ed., New York: Hafner.

Smith, Adam, *An Inquiry into the Nature and the Causes of the Wealth of Nations*, *Selections from Book I*, Ludwig von Mises, ed., Chicago: Gateway, 1953.

Stanlis, Peter J., ed., *Edmund Burke and the Natural Law*, Ann Arbor, Mich.: University of Michigan Press, 1958.

QUESTIONS FOR POLITICAL SCIENCE

13

WHERE DOES MAN BELONG?

Who today is asking those fundamental questions that Socrates asked in his day and that have been asked by the great and influential political scientists, the participants in the Great Conversation, ever since the founding of the discipline? Anyone? Why is there so much talk of the "poverty of philosophy," and not only of political philosophy? What are the questions, rock bottom, fundamental, and yet universal, that should be asked?

One obvious question is this: Where does man belong? Socrates belonged to Athens—all of Socrates belonged to all of Athens. Hence he would not flee after he had been convicted, even though he had the opportunity. But contemporary polities are plural, and each of us is claimed by a vast and complex congeries of overlapping, highly differentiated associations, organizations, groups, and other communities. The sovereign state, which is usually a national state, also makes heavy claims on each human being. Beyond the state itself, there are supranational and even antinational loyalties. We may be Americans and at the same time be Roman Catholics or Protestants, and blacks or whites, and members of other international communities. We are also political and economic and social and cultural men and women. Where do we belong? If we belong in all of these, how then do we reconcile conflicting claims to our loyalties? Neither as simply as Socrates did, nor as radically as theorists of sovereignty would have us do.

In the ancient classics we find the search for the best life and for the best *polis*. Nowadays this search has generally been abandoned. Or else the best life and the best state is defined in some very parochial way; or in a global way, by those persuaded of the universal interdependence of all upon all. Utopia, which means nowhere, is today nowhere or everywhere. Students of politics, perhaps because they feared the responsibilities of their calling, sought to escape into *Wertfreiheit* (valuelessness). They have often ended up in trivia, and they have certainly given up their traditional search for the best.

WHAT IS THE BEST LIFE
AND THE BEST *POLIS*?

Few political scientists today address themselves to Aristotle's questions about the good man, the good citizen, the good *polis*, and the relations between these. Those few who do deal with these eternal questions find themselves unable to join in a meaningful dialogue with one another or to reach agreement. Yet philosophy is becoming more and more political again; this is true even of philosophies and philosophers who start off as explicitly apolitical or even antipolitical, like the Existentialists.

Plato and his followers believed that the truth existed and that it could be known. Even John Stuart Mill believed that. However, today the Marxists, including Mao Tse-tung, as well as anti-Marxists, speak of plural truths and sound relatively skeptical. Probability theory has returned from the physical sciences to politics. In any case, the substance of the future, even for five or ten years, can obviously not be foretold, because of the permanent and institutionalized technological revolution. In such circumstances, can one still formulate guidelines for the good life or the best *polis* in concrete and general terms?

IS THERE A DIFFERENCE
BETWEEN GENERAL AND
SPECIAL INTERESTS?

The founders of the study of politics believed in the distinction between the general interest and selfish interests. Indeed Aristotle based his whole classification of forms of government upon this distinction, and the Utilitarians revived it in more individualized terms. Most of our contemporaries deny this basic distinction, for at least three reasons. First, adherents of Adam Smith's theory of the invisible hand would assert that there is no conflict between selfish and general interests, since the unseen hand guides each man who pursues his own rational happiness to promote an end that is not a part of his intention, namely the wealth and welfare of the nation. Second, adherents of various versions of Marxism do not pin the accusation of subjective selfishness upon people who, as members of classes, are objectively the captives of ideologies. As capitalists, we think and act in terms of capitalist ideology. We have to do so and can escape from this higher form of selfishness—which also makes its contribution to the dialectically evolving welfare of mankind—only through the highest form of consciousness, that is, through Marxism, which, in the present stage, will convert us to captives of a proletarian ideology still somewhat short of perfect substantive truth. Third, followers of Sigmund Freud and other so-called irrationalists tell us that no one knows why he does what he does. All are driven by motives of which no one is aware, at least prior to psychoanalysis. As Martin Buber said, the "I" cannot talk with the "thou."[1] Communication among human beings is impossible in the age of conflicting and complementary beliefs in natural automaticity, of ideologism à la Marx, and of irrationalism à la Freud.

How then can the public interest be defined for any community, of whatever scope and level? Perhaps it is in the public interest to maintain and further a climate in which the sources of human motivation can be exposed, analyzed, and kept in mind by all?

---

[1] Martin Buber, *I and Thou*, Edinburgh: T. Clark, 1958.

Whatever the answer to this question, older notions of the general welfare are no longer adequate, and older classifications of forms of government, based upon the distinction between general and special interests, are obsolete. Even in "genuine democracies," "the people" do not "rule." They do not participate with full pre-Freudian rationality. They do not perceive the general interest in full pre-Marxian objectivity. Nor do members of the power elite in the United States make rational policy designed to promote even their own class interest, according to C. Wright Mills. And we have plenty of evidence that the great dictators, especially Hitler and Stalin, frequently did the opposite of promoting their own most selfish interests of expanding their power.

SHOULD WORLD POLITICS
BE DEVELOPED OR REDUCED?

The most successful constitutions are the ones that are the least engineered and the most naturally grown. Success came in the absence of deliberate efforts to bring about success, that is, without really trying. Those systems whose design was laid down with the greatest deliberation have, on the whole, been the least successful. And students of politics in developing countries find that charisma can neither be planned for, nor produced artificially, nor transferred from one leader to another, or from one set of institutions to another. Some have concluded from this that "social mobilization" should generally be throttled, so that institutions of government, as distinguished from participation in politics, can grow and can grow firmer.

What does all this mean for world politics? Some would reason by analogy from successful constitutional democracies that the social and economic requisites have to be built up first, before one can expect international politics to be either constitutionalized or, eventually, perhaps, democratized. They might also argue that the volume of international politics should not be permitted to expand at the same rate at which it has been expanding since 1945, and probably that this volume should be reduced, especially in the United Nations system, which seems to be overburdened. When told that it will not be possible, as it has not been possible, to keep new states from joining the international system and from participating in it with increasing activity, they might urge the routinization of global politics rather than its further stimulation and development.

But for what end? With what goal or goals in sight? Is either global constitutionalism, and in what sense of the term, or global "totalitarianism" possible? These questions are not really being raised seriously in any fundamental sense. Sometimes, very rarely, they appear at the end of discussions that concern problems of circumstantial substance, as, for example, immediate threats to the peace or nuclear wars or Vietnam.

WHAT IS THE AMERICAN NATIONAL PURPOSE?

The United States of America is the most powerful participant in world politics. Its potential political philosophers, there are no real ones, have made a special contribution to the impoverishment of political philosophy because of their ambivalence toward politics, especially world politics. What does the United States want and what could it get from global politics? In the current century, American politics has made no great contribution to the expansion of the consciousness of the American people. In attempts to interpret American or foreign politics, vulgar materialism has alternated with vulgar teleologism. American thought about politics has displayed a positive dislike of political and institutional inventiveness and of political dialectics except of the rather mechanistic adversary type. American thinking about politics has assumed the constancy of human nature, instead of considering the universals of the human condition. It has shown an odd oscillation between the pragmatism of "playing it by ear" and an almost Prussian preference for order. Official American statements have deplored the disorderliness of the United Nations, of the behavior of new states in the United Nations, and of the new world politics in general. But is not the flow of world politics still so limited that it needs quantitative development regardless of its qualitative style at any one moment (short of nuclear and, therefore, final violence)?

INDIVIDUAL OR COLLECTIVE SELF-PRESERVATION?

To answer that question and all the others, we are always brought back to the basic question behind them: All this for the realization of what values, in pursuit of which goals? Hobbes and Locke gave a partial answer, adequate for their times: self-preservation. But the fundamental law of individual self-preservation has now been converted into the fundamental law of the self-preservation of mankind, since it is now feasible, as it was not before 1945, to annihilate the species. In this respect, the values formulated by a chain of theorists from Hobbes to Locke and the Utilitarians, including John Stuart Mill, have had to have the scope of their applicability extended, in response to technological change. In another respect, however, the positive emphasis given to the originally negative formulation of Hobbes by Locke and his successors, an emphasis on comfort, convenience, property, and ultimately the pursuit of happiness, can no longer serve as a very meaningful normative foundation. This is so for two related reasons. On the one hand, comfort, convenience, and at least the pursuit if not the attainment of happiness have been achieved in countries with mature industrialized economies to a degree far beyond the wildest dreams of the seventeenth or nineteenth centuries. On the other hand, our Freud-induced psychological sophistication and self-awareness are such, that we know or suspect that the achievement of material goals does not really satisfy, perhaps because material goals are not very important when compared to others. Moreover, there are apparently such drives as the death wish. If the pursuit of happiness does not lead to happiness itself, and if even happiness, once attained, and however conceived of, is incomplete so long as it remains the object of the envy of less happy men and lands, what other fundamental values can one posit? We cannot return to property itself as the cement between generations and as the stabilizer of constitutions, both national and international. On the contrary, property has become a great destabilizer.

WHAT ARE ROCK-BOTTOM VALUES?

Within national systems, including new ones in backward countries, governments generally fail to do the jobs they are supposed to do. There is a pervasive *malaise* over almost all the world about government and politics. One cure that has been offered is the improvement of representative institutions. In fact, however, much of what is wrong with governments may be due to the excessive accuracy with which representative institutions represent the represented. In the United States, both the Congress and the President are highly representative. In many ways the personnel of the United Nations is accurately representative too. But neither constitution is doing a job today that satisfies very many people. Neither any one national constitution, nor the international constitution, suffices, unless interdependence, consciousness of interdependence, and procedures for the development of both interdependence and consciousness of it are developed further. Without such development, the dissatisfied within a state and among states can rebel, in the Lockean sense, by appealing to Heaven through war, which if global and nuclear would mean the end for all. No one has empty places to go to any more. All have to accept without possibility of effective dissent an imposed global "constitution" and the covenant upon it.

Again the question must be raised: For what end or ends? What is it that is worth risking war, one life, many lives, all human lives? No global civil religion is desirable or seems possible. No system of international representation is adequate. No general will has been formulated or, if formulated, has been recognized as general by the generality, or even by a majority, of mankind. What can be ends, goals, values capable of eliciting sufficient consensus among those whose dissent could sabotage the system based upon these values to the point of its and everyone's destruction? With reference to what should these values be stated: To the atom of the individual at one extreme? To the mass of mankind at the other extreme? Or to nation, church, class, in between the two extremes?

THE UNIVERSAL COVENANT

Here a possible answer arises to the question raised by the conflict between general and special interests. In a way, it could be said that all human beings have been forced or thrown into participation in a universal covenant. This is a covenant to which no sovereign is a party. It is a covenant of all with all—the converse of Thomas Hobbes's war of all against all. Individuals still have the right to their self-preservation, but they are foiled in the exercise of this right by the very real and growing dangers of universal nuclear destruction. Once a global nuclear war takes place, no individual is likely to be able to preserve himself or his children. Similarly, just as individual preservation has been made meaningless without the preservation of the species, so private, group, or class interests have been broadened into national interest, the interest of a bloc of states, or some other interest that must be considered special because it is opposed to the global interests of mankind as a whole. In this sense, the opposition between special interests and the general interest of humanity has become clearer than ever before, while at the same time the identity between individual self-preservation and the survival of the species has also become more dramatically obvious than in the past.

COMMITMENT OR WITHDRAWAL?

Unfortunately, the existential reality of the universal covenant provides no answer to our first question—Where does man belong?—and no resolution to the individual's dilemma of loyalties. Each of us still belongs to his original community, much as Socrates did. However, unlike Socrates, each of us is aware, some profoundly, of the relativity of "national" values. Plato and Aristotle tried to transcend these merely local conventions, and they, or at least their contemporaries in the Greek *polis*, failed. The Stoics succeeded, but at the expense of the breakdown of the *polis* as a viable political system. Nowadays, men who are forced to act politically, for example, as conscripts in a war, are made very much aware of the relativity of values. Sometimes they reach this awareness on their own, perhaps as a result of participating in a great national debate. Sometimes, they reach it as a result of "enemy" propaganda. They may either do what is required of them, by paying their taxes, serving in the army, participating more or less actively in politics, or they may wish to give minimal compliance, or to withdraw into some kind of "inner emigration" (as it was called in Nazi Germany), or to disobey openly, or to emigrate to some more hospitable political system.

The twentieth century could well be called the century of the refugee. There have been millions of refugees by force, like those who sought refuge from Hitler's persecution before and during World War II, those who fled from religious persecution during the partition of India, those who were refugees from the Israeli-Arab wars. And there were at least thousands of refugees by choice, like Stalin's daughter Svetlana from the Soviet Union, Thomas Mann from Nazi Germany, or Pablo Casals from Fascist Spain. Of course, only relatively few have the opportunity, because of their geographical location and their stature, to make explicit public commitments, either in favor of or opposed to specific political values or a particular political regime. But the spreading awareness of the relativity of merely national values heightens the importance of forging cosmopolitan goals. Everyone, at least everyone within reach of radio and television, must become aware of the fact that what is considered good in his country may be considered evil in some other part of the world. An act that is viewed as heroism in his own country may be considered a war crime by citizens of another land. Hence there is an urgent need to create and popularize globally acceptable and understandable values, in terms of which individuals could decide where they want to belong when conflicting demands are made upon their loyalties. The fact of the tacit universal covenant pushes the dialectic between parochial and universal values ever more toward the goals of greater range.

This answers, to the extent that it can be answered, the question: Where does man belong? It also settles the issue about the development or the reduction of politics, because only the development of politics can lead to the growth of awareness of the possibilities of life, especially life in the interdependent community of mankind. Men can be made more fully aware of the relativity of parochial values and of the need for building up consensus on more widely acceptable goals only through the growth of politics.

THE BEST LIFE AND THE DEVELOPMENT OF POLITICS

It is much more difficult today than it was at any time until World War II to answer the questions about the best life and the best *polis.* Indeed, the rarity with which this question is posed and efforts are made to deal with it can be taken as a reflection not only of the difficulty of answering it but also of the deep *malaise* about government and politics that exists in virtually all parts of the world. Even citizens living under the hitherto most successful, best designed, or most flexibly grown constitutions, and possessed of the most stable representative institutions, feel dissatisfied and frustrated with their political processes today. This was true, for example, in the United States in the 1960s, when the greatest wealth and power ever controlled by a nation was insufficient to prevent the assassinations of a popular president and other leaders, to solve grave racial problems that had beset the nation for more than a century, or to keep the country out of the least righteous war in its history. Similarly, the Communist states were dissatisfied with their institutions, both as they operated within individual countries and as they provided for relations among different Communist states. The ex-colonies, too, had almost without exception failed to achieve the goals for which they had constructed their new constitutions.

All these dissatisfactions and frustrations were related to the reluctance to face up to the most basic questions. Few were the founders of new states or the revolutionaries in old ones who asked themselves and their public: What is the best life? What is the best possible political community? Where do we belong? Where do we want to go? Usually, instead of asking such fundamental questions, they let their answers dictate much more circumstantial questions. They let their situation determine what they wanted to ask of their condition in the world. In wars, and in military jargon, they let their hardware determine their policies, instead of proceeding in the other direction and letting their policies determine the hardware they needed to achieve their goals. On some occasions, the leaders of countries tried to withdraw their communities from world politics. This is no more possible for whole political systems than it is for individuals within modern polities. And, if it were possible, it would be irresponsible. Withdrawal would be irresponsible in a special contemporary, existential sense, because whatever any one political system does or fails to do has repercussions for all other political systems, especially the all-encompassing global one.

The generations of men and women in the world today have signed no social contract, and most of us reject the idea of being bound by our parents' commitments when we did not contribute to their making, even though we are, most of us, enjoying benefits flowing from these commitments. Moreover, there is greater awareness now than perhaps ever before, an awareness to which political science has contributed its fair share, of the fact that even the best designed constitution frequently foils all attempts on the part of its citizens to act responsibly, that is, in awareness of the consequences of one's decisions and in willingness to accept these consequences. Nevertheless, each human being *is* responsible, in a causal sense, for all other human beings. Any single action or lack of it is like a pebble thrown into a pond that sets off waves and ripples in the water. Human capacity to set off ripples in the pond of mankind is constantly expanding, though at the same time and from another point of view, human actions are also becoming more limited in their efficacy. Man seeks power after power unto death, as Thomas Hobbes said. He engages in an ever-continuing pursuit of happiness, as Thomas Jefferson more felicitously put it. In the present century, as a result of the politically guided technological revolutions, man has been getting ever more, and never enough, and more men are living in a greater number of complexly interrelated communities, in an ever-heightening degree of interdependence.

The dialectical tensions between the basic goals that all men, and all political systems, pursue, seem sometimes to be pushed beyond the breaking point. We have available to us a wider range of previously unthought of alternatives than ever before, and we therefore should be able to find satisfaction in the pursuit of the basic goal of flexibility. However, we are limited by our commitments, which are also greater than ever before. Men are capable nowadays of committing not only themselves, but their descendants until doomsday—doomsday literally, in the sense of what a doomsday machine would accomplish—through nuclear tripwire devices, through the testing of hydrogen bombs that leave deposits of deadly materials in the bones of generations yet unborn, or through the despoliation of natural resources. But our commitments are in turn limited by the ever-increasing proliferation of choices available to us. Politicians today command more physical force than ever before, but they control so much power, that power can no longer appear to them as "present means to obtain some future apparent good," Hobbes's definition of power. Just as the range of new alternatives limits our capacity to achieve stability, so the quantum of power at our disposal reduces our achievement of the basic goal of efficiency. And although we have more knowledge, and more and greater foreknowledge of the probable consequences of decisions, our capacity to give stability to our purposes is limited by the expansion of power and the proliferation of alternatives.

All this men can become aware of, and can forever try, and must forever fail, to fit into some meaningful pattern of mutual interrelationships, only through politics, just as they can relate themselves to other individuals and to members of other communities, only through politics. In this sense, what Aristotle said more than two millennia ago has even greater validity today:

> "If then, there is some end to the things we do, which we desire for its own sake (everything else being desired for the sake of this), and if we do not choose everything for the sake of something else (for at that rate the process would go on to infinity, so that our desire would be empty and vain), clearly this must be *the* good and the chief good. Will not the knowledge of it, then, have a great influence on life? Shall we not, like archers who have a mark to aim at, be more likely to hit upon what is right? If so we must try, in outline at least, to determine what it is, and of which of the sciences or faculties it is the object. It would seem to belong to the most authoritative science and to that which is most truly the master science. And politics appears to be of this nature; for it is politics that ordains which of the sciences should be studied in a state, and which each class of citizens should learn and up to what point they

should learn them; and we see even the most highly esteemed of faculties to fall under this, e.g., strategy, economics, rhetoric; now since politics uses the rest of the sciences, and since again it legislates as to what we are to do and what we are to abstain from doing, the goal of this science must include those of the others, so that this end must be *the* good for man. For even if the end is the same for a single man and for a state, that of the state seems at all events something greater and more complete whether to attain or to preserve; though it is worthwhile to attain the end merely for one man, it is finer and more god-like to attain it for a nation or for city-states. These, then, are the goals at which our inquiry aims, since it is political science, in one sense of that term."[2]

---

[2] Aristotle, *Nicomachean Ethics*, book I. 2.

INDEX

6443